W9-AOP-650

www.wadsworth.com

www.wadsworth.com is the World Wide Web site for Wadsworth and is your direct source to dozens of online resources.

At *www.wadsworth.com* you can find out about supplements, demonstration software, and student resources. You can also send email to many of our authors and preview new publications and exciting new technologies.

www.wadsworth.com
Changing the way the world learns®

The Wadsworth College Success Series

Clason and Beck, *On the Edge of Success* (2003). ISBN: 0-534-56973-0

Gardner and Jewler, *Your College Experience: Strategies for Success,* Media Edition, 6th Ed. (2005). ISBN: 0-534-59392-5

Gardner and Jewler, *Your College Experience: Strategies for Success,* Concise Media Edition, 5th Ed. (2004). ISBN: 0-534-60759-4

Gardner and Jewler, *Your College Experience: Strategies for Success,* Expanded Reader, 5th Ed. (2003). ISBN: 0-534-59985-0

Gordon and Minnick, *Foundations: A Reader for New College Students,* 3rd Ed. (2005). ISBN: 0-534-62167-8

Hallberg, Hallberg, and Aschieris, *Making the Dean's List: A Workbook to Accompany the College Success Factors Index* (2004). ISBN: 0-534-24862-4

Hettich and Helkowski, *Connect College to Career: A Student's Guide to Work and Life Transitions* (2005). ISBN: 0-534-62582-7

Holkeboer and Walker, *Right from the Start: Taking Charge of Your College Success,* 4th Ed. (2004). ISBN: 0-534-59967-2

Petrie and Denson, *A Student Athlete's Guide to College Success: Peak Performance in Class and Life,* 2nd Ed. (2003). ISBN: 0-534-56999-4

Santrock and Halonen, *Your Guide to College Success: Strategies for Achieving Your Goals,* Media Edition, 3rd Ed. (2004). ISBN: 0-534-60804-3

Santrock and Halonen, *Your Guide to College Success: Strategies for Achieving Your Goals,* Concise Media Edition, 3rd Ed. (2005). ISBN: 0-534-59346-1

Steltenpohl, Shipton, and Villines, *Orientation to College: A Reader on Becoming an Educated Person,* 2nd Ed. (2004). ISBN: 0-534-59958-3

Van Blerkom, *Orientation to College Learning,* 4th Ed. (2004). ISBN: 0-534-60813-2

Wahlstrom and Williams, *Learning Success: Being Your Best at College and Life,* Media Edition, 3rd Ed. (2002). ISBN: 0-534-57314-2

Study Skills/Critical Thinking

Jenkins, *Skills for Success: Developing Effective Study Strategies* (2005). ISBN: 0-534-63805-8

Longman and Atkinson, *CLASS: College Learning and Study Skills,* 7th Ed. (2005). ISBN: 0-534-62152-X

Sotiriou, *Integrating College Study Skills: Reasoning in Reading, Listening, and Writing,* 6th Ed. (2002). ISBN: 0-534-57296-0

Van Blerkom, *College Study Skills: Becoming a Strategic Learner,* 4th Ed. (2003). ISBN: 0-534-57467-X

Van Blerkom and Mulcahy-Ernt, *College Reading and Study Strategies* (2005). ISBN: 0-534-58420-9

Walter, Knudsvig, and Smith, *Critical Thinking: Building the Basics,* 2nd Ed. (2003). ISBN: 0-534-59976-1

Student Assessment Tool

Hallberg, *College Success Factors Index,* http://success.wadsworth.com

Foundations
A Reader for New College Students
Third Edition

Virginia N. Gordon
The Ohio State University

Thomas L. Minnick
The Ohio State University

THOMSON
WADSWORTH

Australia • Canada • Mexico • Singapore • Spain
United Kingdom • United States

THOMSON
WADSWORTH

Executive Manager: *Carolyn Merrill*
Assistant Editor: *Amanda Santana*
Technology Project Manager: *Joe Gallagher*
Advertising Project Manager: *Linda Yip*
Project Manager, Editorial Production:
  Jennifer Klos
Print Buyer: *Emma Claydon*
Permissions Editor: *Kiely Sexton*
Production Service: *Scratchgravel Publishing
  Services*

Copy Editor: *Carol Lombardi*
Cover Designer: *Bill Stanton*
Cover Image: *Emanuele Taroni/Getty*
Compositor: *Scratchgravel Publishing
  Services*
Text and Cover Printer: *Transcontinental
  Printing/Louiseville*

For more information about our
products, contact us at:
**Thomson Learning Academic
Resource Center
1-800-423-0563**

For permission to use material from
this text, contact us by:
Phone: 1-800-730-2214
Fax: 1-800-730-2215
Web: http://www.thomsonrights.com

Library of Congress Control Number:
2003116812

ISBN: 0-534-62167-8

**Wadsworth/Thomson Learning
10 Davis Drive
Belmont, CA 94002-3098
USA**

Asia
Thomson Learning
5 Shenton Way #01-01
UIC Building
Singapore 068808

Australia/New Zealand
Thomson Learning
102 Dodds Street
Southbank, Victoria 3006
Australia

Canada
Nelson
1120 Birchmount Road
Toronto, Ontario M1K 5G4
Canada

Europe/Middle East/Africa
Thomson Learning
High Holborn House
50/51 Bedford Row
London WC1R 4LR
United Kingdom

Latin America
Thomson Learning
Seneca, 53
Colonia Polanco
11560 Mexico D.F.
Mexico

Spain/Portugal
Paraninfo
Calle Magallanes, 25
28015 Madrid, Spain

This edition of *Foundations* is dedicated
to the memory of
Marilyn E. Hagans
and in honor of
Albert J. Kuhn,
two extraordinary teachers of English.

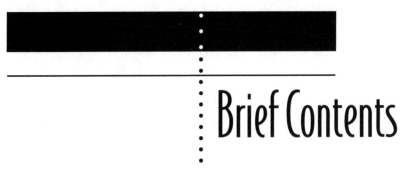

Brief Contents

Contents

UNIT 7
What Is Diversity and Why Is It Important to Me?   185
· ·

UNIT 8
What Should I Know About Careers?   233
· ·

UNIT 9
Life After College: Future Success or Future Shock?   263
· ·

Preface

Students entering college face many important decisions involving academic, career, and personal life choices. The purpose of this anthology is to stimulate the thinking of first-year college students about issues they will likely confront during their college years. We hope that, by reflecting on the ideas and insights provided by the writers included, students will recognize and perhaps be comforted by the universal character of the issues they face and will be better prepared to address and resolve them.

This anthology is designed to serve courses that help orient students to college life. In some colleges this text may also be suitable as a reader in first-year composition, and some high schools might find it useful in courses that introduce college issues to prospective college students. In compiling these essays, we have sought to incorporate topics in higher education about which entering college students should have some knowledge as they begin their journey to graduation.

The reader format provides a diversity of opinions and perspectives on a variety of topics. Consequently, it encourages dialogue among different points of view. Because such dialogue is essential to a learning community, students are encouraged to participate in the exploration of ideas, which is how their journey toward knowledge and self-knowledge can best proceed. Instructors are also encouraged to participate in the dialogue, because students will benefit from their example. Journaling activities encourage students to reflect on what they read and how the topics may be relevant to their college life.

The topics are drawn from the common experiences of entering college students. Unit 1 examines the value of a college education by raising such questions as "What is a truly educated person?" and "Is a college education an investment for the future or an end in itself?" It also offers a brief history of higher education and the contemporary American university as they have evolved through the last century. Unit 2 focuses on what you can reasonably expect of college work and how you are likely to change during your college experience. Among the questions discussed are "How will you change intellectually and personally through the college years?" and "How can you learn to become personally effective in college, work, and life?" Unit 3 takes up very practical topics—such as using the library, selecting your major, attending classes, and turning in assignments on time—that relate to the general question of "How can you succeed academically?"

Because the act of learning is such an integral part of student life, the writings in Unit 4 offer a variety of perspectives on this important process. Included are practical matters such as how to understand your own learning style and how to take an active role in shaping how you learn. New forms of learning that have taken root on many campuses—service learning and distance learning—are also discussed in Unit 4. Unit 5 complements Unit 4 by raising issues about technology—namely, how it can and will affect how you think, learn, and associate with others. The readings in Unit 5 cover different aspects of technology's influence that now permeate our academic, work, and personal lives. From a historical perspective on how technology has evolved to a futuristic view of tomorrow's workplace, the writers in this unit offer a fascinating picture of where we have been and where we might be headed.

Unit 6 introduces the idea of college as a special kind of community, one defined by the common mission of its members: the search for knowledge and truth. Academic freedom (the freedom to express any point of view so that it can be studied and evaluated) is the essential condition of the college community. Because the search for truth is at the heart of the academic experience, certain kinds of behavior are intolerable within it, including, for example, cheating or plagiarism. Unit 7 discusses the value of diversity in a college setting. The dialogue essential to discovering truth places a high value on diversity because, through their diverse opinions and experiences, the varied members of an academic community enrich that dialogue and make it likelier to uncover many truths. Behavior that limits or undervalues diversity, especially discrimination against individuals based on minority group status, weakens an academic community and its ability to serve its primary mission.

The essays in Unit 8 will help you better understand how your professional life is likely to develop and, therefore, how best to prepare for your chosen career in the changing world of the 21st century. Unit 9 looks forward to life after graduation. We believe that post–high school education needs to prepare students for lifelong learning. The essays in Unit 9 encourage you to think about the future so that, even in your first year of college, you begin to lay the foundation for the days after graduation.

In compiling this anthology we have been helped by many students, colleagues, and friends, and we thank them. Dr. Mac A. Stewart, Vice Provost for Minority Affairs at The Ohio State University, supported us through his encouragement and by making time and resources available to us. Mary Ellen Jenkins, assistant dean of the Colleges of the Arts and Sciences, undertook the essential task of securing permissions for reprinting material under copyright and contributed important biographical information about the authors included here. Edie Waugh helped prepare the manuscript and patiently endured frequent editorial reconsiderations. Students Michael Gifford and Dane Terry cheerfully undertook aspects of the manuscript preparation, working with remarkable speed and accuracy. The following reviewers provided input on improvements for this third edition: Barbara Colby, Arizona State University; Juan J. Flores, California State University, Sacramento; Laureen O'Hanlon, California State University, Sacramento; and Judith Termini, Gallaudet University. Finally, we want to acknowledge the lessons we have learned from generations of colleagues and students in University College at Ohio State who enrolled in and taught University Survey, a course we have been associated with for more than 25 years that has, in that time, introduced more than 250,000 first-year students to the values and challenges of living and learning in an academic community.

How to Keep a Journal

A fter most of the readings in this textbook, you will find Suggestions for Your Journal. We strongly encourage you to get into the habit of keeping a written journal of your reactions to and reflections on your assigned readings. Such journaling will result in a record of your development as you think through both the essays and your experiences as a new student at your college or university. Because many new college students may not know what a journal at its best can be, or how to keep one, we offer the definition and suggestions that follow.

Why keep a journal? The type of journal we are suggesting that you write is a "response" journal in which you will record your ideas and feelings in response to the readings that you are assigned in each unit. Writing a journal can reveal how your thought processes work and how they develop or change, serve as a memory aid, and provide an informal way of keeping track of your ideas that may be less threatening than more formal writing assignments like essays and research papers. Writing in your journal means working to find the right words to express yourself, and so keeping a journal can help you make your ideas more specific, more concrete.

The purpose of a journal is usually to provide a record, often day by day, of the writer's own internal or spiritual growth. In this regard, both journals and the closely related form, diaries, are similar to a document once needed on every sailing ship, the captain's log. The log was a book in which the chief officer of the ship kept a daily record of the ship's travels. Entries were usually brief, providing the ship's location in longitude and latitude and perhaps a sentence or two about important events of the voyage: "Sighted a large group of whales to the west," for example, or "Finished the last fresh provisions today." The ship's log therefore became the skeleton of a history. For some writers, a diary can be very similar to a log. Depending on how much detail an author chooses to include, a diary can be as lean as a ship's log or substantially more informative. An important difference is that the ship's log was intended to be available to others, such as the ship's owners. A diary is almost always intended to be a private document. A journal, in the sense that we hope you will use the word, is similar to a log or diary in that the entries can be made daily and should be dated. Unlike a personal diary, the best journals are written with the expectation that sometime, someone besides the writer will probably read them. Yet they retain a sense of ease and intimacy as though the prospective readers were the author's good friends.

Keeping a journal can encourage you to think more critically by helping you to make connections between what an author has written and your agreements or disagreements with that author's point of view. For example, a typical journal entry may note:

> Date: September 30, 2004 [Most journal entries should be dated!]
> Essay: "College Major Doesn't Mean That Much" by William Raspberry
>
> As I read Raspberry's advice to his daughter about not choosing a major right away, I wished that my parents had told me this. I felt really pressured to choose a major during orientation since everyone else seemed to know what they were doing. Now that I have been in college for a few weeks, I'm beginning to have second thoughts about majoring in engineering. The trouble is, I don't know what else to major in or even what I might be good at. I don't have to worry about a "career," as Raspberry puts it, if I stick with engineering. But I am not sure what an engineer does all day. Raspberry says to pick a major "on the pleasure principle" for what I enjoy studying. That sure isn't math and physics. And yet I was good in these subjects in high school, and so far in my college classes I have been doing at least average with everyone else in my classes. I think a good way to proceed is to stay in general with the engineering plan but add some other classes in areas— like Theater!—that I really enjoy. Maybe I can find a way to balance both options.

This entry starts with an idea from an assigned essay and develops it with the student's personal point of view, including her examples, generalizations, and relevant personal experiences. A journal entry is usually this length or longer: One perfect sentence might be adequate and expressive, but usually a reflective response will require some development. A paragraph is a common length for an entry, but some may be as long as several paragraphs—even amounting to an essay.

We recommend that you read every essay with an eye for what you personally can learn or take from that essay. Can you apply some comment or suggestion from that reading to your experience? How? Or why not? Our suggested topics are not meant to limit you but merely to serve as possible starting places. In addition, here are some practical tips for keeping a journal that many writers find helpful:

- In journal writing it is permissible to write as you would talk to a friend or trusted adviser. The content is more important than perfection of style, and you will often find the entries are more informative if you think about what you want to express without worrying too much about the style or form of expression you use.
- Write about the insights, feelings and emotions, or problems that you think about when reading the assigned essay. Don't worry if you may seem more negative than positive: It is entirely all right to disagree with an author.
- Sometimes as you are reading an assignment, it is handy to jot down notes with your reactions in a very brief form (just so you can understand them

later!). Your journal entry can then be developed from these notes, as you think about them and put them into your own organization.

- Interact with and expand upon what the author is saying but do so in your own words, adding your own ideas.
- Use any creative format that you think best expresses your responses. You may want to write in the form of a dialogue between you and the author or of a letter to a friend or to your parents.

Your course instructor will tell you how your journal entries will be used in class—that is, how they will fit into the course structure and count in your final grade. Some students find that they enjoy keeping a journal and continue the practice even after they are required to do so by a class. Many successful authors keep journals for decades and take from them their ideas for longer essays or books. And some journals have become important historical documents because, like the captain's log of an important voyage, they help others to navigate along one of the paths that eventually we all must find and follow.

UNIT 1

The Value of a College Education: Why Am I in College?

Students attend college for many reasons. In a national survey by Alexander Astin of UCLA, who has studied each class of first-year students for many years, the largest number of entering students (73 percent) indicated they were coming to college to prepare for a better job. Other common reasons that students gave were to make more money, find a philosophy of life, become a more cultured person, or satisfy their parents' wishes.

Examining your reasons for enrolling in higher education can help you determine what you can realistically hope to accomplish as a student. Because new students may find it difficult to set tentative educational and occupational goals, they usually find it helpful to understand what the college experience is intended to, and can, provide. Such an understanding establishes a foundation on which to shape your personal expectations.

College will open for you an unbelievable range of opportunities to explore diverse fields of knowledge, along with a variety of activities that will help you grow personally

Enter to grow in wisdom. Depart to serve better thy country and mankind.

—INSCRIPTION ON THE 1890 GATE TO HARVARD YARD

1

and socially. Although you could educate yourself outside the college environment, it is much more expedient and satisfying to learn with other students and from teachers who are committed to creating an environment that supports learning.

In college you will have the time and freedom to delve into many areas of interest that you may not have explored. You will also be exposed to areas of the human experience that you did not know existed. Imagine! In a four-year (now often longer) span of time, you can acquaint yourself with a wide range of human knowledge and experience. Even in a two-year institution, these same opportunities exist, although they will be more focused.

At no other time in your life will you have such a concentrated opportunity for learning. In high school, most of the courses you took were prescribed for you by others. In college, although some majors are more rigidly structured than others, you have more freedom to pursue your personal interests. You are in control of your own learning.

On the other hand, if one of your reasons for being in college is to obtain a job, consider what college can offer you in preparing for your future career. A U.S. Department of Labor study, done with the American Society for Training and Development, identified the following seven basic skills that workers in the future must possess if they are to be successful: learning to learn, competence, communication, personal management, adaptability, group effectiveness, and influence. Many people feel that you will be able to acquire and perfect these basic skills through your college experience. Consciously working to acquire these skills in the classroom, in campus activities, and in social and other contacts will enhance your effectiveness with them by the time you graduate.

The readings in this unit are intended to stimulate your thinking about why you are in college and what you expect from it. The essays present a broad perspective on higher education and its value to the individual, not only intellectually but also as the beginning of a lifelong pursuit of learning. The essays in this unit by Bennett and Cicarelli attempt to reconcile the notion of learning for its own sake with a practical question about careers that students frequently and justifiably ask: "But what can I do with a major in _____?" Gardner tackles the same question in a different way, by defending the (to him) universal value of liberal learning. Rhodes briefly summarizes the history of American higher education in an essay included here because, when you want to know where you are, it can be helpful to know where you have been. These readings can help you compare your reasons for enrolling in college with some of the goals and objectives of higher education in general. You might also want to discuss with faculty, administrators, and other students your institution's mission and goals for preparing its students for the future.

The Lure of Learning
William J. Bennett

William J. Bennett is an accomplished scholar, teacher, and academic administrator. He was chair of the National Endowment for the Humanities in the early 1980s, Secretary of Education in the Reagan administration, and the nation's "Drug Czar" in the George H. W. Bush administration. Since leaving government service, Bennett has remained an active commentator on cultural issues, publishing more than a dozen books. He has stated that students should be taught "patriotism, self-discipline, thrift, honesty, and respect for elders." He received a Ph.D. in philosophy from the University of Texas and a law degree from Harvard.

This essay reflects Bennett's strong belief in the value of college teaching and its effect on students' learning. His career as an outstanding professor was obviously influenced by those who taught him and brought life to the subjects.

W hen I arrived at college as a freshman some time ago, I had definite ideas about how I wanted to use my four years of higher education. I wanted to major in English because I wanted to become *sophisticated*.* I wanted to become sophisticated because I wanted to land a good job and make big money.

But because of my college's course requirements, I found myself in an introductory philosophy class, confronted by Plato's *Republic* and a remarkable professor who knew how to make the text come alive. It seemed to me and many of my fellow classmates as if we had come face to face with a reincarnation of Socrates himself. Before we knew it, we were ensnared by the power of a 2,000-year-old dialogue.

In our posture of youthful cynicism and arrogance, we at first resisted the idea that the question of justice should really occupy our time. But something happened to us that semester as we fought our way through the *Republic*, arguing about notions of right and wrong. Along the way, our insides were shaken up a little bit. Without quite knowing it, we had committed ourselves to the serious enterprise of raising and wrestling with questions. And once caught up in that enterprise, there was no turning back. We had met up with a great text and a great teacher; they had taken us, and we were theirs.

Every student is entitled to that kind of experience at college. And if I could make one request of future undergraduates, it would be that they open the door to that possibility. College should shake you up a little, get you breathing, quicken your senses and animate a conscious examination of life's enduring questions. Know thyself, Socrates said. Higher education worthy of the name aspires to nothing less than the wisdom of that *dictum*.

---

*Vocabulary words are italicized in each essay—ED.

These are lofty ambitions. What do they mean in the context of four years of campus life?

A college is many things. It is a collection of dormitories, libraries, social clubs, *incorrigibly* terrible cafeterias. But above all, it is a faculty. It used to be said, when this country was much younger, that a log lying on the side of the road with a student sitting on one end and a professor on the other was a university.

That essence has not changed. It is the relationship between teachers and their students that gives a campus its own special genius. "Like a contagious disease, almost," William James wrote, "spiritual life passes from man to man by contact." Above all, a student should look for—and expect to find—professors who can bring to life the subject at hand.

What else should students find at college? They should discover great works that tell us how men and women of our own and other civilizations have grappled with life's relentless questions. What should be loved? What deserves to be defended? What is noble and what is base? As Montaigne wrote, a student should have the chance to learn "what valor, *temperance,* and justice are, the difference between ambition and greed, loyalty and servitude, liberty and license; and the marks of true and solid contentment."

This means, first of all, that students should find wide exposure to all the major disciplines—history, science, literature, mathematics and foreign language. And it means that they should be introduced to the best that has been thought and written in every discipline.

College is, for many, a once-in-a-lifetime chance to discover our civilization's greatest achievements and lasting visions. There are many great books, discoveries and deeds that record those achievements in unequaled fashion. There are many more that do not. A good college will sort the great texts and important ideas from the run-of-the-mill and offer the best to its students. And that offering will be the institution's vision of a truly educated person.

All students have different notions about where they want a college degree to take them. For some, it is law school or journalism. For others, it's public service. That's fine. College *should* be a road to your ambitions. But every student should take the time to tread the ground outside his or her major and to spend some time in the company of the great travelers who have come before.

Why? Put simply, because they can help you lead a better and perhaps happier life. If we give time to studying how men and women of the past have dealt with life's enduring problems, then we will be better prepared when those same problems come our way. We may be a little less surprised to find treachery at work in the world about us, a little less startled by unselfish devotion, a little readier to believe in the capacity of the human mind.

And what does that do for a future career? As Hamlet said, "Readiness is all." In the end, the problems we face during the course of a career are the same kind that we face in the general course of life. If you want to be a corporate executive, how can you learn about not missing the right opportunities? One way is to read *Hamlet.* Do you want to learn about the dangers of overweening ambition? Read *Macbeth*. Want to know the pitfalls of playing around on the job? Read *Antony and Cleopatra*. The importance of fulfilling the responsibilities entrusted to leadership? Read *King Lear*.

Even in the modern world, it is still that peculiar mix of literature, science, history, math, philosophy and language that can help mature minds come to grips with the age-old issues, the problems that *transverse* every plane of life. Students who bring to college the willingness to seek out those issues, to enliven the spirit and broaden the mind, will be more likely to profit in any endeavor.

Reprinted by permission of the author.

 Vocabulary

As you think about this essay, these definitions may be helpful to you:
1. **sophisticated**   worldly, wise, knowing
2. **dictum**   a formal authoritative pronouncement of a principle or opinion
3. **incorrigible**   not capable of being corrected, permanently wrong, stubborn
4. **temperance**   moderation in action, thought, or feeling
5. **transverse**   set crosswise

 Discussion Questions

1. How did Bennett and his fellow students initially react to their philosophy class? How did their reactions change?
2. What does Bennett ask undergraduates to do in order to expose themselves to the same wonders of learning that he enjoyed?
3. According to Bennett, what gives each campus its own "special genius"? Have you found this in your classes? Describe.
4. What should students find at college in addition to good teaching?
5. What does the college experience do for a future career, according to Bennett?

 Suggestions for Your Journal

Did you decide to come to college because of the "lure of learning"? If so, how do you think that element arose in you? Have you always planned to attend higher education? Did your expectations for college fit the reality you have already found? Be specific in considering these questions, because the details of your experience may fade as time passes.

Have you begun to discover your institution's "vision of a truly educated person"? Write about that vision and the evidence you have already found for it.

A New Debate Is Joined over an Old Question: Is College an Investment or an End in Itself?

James Cicarelli

James Cicarelli is currently dean of the Walter E. Heller College of Business Administration at Roosevelt University in Chicago, Illinois.

In this essay, Cicarelli discusses the objectives of higher education and how to measure its impact on students. He outlines two philosophies and discusses how each is supported by different types of disciplines and institutions.

The seemingly endless debate about higher education is now focusing on the question of what the purpose of higher education is and how best to determine how well colleges and universities are achieving it. Particularly heated right now is the discussion over the pros and cons of so-called value-added *assessment.*

On one side of the debate are proponents of the relatively new view of college as a place where students go to add to their individual reservoirs of information. This philosophy of education emphasizes quantifiable knowledge that can be measured by student performance on nationally standardized tests. The idea is that by testing students before, during, and at the end of their college careers, an institution can discover its educational strengths and weaknesses through "outcomes evaluation"—measuring exactly how much has been added to each student's store of knowledge by the education he or she has received.

On the other side of the debate are those who hold a more traditional view of college as a place where students go to learn to appreciate their cultural heritage, *hone* their skills in critical thinking and communication, and otherwise transform themselves from self-centered individuals into decent and caring citizens. In this view, the emphasis in college should be more on the development of moral principles than on the accumulation of knowledge, per se. Since that sort of outcome is difficult, if not impossible, to measure, the *traditionalist* institution looks to "input" rather than "output," measuring success in terms of the variety and depth of experience to which its students have been exposed.

Despite obvious differences, the two philosophies are not mutually exclusive. Actually, both can be seen as variants of "*developmentalism,*" an approach to education concerned with both the content and the *cognitive* aspects of learning. What set the two views apart are their conflicting methods of assessment, and the resulting controversy is going to dominate the discussion of evaluation for the foreseeable future.

While each side aims to improve higher education, both systems have disadvantages that would make them less effective than their proponents promise. For example, it is foolhardy to judge the success of a college education in terms of how much information the students have accumulated, because so much of it is already obsolete by the time they graduate. Students need to learn how to learn and how to teach themselves—talents that are nurtured by the ability to think clearly and read and write effectively, rather than by the mastery of information whose half-life is often measured in months.

On the other hand, it is pretentious to suppose that a college can teach values or should even try to do so. While most people can accept the broad principles embodied in the old Superman motto—"Truth, Justice, and the American Way"—it's difficult to translate them into working precepts. *Whose* truth? *What* system of justice? *Which* American way? Only in a dictatorship is one set of values taught to all. Yet simply exposing students to competing value systems, without discrimination, leads to confusion, if not anarchy.

Contributing to the controversy are the differences between professional, career-oriented education and general, liberal arts education. The former readily lends itself to the value-added approach because a profession is based on a body of knowledge that must be mastered before the student becomes a practitioner. Mastery of factual information can be demonstrated by passing a standardized test. Such a test shows how well an institution has prepared its students for entry into a profession. In other words, it measures the effectiveness of the education provided. Thus, prospective students interested in a particular career might consider such test results when deciding which college to attend. Unfortunately, that is not foolproof.

A decade ago, for example, when the boom in the oil industry led many colleges to expand their geology programs and others to begin new ones, a bachelor's in petroleum engineering was the hottest degree an undergraduate could earn. Today, most of those programs are as inactive as the West Texas oil fields where all the new geologists and engineers were supposed to find work. Educating for a job can produce graduates who are fit for that job and little else. A liberal arts education, on the other hand, can provide students with skills that transcend specific jobs and can be usefully applied in virtually any occupation.

The general-vs-professional issue is part of the larger question of whether college should be seen as an investment or as an end in itself. Advocates of the value-added philosophy tend to consider higher education an investment, an expenditure of time and resources that should yield a payoff large enough to justify the initial cost. In their view, society invests a great deal in education, in part because of the hope that the schools and colleges will produce productive citizens who will then ensure that the next generation has the wherewithal to renew the investment. Traditionalists are more apt to view higher education as something one acquires for its own sake, not because it may lead to a good job or some other material gain. If it does result in enrichment in monetary as well as intellectual terms, fine; but the purpose of a college education is to make one better, not necessarily richer.

Whatever else is involved in the debate, a big part of it, for me, has to do with romanticism versus realism. My romantic side, the one that envisions college as a mind-expanding experience, sees the value-added philosophy as an educational straitjacket that demands curriculum conformity at the expense of individualism and experimentation. Reducing the purpose of college to producing graduates who can demonstrate their proficiency on national examinations risks our turning out intellectual clones whose creativity and imagination are suppressed, if not obliterated. Only the traditional approach promises to develop free-thinking citizens who cherish liberty and, therefore, are willing to question authority rather than just accept it blindly.

My realistic side, however, characterizes this line of reasoning as so much drivel. The colleges and universities in the United States represent the entire spectrum of values, from secular liberalism to religious fundamentalism. Students are free to choose the institution that best fits their individual preferences, and national value-added tests would not restrict their choice one iota. In fact, such a system would take some of the guesswork out of choosing a college, because it would show prospective students just how well an institution has done in delivering what it promises.

At this point, it's hard to tell how, if at all, the debate will be resolved. Institutions with no national reputation and few resources will probably embrace the value-added philosophy, since they have everything to gain by doing so and little to lose. Conversely, the better-known, better-endowed institutions will tend to stick with tradition, because they have little to gain and a lot to lose. If the students from the nation's top colleges do well on national standardized tests, they will simply be performing as expected. Should they do poorly, however, even in relative terms, their performance would be taken as a sign that the college or university was doing a poor job, and its reputation would suffer accordingly.

The unknown quantity so far is which side the institutions in the middle, the ones with "average" students and reputations and resources, will take in the controversy. They constitute the majority, after all, and it is their response that will determine the outcome of the debate. Should they tilt toward the value-added side, then evaluating educational results by numbers will become an integral part of the American college system. If, however, they stay on the side of tradition, then "value-added" will, like "relevance," become an interesting footnote in the history of higher education.

Reprinted by permission of the author.

 # Vocabulary

As you think about this essay, these definitions may be helpful to you:
1. **assessment**   a determination of the importance, size, or value
2. **hone**   to make more acute, intense, or effective
3. **traditionalists**   people who believe an inherited or established pattern of thought
4. **developmentalism**   belief in a process of growth, differentiation, or evaluation by successive changes
5. **cognitive**   capable of being reduced to empirical factual knowledge

 # Discussion Questions

1. What do advocates of the value-added philosophy consider to be the worth of a college education?
2. According to Cicarelli, how do traditionalists view higher education?
3. What are the differences between a specific, career-oriented education and a general, liberal arts education?
4. How does Cicarelli distinguish between romanticism and realism? Which do you think is the better view? Why?
5. Does Cicarelli think the question of value-added assessment will be resolved? How?

 # Suggestions for Your Journal

Write about your current thinking on the major question that Cicarelli addresses: Do you think of your college education as primarily a way to get a better job, or do you seek a more general liberal arts education? What factors might change your thinking on this important question?

You probably have some general education courses to complete as part of your intended degree program. Do you agree that they will help to make you knowledgeable about areas of study and thought that you would normally not be exposed to?

Assume that you have a younger relative or friend who will be entering college next year. Consider writing a journal entry in which you argue for or against general studies courses using that relative or friend as your primary audience.

An Uncluttered Perspective: The True, the Beautiful, and the Good

Howard Gardner

Howard Gardner is the John H. and Elizabeth A. Hobbs Professor in Cognition and Education at Harvard. The author of 18 books and several hundred articles, Gardner has argued that there are many kinds of intelligence, not just one, and therefore that there cannot be only one way to measure intelligence. This selection is from his book, *The Disciplined Mind: What All Students Should Understand.* In this essay, he describes three important ideals that should inspire education.

• • • • • • • • • • • • • • • • • •

I want everyone to focus on the content of an education—the meat and potatoes: on how that content should be presented, mastered, put to use, and passed along to others. Specifically, I believe that three very important concerns should animate education; these concerns have names and histories that extend far back into the past. There is the realm of truth—and its underside, what is false or indeterminable. There is the realm of beauty—and its absence in experiences or objects that are ugly or *kitschy.* And there is the realm of morality—what we consider to be good, and what we consider to be evil.

To make clearer what I include in these realms, let me mention three topics that I would like individuals to understand in their fullness. My example in the realm of truth is the theory of evolution, as first articulated by Charles Darwin and as elaborated upon by other scientists over the last one hundred and fifty years. This is an important area of science, with particular significance for a developmental psychologist like me. Unless one has some understanding of the key notions of species, variation, natural selection, adaptation, and the like (and how these have been discovered), unless one appreciates the perennial struggle among individuals (and populations) for survival in a particular ecological niche, one cannot understand the living world of which we are a part.

The processes of evolution are fascinating in their own right, as countless budding scientists have discovered. But such understanding has also become necessary if one is to participate meaningfully in contemporary society. Absent a grasp of evolution, we cannot think systematically about a whole range of topics that affect human beings today: the merits and perils of cloning; the advisability of genetic counseling, gene therapy, and various forms of *eugenics*; assertions that "lifelike entities" have been created computationally and that these entities evolve in a manner similar to organic matter; claims that human behavior is best explained by sociobiology or evolutionary psychology.

As my example in the realm of beauty, I select the music of Mozart: to be specific, his opera *The Marriage of Figaro*. This choice begins in the personal. I love classical music, and in particular the works of Mozart; for me, at least, they represent the pinnacle of beauty fashioned by human beings. I believe that everyone ought to gain an understanding of rich works like *Figaro*—their intricate artistic languages, their portrayals of credible characters with deeply felt human emotions, their evocation of the sweep of an era.

Again, such understanding is its own reward; millions of people all over the globe have been enriched by listening to Mozart or immersing themselves in other artistic masterpieces from diverse cultures. Moreover, a sophisticated grasp of Mozart's achievement can be brought to bear on unfamiliar works of art and craft and perhaps also inspire beautiful new creations. And such understanding also proves relevant to the decisions that we make as citizens; which arts, artists, and other creative individuals to support; how to support them; how best to encourage new works; whether there are artistic creations that ought to be censored or regulated, and, if so, by whom; whether the arts should be taught in school, after school, or not at all.

Finally, as my example in the realm of morality, I would like individuals to understand the sequence of events known as the Holocaust: the systematic killing of the Jews and certain other groups by the Nazis and others, before and especially during the Second World War. This event has personal significance, since my family came from Germany and several of its members were victims of the Holocaust. But every human being needs to understand what it is that human beings are capable of doing, sometimes in secret, sometimes with pride. And if the Holocaust is mostly an account of unprecedented human evil, there are scattered incidents of goodness and heroism even in that grim chapter.

Like the study of science and art, accounts of historical events can be intrinsically fascinating. But they have a wider significance. I believe that people are better able to chart their life course and make life decisions when they know how others have dealt with pressures and dilemmas—historically, contemporaneously, and in works of art. And only equipped with such understanding can we participate knowledgeably in contemporary discussions (and decisions) about the culpability of various individuals and countries in the Second World War. Only with such understanding can we ponder the responsibility of human beings everywhere to counter current efforts at genocide in Rwanda and the former Yugoslavia and to bring perpetrators to justice.

The understanding of striking examples of truth, beauty, and goodness is sufficiently meaningful for human beings that it can be justified in its own right. At the same time, however, such an understanding is also necessary for productive citizenship. The ways of thinking—the disciplines—that have developed over the centuries represent our best approach to almost any topic. Without such understanding, people cannot participate fully in the world in which they—*we* live.

One might think that at least some understanding of these well-known topics is widespread. It is therefore sobering to discover that the theory of evolution is considered to be false by one out of every two Americans, and even by 20 percent of science educators. According to the noted scientist Carl Sagan, only 9 percent of Americans accept that humans have evolved slowly from more ancient beings without any divine intervention. As for the Holocaust, about one-third of all Swedish high school students believe that the Holocaust did not take place. Comparable skepticism (if not outright denial) is expressed by various American groups; 20 percent of Americans admit that they do not know what happened in the Holocaust and 70 percent wish that they were better informed about it. Robert Simon, who teaches philosophy at Hamilton College, reports that anywhere from 10 to 20 percent of his American students cannot bring themselves to say that the Nazi attempt at genocide was wrong.

It is not difficult to anticipate a response to this trio of topics: How can one call this an education for all human beings? It is time-bound (the modern era); it is place-bound (Western Europe and places influenced by it); and it is even linked to the author's personal concerns.

"Right and not right," as they say, I would indeed be pleased if all human beings became deeply immersed in the themes of evolution, Mozart, and the Holocaust. There are worse ways to enlarge one's universe. *But—note well— these choices are not privileged, and certainly not uniquely so.* Within the West, there are numerous other scientific theories of importance (Newtonian mechanics and plate tectonics, to name just two examples); other singular artistic achievements (the works of Michelangelo or Rembrandt, Shakespeare or George Eliot); other morally tinged historical events (the French and Soviet revolutions; the American struggle over slavery). And within other cultural traditions, there are abundant examples of the true (these would include folk theories about healing or traditional Chinese medicine); the beautiful (Japanese ink and brush painting; African drum music); and good and evil (the precepts of *Jainism,* the stories of Pol Pot and Mao's Cultural Revolution, the generosity of bodhisattvas).

I am not contending, then, that everyone needs to be able to explain what constitutes a species or to discern the development of melodies and the intermingling romances in a work like *Figaro,* or to analyze the reasons why so many Germans were complicitous in the Holocaust. Rather, what I claim is that "an education for all human beings" needs to explore in some depth a set of key human achievements captured in the venerable phrase "the true, the beautiful, and the good."

Another possible objection. Aren't the categories "true," "beautiful," and "good" themselves time- and culture-bound? Again, this is a valid point, but not a decisive one. The articulated concepts of "truth," "beauty," and "goodness" reflect a philosophically oriented culture; indeed, our first records of explicit discussion of these virtues are the dialogues recorded by Plato in Greece nearly 2500 years ago. Other cultures have developed similar notions, although how they parse the three domains may well differ. However, the beliefs and practices of cultures—the beliefs and practices that they value, transmit, punish, or prohibit—reveal that each culture harbors specific views of how the world is and how it should (and should not) be. And these views embody implicit senses of truth, beauty, and morality.

There is another, more important reason for my endeavor. In the end, education has to do with fashioning certain kinds of individuals—the kinds of persons I (and others) desire the young of the world to become. I crave human beings who understand the world, who gain sustenance from such understanding, and who want—ardently, perennially—to alter it for the better. Such citizens can only come into existence if students learn to understand the world as it has been portrayed by those who have studied it most carefully and lived in it most thoughtfully; if they become familiar with the range—the summits, the valleys, the straight and meandering paths—of what other humans have achieved; and if they learn always to monitor their own lives in terms of human possibilities, including ones that have not been anticipated before....

I've selected my three textbook examples because they are familiar to me, and because they will be familiar to many readers. But I must repeat: there is nothing *sacrosanct* about this trio. Another book, on another day, could focus upon relativity, revolutions, and the *ragas* of southern India. And I would devour such a book....

Reprinted by permission of Simon & Schuster Adult Publishing Group from *The Disciplined Mind*, by Howard Gardner. © 1999 by Howard Gardner.

· ·

 Vocabulary

As you think about this essay, these definitions may be helpful to you:
1. **kitschy**   adjective form of *kitsch,* which means sentimentality or tastelessness in decoration or the arts
2. **eugenics**   the science that deals with the improvement of races and breeds through the control of hereditary factors and mating
3. **Jainism**   a Hindu religious sect that teaches reverence for wisdom and respect for animals
4. **sacrosanct**   very holy or sacred
5. **ragas**   musical works that follow a traditional form of the classical music of India

 Discussion Questions

1. What is the purpose of education, according to Gardner?
2. What does Gardner mean when he says "the range—the summits, the valleys, the straight and meandering paths—of what other humans have achieved ..."? Is his metaphor from geography useful?

3. Gardner chooses Charles Darwin's theory of evolution as his example of "the true." Explain why this is a controversial choice.
4. Gardner says that his selection of examples is based in his cultural framework. Using the examples as your clues, characterize Gardner's personal cultural background.

 Suggestions for Your Journal

You can apply Gardner's ideas to yourself in several ways. For example, select one new example for each of Gardner's three categories (the true, the good, and the beautiful) but draw them from a very different cultural context than the Western culture that Gardner refers to. Does modifying the cultural context confirm or dispute Gardner's ideas? Gardner's examples for "the true" are based in science. Can you give examples that are not based in modern scientific knowledge?

Assuming that Gardner is right about the purpose, or "end," of education, what steps do you anticipate you will have to take in order to reach that goal for yourself?

The Rise of the American University

Frank H. T. Rhodes

A geologist by training, Dr. Frank H. T. Rhodes was president of Cornell University for
18 years. This reading is from the first chapter of his 2001 book entitled *The Creation
of the Future: The Role of the American University*. In it, Rhodes discusses the
challenges confronting the modern research university in the 21st century, basing his
account on the past and present states of these remarkable and varied institutions.

The quality of life enjoyed by the people of the United States rests in substantial part on the broad foundation provided by the American university during the twentieth century. Higher education has been the doorway to advancement and participation for countless citizens and dozens of immigrant groups.
It has been the path to social attainment for millions from impoverished backgrounds, the generator of the nation's leaders in every area of life, the key to
vastly improved professional services from health care to technology. It has
been the foundation of growing national economic prosperity and manufacturing success, vast improvements in the products of agriculture and industry, and
undreamed-of access to new means of communication. And beyond all those
benefits, it has provided to successive generations the opportunity for meaningful careers, for service in a free society, and for access to the riches of human
experience, aspiration, and achievement. For all its shortcomings, the American
university has been an *unambiguous* influence for good. To a degree unknown
elsewhere, it has educated a steadily growing proportion of the population and
thus nurtured the democratic spirit and enlivened the nation. It has trained the
workforce, enriched the individual experience, and enlightened public life. It
has quickened the social conscience and empowered and inspired each rising
generation.

What accounts for the distinctive strength and singular contribution of the
American university? How did it come into existence? What forces have shaped
its development? What is possible is to pick some conspicuous milestones on
the path of development, turning points on the long, unfolding journey to the
present. Perhaps we might choose five universities to mark the path by which
the modern American university came into being: Bologna, Harvard, Virginia,
Cornell, and Johns Hopkins.

The University of Bologna

Lying at the base of the Apennine foothills, on the fertile plain between the
Reno and Savena Rivers of Italy is an *unassuming* city, carrying its ancient history lightly under a facade of mellow brick. It was here in the eleventh century
that the Western university, represented by the University of Bologna, came into

existence. Students from all over Europe came to Bologna, and by the middle of the twelfth century students are said to have numbered nearly ten thousand. The names and arms of those elected as representatives of their nations are still preserved in the ceiling of one of the city's oldest buildings.

The ancient university had no campus; it owned no buildings. It was a loose community of professors and students with the professors often teaching in their own apartments, paid by the students lecture by lecture for their services. It was five hundred years before the University of Bologna had its own buildings. So Bologna, like other older universities, was—to use modern jargon—a virtual learning community, long before it was formally recognized as an educational institution. Formal recognition came first from the chancellor of the local cathedral, who licensed instruction outside the *cloister,* but in time the reigning pope or emperor recognized the older and more distinguished institutions as *studia generale*, whose graduates had the right to teach at any institution, without further examination.

A flowering of legal studies in Bologna about the year 1000, spurred in part by legal disputes between the pope and the emperor, led to the rise of the university. So studies in both canon and civil law flourished side by side. By about 1200, faculties of medicine and philosophy (the liberal arts) came into being, while theology followed later.

Bologna is not the oldest university-like institution. Salerno, for example, had a famed school of medicine at least as early as the ninth century. Centers of higher learning were associated with some of the larger mosques of the Islamic world. But Bologna was the first to develop a comprehensive range of studies, balanced faculties, both professional and liberal arts, and perhaps the first to create student colleges and a deliberative assembly, presided over by a rector.

The founding of Bologna was followed by a remarkable growth of universities in other Italian cities—among them Reggio nell'Emilia, Modena, Vicenza, Padua, and Naples. Elsewhere, in such places as Paris, Oxford, Cambridge, Valladolid, Salamanca, Seville, Coimbra, Prague, Cracow, Vienna, Heidelberg, Cologne, Louvain, Leipzig, and St. Andrews, others followed. In a span of two centuries, the university came into being across the length and breadth of Europe.

Harvard University

In 1636, the new institution reached North America, when the first American college was established in New Towne, Massachusetts, lying on the Charles River across from the city of Boston. It was in this same place, on July 3, 1775, that Washington was to take command of the Continental army. The general court of the Massachusetts Colony voted £400 to create a "schoale or colledge." Two years later, the site of its founding was renamed "Cambridge," in honor of the university where many leaders of the colony had been educated. John Harvard, a Cambridge graduate and Puritan minister, left half of his estate ... and his library of 260 books to the fledgling college. The purpose of Harvard's founders is touchingly summarized in their statement: "After God had carried us safe to

New England and we had builded our houses, provided necessaries for our livelihood, rear'd convenient places for Gods worship and settled the Civill Government; One of the next things we longed for, and looked after was to advance Learning and perpetuate it to Posterity; dreading to leave an illiterate Ministry to the Churches, when our present Ministers shall lie in the Dust." In 1642, Harvard awarded its first degrees—the degree of bachelor of arts—to nine young men. The charter of 1650 established the college for "the advancement of all good literature, arts and the sciences" and "the education of the English and Indian youth in knowledge and godlynes."

The foundation of Harvard was followed by the creation of other colonial colleges. The student experience at these various colleges was remarkably similar, including compulsory attendance at the college chapel, pursuit of the classical curriculum, participation in the extracurricular literary societies (which encouraged debates, readings, lectures, and other activities), and the senior capstone course in moral philosophy—the "great glory" of the curriculum—taught generally by the president.

As the young nation grew in numbers and expanded its frontiers, it faced a steadily growing need for both educated citizens and trained professionals, and public funding was contributed by a number of states—Virginia, North Carolina, and Michigan among them—to meet this need.

The University of Virginia

This led to the creation of public universities, funded largely by the states. The best known of these—though not the most typical—is the University of Virginia, founded by Thomas Jefferson at Charlottesville, in the shadow of the Blue Ridge Mountains. The campus echoes the Jeffersonian dream. Jefferson planned every aspect of its development, choosing the site, planning the layout of the "academical village": designing the buildings, creating the curriculum, selecting books for the library, appointing the founding faculty, and serving as the first rector. "Mr. Jefferson's University" was chartered in 1819, and opened in 1825 with eight members of the faculty. Forty years later, it was second only to Harvard in size.

The University of Virginia had two distinctive features. Unlike other universities of its time, it had no religious affiliation and required no religious assent of its students.

It also broke from the classical curriculum, which was then dominant, by creating eight schools, each headed by a professor: ancient languages, modern languages, anatomy and medicine, law, natural history, mathematics, natural philosophy, and moral philosophy. These schools, designed to grow as funds permitted, were later to be joined by commerce, diplomacy, and manufacture. This rich assortment of offerings was to allow an elective program of study, in contrast to the rigid requirements of other colleges. The architecture matched the curriculum, with each school housed in its own pavilion, with students living on the campus, "in watchful proximity" to their professors' residences.

Cornell University

But the massive growth of public funding of higher education began with the Morrill Act of 1862, signed into law by Abraham Lincoln, which provided grants of federal lands to the states for the establishment of public universities and colleges. These "land-grant colleges and universities" were to provide for "the liberal and practical education of the industrial classes in the several pursuits and professions of life." This act led to the creation in every state of a new kind of college that was distinctively American. Perhaps no university is more typical of the fusion of scholarly inspiration and worldly practicality, on the one hand, and of the joint power of private philanthropy and public expenditure, on the other, than Cornell University.

Frederick Rudolph, in his magisterial book on the university curriculum, describes the impact of the founding of Cornell as follows:

> Cornell brought together in creative combination a number of dynamic ideas under circumstances that turned out to be incredibly productive. Andrew D. White, its first president, and Ezra Cornell, who gave it his name, turned out to be the developers of the first American university and therefore the agents of revolutionary curricular reform. Ezra Cornell, whose wealth and imagination allowed him to be Western Union's largest stockholder, turned these same assets into a few words that transformed the American college curriculum: "I would found an institution where any person can find instruction in any study." Andrew D. White, the university's first president, translated a classical education at Yale, scholarly training in European universities, and experience on Henry Tappan's faculty at the University of Michigan into a resolution to create a great American university (Rudolph 116).*

So, with the founding of Cornell, a new kind of university came into existence. When Ezra Cornell spoke of "any person" he meant poor as well as rich, as he provided work and scholarships; women as well as men, as he built a women's college as an integral part of the university; "the whole colored race and the whole female sex" in White's words (Bishop 42). Ezra Cornell was equally serious when he spoke of "any study," leaping over the weary debate on the traditional classical curriculum in relation to more modern studies. Law and languages, agriculture and architecture, engineering and English jostled together, with the student encouraged to make informed choices within a range of nine "departments" broadly aimed at professional careers, while the division of literature, science, and the arts allowed nonprofessional students five routes toward a general course of study. "Discipline comes," White declared, "by studies which are loved, not by studies that are loathed" (Rudolph 120).

"In walking away from choice and embracing all alternatives, White made an American decision consistent with Ezra Cornell's democratic intentions and

---

*Rhodes uses a variant of APA (American Psychological Association) style to cite references. He gives an author's last name and a page number within parentheses in the text and lists his sources in a "Works Cited" section at the end of the article—ED.

the imprecise, but clear obligations of the Act of 1862," Rudolph wrote. "Practical vocationalism, scientific research, applied technology, classical learning, and university scholarship all found a welcome" (Rudolph 117–19). "The Cornell curriculum brought into imaginative balance the openness of American society, the temporary nature of its directions and opportunities; it multiplied truth into truths, a limited few professions into an endless number of new self-respecting ways of moving into the middle class" (Bishop 190–91).

Ezra Cornell and Andrew Dickson White insisted on one other concept; their university was to be *nonsectarian,* with a board of trustees in which members of no one denomination should have a majority. So Cornell was to become hospitable to all religious persuasions, but committed to no one denomination.

Johns Hopkins University

To the Morrill Act of 1862, two other pieces of federal legislation were later added: the Hatch Act of 1887 provided federal funds for research and experiment stations, while the Smith-Lever Act of 1914 provided additional funds for extension programs, designed to bring to their communities the benefits of new campus-based research.

But when Cornell was founded, there was precious little research to extend. The universities of the mid-nineteenth century were teaching institutions, in which scholarship, though prized, was generally understood to mean high competence in one's field, whether in theory or in practice. In contrast, the German universities of this period became centers of research and graduate study, spurred on, to some extent, by industry's need for technical and scientific research. Many of the professors of America's new universities had themselves been students in these German graduate schools, and, almost imperceptibly, the Germanic scholarly influence, and the new knowledge it created, seeped into the American curriculum.

Our fifth landmark is Johns Hopkins in Baltimore, Maryland. It was Baltimore's importance as a port and center of communication that led indirectly to its distinctive contribution to the growth of the American university. Its excellent harbor had long made Baltimore a leading shipping center, while its position on the *National Road* contributed to its early eighteenth-century growth. But the completion of the Erie Canal threatened its prosperity, and a group of wealthy local investors chartered the Baltimore & Ohio Railroad—the first public U.S. railroad—to strengthen its access to the west. Among these investors was Johns Hopkins (1795–1873), who gave his fortune of $7 million and his name to a new university; Johns Hopkins's first president, Daniel Coit Gilman, made advanced scholarship, scientific research, and graduate study the university's main purpose, though it also included an undergraduate college. The Hopkins model—serious scholarship, graduate study, the Ph.D. degree, the specialized academic major and expansive minor, a pervasive spirit of inquiry and an earnestness of purpose that went with it—soon influenced the new universities and aspiring colleges, both private and public.

"The presidents of state universities knew that they could not be universities in reality until the spirit of Johns Hopkins had become as pervasive as that of Cornell," concluded Rudolph (Rudolph 131). Opened to great acclaim in 1876, Hopkins in its preoccupation with research served as the model for a number of other embryonic universities—Clark University, Catholic University of America, and the University of Chicago among them. But though total immersion in research to the exclusion of substantial concern for the well-being of undergraduate students and professional studies proved an unsuccessful recipe, Hopkins's great contribution to the development of the American university was to inject a spirit of advanced study, serious inquiry, and scholarly emphasis into the Cornell model of wide access, expansive scholarly and professional programs, and institutional autonomy. Its influence remains strong today.

The Contemporary University

By the final quarter of the nineteenth century the general form of the American university had taken shape. It had become a learning community with a largely residential campus, embracing both a college of liberal arts and sciences and graduate and professional schools, devoted to both teaching and research, committed to widening access and expanding public service. That structure continues into the twenty-first century.

The contemporary American university, however, is a distinctive product of the twentieth century and especially of the last fifty years. There are several particular trends that have altered the shape, though not the structure, of the university.

The university has seen a deliberate growth in social inclusiveness, with a major expansion in the proportion of the traditional college-age population attending college and a more recent but rapid increase in lifelong learning, including both continuing professional education and distance learning.

There has been a growth in number and size of institutions to accommodate this growing student enrollment and the differentiation of institutional style to respond to differing educational needs and opportunities.

The university has seen increasing intellectual inclusiveness, with growing professionalism both in the "established professions" such as law, medicine, and engineering and in new ones such as architecture, city planning, and business, as well as the specialization and growing professionalization of the traditional disciplines.

Finally, universities have experienced the disproportionate expansion of science and the science-based professions, supported by infusion of federal funding for research, and their growing influence in shaping the culture of the campus.

In 1900, only 237,592 men and women attended college, about 4 percent of the college-age population. By 1940, total enrollment had reached 1.5 million, about 12 percent of the college-age population. The passage of the G.I. Bill at the end of World War II represented a national decision to extend the benefits of a college education to a greater proportion of the population, offering support to returning veterans, and thus giving a major boost to college attendance. By 1998, a record 67 percent of the graduating high school seniors were enrolled in college, most of them as full-time students at four-year institutions.

Today's 4,096 colleges and universities represent a bewildering variety of institutions, and that huge number does not include another 6,737 vocational institutions. All of them, however, have deliberately improved access for students and have sought to increase the enrollment from groups previously underrepresented. Flexible attendance schedules, financial aid, and a wealth of institutional programs and types have facilitated this access. Of the 14.6 million students enrolled in universities and colleges, more than 5 million are enrolled in community colleges, which offer open access, remedial education, and a vast range of programs to those from nontraditional backgrounds or those who have not pursued or qualified in the typical precollege curriculum, and they also provide well-established transfer opportunities to four-year colleges and universities. As colleges and universities have increased in number and size, one might suppose there would also have been an increase in variety and richness of offerings. In some colleges, there has. The rapid increase in community and junior colleges reflects a recognition of the value of providing technical skills linked to local employment opportunities, as well as more general educational offerings. In these colleges there is a rich variety and creative experiment. They are one of the nation's unwritten success stories.

Increased inclusiveness involved more than attendance ratios. Thirty years ago, universities set out to make their campuses look more like America. It was a mission supported, monitored, and overseen by federal and state governments on the basis of widespread agreement on this threefold premise: education provides a foundation for personal growth, professional training, and social mobility; women and minority groups have been historically underrepresented on college campuses and in professional and leadership roles in society; and universities should pursue affirmative policies to recruit these groups and so remedy past underrepresentation.

Although the concept of affirmative action is now the topic of litigation and lively public debate, the striking growth in numbers of women and previously underrepresented minorities in both higher education and public life is evidence of the success of this venture. Also notable are the growing presence of students from families of lower income levels and the growth in numbers of female and minority faculty. Until recently, university admissions were guided by the *Bakke* case, a 5–4 decision of the Supreme Court that prohibited discrimination by race, but allowed race to be used as one positive criterion, among others, in college admissions.

Many factors have shaped the history of the American university over the last century. It would be rash, of course, to suppose that any one factor has been decisive. Quite different patterns of organization and oversight, for example, have been used by the various states in their support of the great flagship public universities. But collectively these features have defined the characteristics of the most successful universities. Unplanned, opportunistic, well governed, well led, as conservative in some respects as it has been entrepreneurial in others, the university is one of the great success stories of America's twentieth-century history.

Works Cited

Bishop, Morris. *A History of Cornell*. Ithaca, NY: Cornell University Press, 1962.
Rudolph, Frederick. *Curriculum: A History of the American Undergraduate Course of Study Since 1636*. San Francisco: Jossey-Bass, 1977.

From Frank H. T. Rhodes, *The Creation of the Future: The Role of the American University* (Ithaca and London: Cornell University Press, 2001).

• •

 Vocabulary

As you think about this essay, these definitions may be helpful to you:
1. **unambiguous**   having a clearly defined meaning
2. **unassuming**   modest, not pretentious
3. **cloister**   a monastery or convent
4. **nonsectarian**   not affiliated with or restricted to a specific religious group
5. **National Road**   Today called U.S. Route 40, this was the first highway built entirely with federal funds. The road was authorized by Congress in 1806 and construction began in Cumberland, Maryland in 1811.

 Discussion Questions

1. Rhodes correctly points out that religious institutions were highly important in the history of universities. Cite some examples from his account. Then discuss whether your own college or university has a religious history or affiliation and what that means in the modern life of your school.
2. A subject of debate in colleges is "What should be taught?" The curriculum, or course of study, at most universities includes some requirements intended to broaden your general understanding and other requirements to provide depth and focus for some part of your training. How does this work at your institution? What is the right balance between these components?
3. The first president of Cornell University, Andrew D. White, is quoted as saying, "Discipline comes by studies which are loved, not by studies that are loathed." Does this mean students should never be required to study subjects that they don't like? What do you think he meant?
4. Talk about some of the changes Rhodes identifies that have come about in the contemporary university. In your view, are they improvements?

 Suggestions for Your Journal

Write about why the history of universities and specifically of your university or college matters to you. Many individual colleges often speak about their traditions: What are some that you have learned about at your school? Do they matter as history?

UNIT SUMMARY

In this unit you have examined many different perspectives about college as an American institution and its meaning and value to you as a student. The following questions can help you think about the viewpoints represented in these readings.

Summary Questions

1. What is a liberal education according to the authors in this unit? How will it prepare you to become a lifelong learner?
2. What are some general goals and objectives of higher education according to these readings? How do they compare with your personal reasons for being in college?
3. Many college students have traversed your campus in the past. What aspects of the history and traditions of your campus are most interesting and important to you?

Suggested Writing Assignments

1. Write an essay about your reasons for being in college. In it describe five goals you wish to accomplish during your first year.
2. How is college different from high school (e.g., teachers, assignments, classroom behavior, course content, learning expectations)? Write about your most difficult academic adjustment.
3. Interview a college teacher in whose class you have learned a great deal. Discuss learning from this teacher's perspective. How does this teacher think learning his or her subject matter can be useful in life?

Suggested Readings

Bloom, Allan. *The Closing of the American Mind.* New York: Simon & Schuster, 1987.

Gardner, Howard. *Multiple Intelligences: The Theory in Practice.* New York: Basic Books, 1993.

Hutchins, Robert M. "The Autobiography of an Uneducated Man." In Robert M. Hutchins, *Education for Freedom,* 1–18. Baton Rouge: Louisiana State University Press, 1943.

Rudolph, Frederick. *The American University and College: A History.* New York: Knopf, 1962.

Willie, Charles. *The Ivory and Ebony Towers.* Lexington, MA: Heath, 1981.

What Can I Expect from College and How Will I Change?

What we anticipate seldom occurs;
what we least expect generally happens.

—Benjamin Disraeli

What do you expect will happen to you during your college years? The college years are known for the personal and social changes that take place in individuals. New students are likely to notice, first, the academic challenges in the classroom and the social opportunities present at every turn. For many, the increased difficulty of college course work comes as a surprise, and the social freedom, which may have been predictable, is more overwhelming than expected.

Furthermore, students usually expect that college will prepare them for a career and will accomplish this in some very specific ways. Students often expect a direct-line or one-to-one relationship between what they study in college and the job that follows graduation. Direct relationships do occur in such fields as engineering and nursing, but more often, college courses teach general skills, not specific job tasks. Students who expect specific training may not see the relevance or importance of this more general instruction.

As time passes, they may become even more confused. For many first-year students, uncertainty about their future career and life is unsettling and worrisome. Their expectations for clear-cut decisions regarding their future may not be fulfilled.

According to many student developmental theorists, these unsettling feelings are common and can be considered normal. Most students need time to master certain developmental tasks that lead to a mature way of thinking and being. For example, as far as personal development is concerned, students need to cope with leaving home, perhaps for the first time. Often both parents and students find this transition difficult.

Some of the best features of college life are the opportunities to make new friends and to meet people who are different from yourself. Some students may find it easy to strike up new friendships, while others struggle with shyness and uncertainty. However, in time these relationships can become one of the most rewarding aspects of college life.

In classes, students are thrust into new experiences with demanding course work. They need to master rapidly moving and complex course content, and some will find they need help with basic learning skills. Academic freedom and the occasional need to drop a course may be new to many students. Some think they can succeed if they work harder, a strategy that doesn't always work. A student's expectations for academic success may take a few detours.

All these developmental concerns are in some sense predictable, as the essays in this section demonstrate. Gordon's essay outlining the theories of Perry and Chickering describes the importance of mastering the various developmental tasks. Another essay outlines how one professor (Finster) has adapted his teaching methods to challenge this development in his students.

Family members can be an important support group when students enter college. Bell describes the experiences of both students and their parents during this transition. The essay by Newman and Newman deals with the feelings of loneliness that some students may experience, especially as they begin college. Sears offers suggestions for ways to become personally effective in college, work, and life.

Setting goals, both short-term and long-term, is an important element in the evolution of this highly personal process. Your expectations for what you want to receive and accomplish during the college years will probably change. It will be natural for you to expand and refine your expectations. The essays in this unit may give you some appreciation for the experiences and tasks that others consider important as you progress toward graduation.

The Developing College Student

Virginia N. Gordon

Virginia N. Gordon, who has been a college teacher and administrator, is best known as a researcher, academic adviser, and counselor for undecided students. She received her Ph.D. in counseling from The Ohio State University.

This essay describes two theoretical perspectives on how students change intellectually and personally during the college years. These theories are based on what students have experienced and related to researchers through personal interviews.

• • • • • • • • • • • • • • • •

By entering college you begin a very exciting and challenging period in your life. Although it may be difficult for you to imagine now, think about yourself on the day you graduate with a college degree. In addition to being a college graduate, what kind of person will you be? How do you expect to change during your college years?

After careful research, many theorists have described how students change and develop throughout the college experience. Social scientists who have studied college students have discovered some patterns and common themes in the way they change. One such theorist, Professor William Perry, of Harvard University, has studied how college students change intellectually and ethically. He developed a scheme to describe the development of the thinking and reasoning processes that takes place naturally as students mature and grow intellectually. Each phase of this development may be likened to a set of filters through which students see the world around them.

Dualistic students see the world in polar terms; that is, they believe that all questions have a right answer and, therefore, that all answers are either right or wrong. Such students are happiest when they find simplistic answers to their questions about the world, and they want to view their teachers and advisers as experts who can give them the right answer. They believe that hard work and obedience pay off. They depend on others to make important decisions for them. Many freshmen begin their college experience seeing through this dualistic lens.

As students develop, however, Perry says they become capable of more complex reasoning and dissatisfied with simplistic answers. They are moving into a "*multiplistic*" view of the world. They begin to see and understand cause and effect relationships. Diversity becomes legitimate because they realize that no one has all the answers. They believe everyone has the right to his or her opinion. They still, however, depend on others to make decisions for them. Some freshmen and sophomores view their experiences through this multiplistic lens.

Perry identifies the next phase, "relativism," as the time when students begin to synthesize diverse and complex elements of reasoning. They are able to view uncertainty as legitimate. They see *themselves* as the principal agent in decision making and acknowledge that they must not only make their own decisions, but also take responsibility for those decisions, regardless of how well or badly those decisions may turn out. Many juniors and seniors fall into this category of "relativistic" thinkers. Because the emphasis in Perry's system is always on how college students tend to think and reason, his theory is called a theory of *cognitive* development.

For Perry, the most advanced phase of cognitive development is one in which students make a commitment to a personal identity and its content and style. Each develops a sense of being "in" one's self, along with an awareness that growth is always transpiring, that change is inevitable and healthy. Students also make a commitment to a defined career area and are able to develop a lifestyle that is appropriate for them. Many students continue in this state of personal growth and development after college.

Through his theory of cognitive development, Perry helps us understand how students view, react to, and assimilate knowledge as they progress through college. It is important to recognize that while college experiences encourage and foster this development, non-college students also mature and develop in much the same way. (It is also important to remember that any theoretical model, no matter how carefully established, is just that: a model. Judgments about how individuals may be measured against a model require great care. And, as you see later, other models are also well established.)

Perry theorizes that growth occurs in surges, with pauses between the surges when some students might need to detach themselves for a while, while others even retreat to the comfort of their past ways of thinking. Ask five seniors to look back on how they have changed intellectually. While they will be able to reflect on their intellectual development in unique and personal terms, the patterns of growth that Perry describes will usually be evident. However, it sometimes takes courage to confront the risks each forward movement requires. Every student has the freedom to choose what kind of person he or she will become, but the forces of growth, according to Perry, will not be denied.

Developmental Tasks

Another theorist, Arthur Chickering, suggests that college students develop in an orderly way on many dimensions: intellectually, physically, psychologically and socially. He describes several developmental tasks, or *"vectors,"* through which students move during their college years. A vector, according to Chickering, is a developmental task that (1) has specific content, (2) shows up at certain times in our lives, and (3) takes two to seven years to resolve. The process is ongoing throughout our lives, and even though we may resolve a task once, it may resurface later. These tasks build on each other; how we resolve one may affect the ones that follow. While these tasks develop in order, they may also be concurrent, so we may be dealing with several at one time. The seven developmental tasks that Chickering has proposed are described next.

1. Achieving Competence

The first task is achieving competence. College students need to achieve competence in several areas: intellectually, physically, and interpersonally. Chickering likens this to a three-tined pitchfork, since all three happen simultaneously.

Intellectual competence involves the skill of using one's mind in "comprehending, analyzing and synthesizing." It means learning how to learn and acquiring knowledge. Most students enroll in college in order to develop intellectual competence. They begin to develop good study habits and the skills of critical thinking and reasoning. They will be able to appreciate and integrate many points of view in their thinking. Ideally, they will enjoy learning for its own sake and feel the excitement of entering new realms of knowledge. Physical competence involves manual skills as well. The recreational value of, and prestige associated with, athletic skills or the creative value of arts and crafts are important to many students. More and more we are concerned that lifelong fitness is important. Recreational skills and interests that one develops in college continue throughout life. Colleges provide many physical facilities for students who seek to develop competency in this area.

Probably the greatest concern of many students is how to develop interpersonal and social competence. They feel a need for communication skills, such as listening and responding appropriately, so they can relate to others individually or in groups. Learning the social graces and how to interact with peers is an important task that most students accomplish early in their college years. Much of this learning happens as a result of observation, feedback from other students, and experience.

When these three competencies are achieved, students feel a *sense* of competence; they sense that they can cope with whatever comes. They are confident of their ability to achieve successfully whatever they set out to do. They respond to new challenges by integrating old learning with new. The task of developing competence is especially important during the freshman year.

2. Managing Emotions

Two major emotional impulses that need to be managed during college are sex and aggression. Maturity implies that legitimate ways have been found to express anger and hate. Sexual impulses are more insistent than ever. Students feel pressured to find answers to questions concerning interpersonal relationships. They move from being controlled by the external rules of their heritage to control by internal norms of self. (Students from rural areas may have different sets of rules, for example, than inner-city students.) Many students are still controlled by the external norms of their peers. Exaggerated displays of emotion are not uncommon: in the past, for example, college students initiated panty raids or held contests for swallowing the greatest number of goldfish.

People often feel boredom, tension and anxiety as normal emotions while their impulsive feelings need to be controlled. Becoming aware of positive emotions such as sympathy, yearning, wonder and awe is also important.

Eventually, students learn to be controlled by their own internal set of norms. Achieving competence in the management of emotions means moving from an awareness of the legitimacy of emotions, to acting on them, to controlling them internally.

3. Moving Through Autonomy Toward Interdependence
Another important task for new college students during the first months of college is to achieve independence. A student may be hesitant to try certain new experiences or to approach new people. Such a student is trying to become independent but, as Chickering says, is like a "hog on ice," a little shaky at first. For probably the first time in their experience, many students may be living with no restraints or outside pressures, with no one to tell them when to study or to be home by 11 o'clock. As they act on their own, they may flounder at first. Beginning students may wonder, for example, why they have so much free time. They attend classes for only three or four hours a day and then may squander the rest of the day—until they realize the importance of quality study time.

The student who achieves *emotional* independence has learned to be free of the continual need for reassurance, affection or approval. Such a student has learned to deal with authority figures and feels comfortable with professors or other very important people on campus. There is less reliance on parents and more on friends and nonparental adults. Achieving *instrumental* independence means students can do things for themselves that parents used to do, such as washing the laundry or managing money. They are able to solve problems and use resources on their own.

When the student finally comes to recognize and accept *inter*dependence, the boundaries of personal choice become clearer and the ranges within which one can give and receive become more settled. Autonomous students feel less need for support from their parents and begin to understand that parents need them as much as they need their parents. They begin to see their parents for what they are: middle-aged people with weaknesses just like themselves. Becoming autonomous is a very important task for freshmen to accomplish.

4. Developing Mature Interpersonal Relationships
Developing mature relationships means that students become less anxious and less defensive, more friendly, spontaneous and respectful. They are more willing to trust and are more independent. They develop the capacity for mature intimacy. They can participate in healthy relationships that incorporate honesty and responsiveness. They finally realize that perfect parents don't exist and that Prince or Princess Charming is not coming to sweep them off their feet. They also have an increased tolerance for people culturally different from themselves. They have acquired increased empathy and altruism and enjoy diversity. They are able to develop mature relationships with many types of people.

5. Establishing Identity
The fifth vector, according to Chickering, is establishing identity. This task is really the sum of the first four vectors: developing competence, managing emo-

tions, developing autonomy through interdependence, and developing mature interpersonal relationships. Success at achieving identity will often hinge on how these former tasks have been accomplished. Studies suggest that students generally achieve a coherent, mature sense of identity during their sophomore or junior years.

In addition to these inner changes, students need to clarify their conceptions of physical needs, personal appearance, and sex-appropriate roles and behavior. They identify a personal life-style that is theirs. Once such a sense of identity is achieved, other major vectors may be approached. Establishing an identity is the hinge on which future development depends.

6. Developing Purpose

Developing purpose is the vector related to career choice. The questions to be faced for this vector are not only "Who Am I?" but also "Where Am I Going?" Interests tend to stabilize; vocational exploration becomes a serious task. A general orientation toward a career area is achieved first, and then more specific career decisions are made. Students begin to formulate plans and integrate vocational and lifestyle considerations into those plans. An initial commitment to a career goal is made with the move into adulthood.

7. Developing Integrity

Students also need to clarify a personally valid set of beliefs that have some internal consistency. This happens in three stages, according to Chickering. Their values are first (1) humanized, then (2) personalized, and then (3) their beliefs and actions begin to suit each other. During childhood, students assimilate their parents' values. In college, students begin to examine these inherited values to see if they fit them personally. Some values may be rejected while others may be retained. The student's task is to personalize these values by achieving behavior consistent with them and being willing to stand up for what he or she strongly believes. Such a degree of commitment leads to congruence between one's beliefs and values and one's actions. Standards for assessing personal actions are set and are used as guides for all behavior.

Working through these seven developmental tasks is crucial to the college student's successful passage into mature adulthood. How will you be different on graduation day? I hope that you will have no regrets about missed opportunities to become involved in your own development. The college environment offers an almost unbelievable assortment of opportunities in and outside the classroom. There are many resources, including people, who stand ready to challenge and support you. As you move into the world you will be willing to assert the convictions and values you carefully (and sometimes traumatically) learned during your college years. Knowing that everyone moves through these passages of development and that change is inevitable can help you see the more difficult times as periods of growth. In this way you will be able to react positively and productively.

Reprinted by permission of the author.

 # Vocabulary

As you think about this essay, these definitions may be helpful to you:
1. **dualistic**   consisting of two irreducible elements or modes; a way of thinking that sees issues as black or white, rather than as shades of gray
2. **multiplistic**   numerous or various
3. **cognitive**   involving the act of knowing, including both awareness and judgment
4. **vector**   a course or direction
5. **instrumental**   serving as a means, agent, or tool; in this essay, instrumental independence is the ability to live and work on your own

 # Discussion Questions

1. What aspect of student development does Perry's scheme address? What is its primary thesis? Do all students fit these patterns?
2. How does a dualistic student view the world?
3. How does Perry describe commitment, which he considers the most advanced phase of cognitive development? How do you reach commitment?
4. What are the seven developmental tasks of college students as proposed by Chickering? Which are most relevant to first-year, traditional-age college students?
5. What, says Chickering, is required to develop an identity? How are the last two tasks of developing purpose and integrity related to identity?

 # Suggestions for Your Journal

Sketch your own intellectual development from the time you were a child until now. Where do you think you fit into Perry's scheme? Have you ever consciously experienced a period of intellectual growth? How would you describe it?

Which of Chickering's developmental tasks have you completed? Which will be the most difficult to master?

Freshmen Can Be Taught to Think Creatively, Not Just Amass Information

David C. Finster

Dr. David C. Finster is professor of Chemistry and chair of the Chemistry Department at Wittenberg University of Springfield, Ohio. He has been a recipient of the Wittenberg Distinguished Teaching Award.

Finster describes how he applies Perry's theory of cognitive development to his teaching methods and how he uses student-based teaching in his classes. He challenges his students to think about *how* they solve a chemistry problem in addition to finding the solution.

Not long after I embarked on my teaching career, I realized that to be an effective teacher one must first know something about learning. To try to convey knowledge with no understanding of the process of receiving it is to forget the principles of communication. My questions about learning led me to the work of the educational psychologist Jean Piaget on *cognition* in children. His insights, which beautifully explain how children learn to think about problems and to make sense of the world around them, were critical for me. Indeed, understanding how to foster a child's natural growth from simplistic to more complex and abstract thinking processes seems to me vital for any teacher.

But what about college freshmen? Are they just "big children"? In the sense that they are still wrestling with the turmoils of adolescence, now compounded by the independence and responsibility of college life, perhaps so. But in the sense that they are making the transition to what Piaget calls formal *operational* thought, they are not.

A clearer view of cognition in college students came to me from the work of William Perry. He studied the college experience through lengthy interviews with students over several years and then formulated a "developmental scheme" based on his findings. His charting of the intellectual and ethical growth of college students reveals much about the processes of learning and teaching.

Perry's scheme describes progressive stages of development in young people of the ability to comprehend the difference between information and knowledge, to understand the roles of teacher and student, and to make considered decisions in resolving life's simple and complex dilemmas. At the first stage, they are "dualists," with a right-or-wrong view of the world. They see knowledge as a collection of facts to be memorized and authority figures as having all the answers. At the middle stage, they develop a more complex worldview, recognizing that there can be a variety of opinions and viewpoints on an issue. Later they become capable of evaluating those different perspectives through reasoning and judgment, and, finally, they are able to make decisions and commitments based on their own value system. This latter stage is crucial in the formulation of individual identity.

Perry notes nine distinct developmental "positions" along the way to maturity, which must be gone through sequentially—that is, one cannot advance from the second to the fifth position without going through the third and fourth. Most students come to college in "late *dualism,*" or at the third position, believing that the purpose of education is to accumulate information and that people in authority have the right answers. Their ability at that stage to see multiple perspectives on an issue is very limited. The way to promote their progress along Perry's scheme is to challenge them to think of the stage just beyond their current level while providing the necessary support to help them do so.

A good teacher seeks not only to build students' knowledge of the content of a discipline but also to teach them to think critically as they learn. The second aim may explain the difficulty some students have in learning at the college level. Critical thinking—that is, the ability to evaluate different perspectives and challenge assumptions—comes at a stage in the Perry model that is beyond students in the "dualist" position. Teachers naturally prefer teaching their disciplines at that level, however, and many expect their students to welcome this broadening aspect of their education. Dualists, on the other hand, see education differently.

A problem arises when the gap between where students are in their intellectual development and where their teachers teach is too large. Most teachers are aware of the gap, but find that time-honored teaching methods do not readily bridge it. Some choose to ignore it, because they are loath to "water down" their courses. Others eliminate it by reducing their goals to a more elementary level and teaching information rather than thinking skills.

The latter tactic is encouraged in our educational system, because content is readily measured by testing, and so "mastery" of a subject can be easily demonstrated. Unfortunately, teachers who resort to it *entrench* their students in the early stages of development by reinforcing a simplistic view of education.

An alternative solution to the problem would be to adopt a developmental instructional method. Using that approach, a teacher begins by recognizing where students are in their ability to understand the purpose of education, to see a difference between information and knowledge, and to think for themselves in the classroom. The aim is then to foster their intellectual growth from that point on.

A favorite saying of mine is that the purpose of college is to calm the disturbed and disturb the calm. Part of good teaching is challenging the way students think, while at the same time providing them with mental and emotional tools to resolve the dilemmas they face. In this manner, we help them grow *incrementally* and become mature adults.

Developmental-instruction theory holds that success in fostering intellectual growth depends in large part on the degree of personal interaction in the educational environment. Small classes are therefore important, because in addition to avoiding the impersonal atmosphere of large lectures, they allow a two-way exchange between teacher and student. Such exchanges play a vital part in active participatory learning and in the development of critical-thinking skills.

Another tenet of development theory is that the first year of college is crucial in tapping students' potential to grow intellectually. So, while large sections of introductory courses are efficient in terms of allocating teaching resources, the freshman year is the worst time for "mass education" because it reinforces the early stage idea that the purpose of education is to amass information.

As a chemistry professor, I have adopted developmental theory in teaching science courses. I begin by challenging the notion that science is Truth—a classic dualistic belief woven into our culture from the time of Galileo and Newton. There are multiple perspectives possible in many aspects of science, and, while I point out that in some cases only one answer to a scientific question is the right one, I present alternative perspectives as often as I can in class. Discussing applications of science that both create and solve special dilemmas provides ample opportunity for examining different perspectives.

In teaching my chemistry classes, I focus on process as much as on content. *How* one solves a problem in chemistry is as important as the solution, particularly when one is learning. I therefore avoid multiple-choice tests in favor of examinations that force my students both to solve the problem and to explain how they approached it. I try to lecture in an interactive way also, by engaging students in the process of thinking through an argument rather than just presenting them with the facts and theories. They begin to become educated scientists by discussing historical and current scientific issues in class, in assignments, and on tests.

Writing is a well-recognized method of exposing students' thought processes to themselves, and I assign my students term papers that require them to investigate a contemporary, controversial issue in science and then present their conclusions clearly. In fact, I "think developmentally," even when I am prescribing the format for writing up their lab reports.

The changes in the way I approach my classes that have resulted from my study of developmental theory may seem insignificant individually, but in combination they have added, for me, a new and exciting dimension to my teaching. As I listen to students talk about learning and life, I hear Perry's positions and stages review themselves. His model has given me a framework for understanding my students' assumptions about education—particularly as they conflict with mine. It helps me guide their progress with a sense of direction. Student-based teaching has worked for me, and I am convinced that the Perry model can be applied profitably to any discipline.

Reprinted by permission of the author.

 Vocabulary

As you think about this essay, these definitions may be helpful to you:
1. **cognition**   the process of knowing, including awareness and judgment
2. **operational**   ready to undertake a destined function
3. **dualism**   a theory that considers reality to consist of two irreducible elements or modes
4. **entrench**   to establish solidly
5. **incrementally**   changing by small amounts or degrees

 Discussion Questions

1. How has the work of Piaget, a French psychologist and philosopher, influenced Finster's understanding of cognition, or how individuals learn in the broadest sense?
2. Describe the "dualists'" way of thinking according to Perry.
3. How can students be encouraged to progress beyond their current level of thinking, according to Perry?
4. How does Finster describe a "good teacher"? How do his ideas compare to your definition of a good teacher?
5. What specific steps does Finster take to apply Perry's ideas in his teaching chemistry?

 Suggestions for Your Journal

Write about some of the good teachers you have had over the years. Do they fit Finster's definition of a good teacher? What do you think of Finster's description of "mass education"? Do you think his teaching methods are effective?

Trouble with Parents

Inge Bell

Inge Bell is a Sociology professor at Pitzer College. In this essay, she discusses the transition of students as they enter college and the changing roles that develop between them and their parents. The sentences in quotation marks used as examples in this reading are directly from students that Bell talked with in her research.

• • • • • • • • • • • • • • • • • • •

The last time I went home, I realized that I was visiting my parent's house—not coming home. It was a sad feeling, but also a feeling of independence and maturity. I had to say goodbye to my childhood and the familiarity of my home town, but I realized that I have a whole adult life of my own to look forward to.

Next to grades and love, parents are surely the most frequent cause of *vexation* among students. When I opened up this subject with some classes, the response was immediate. When I asked who was having difficulties with parents, most hands went up.

One young man says, "You come home and they think you are still the same age as when you left. I've been living at school since I was 15 and my parents still treat me like they did when I was 15."

A young woman chimes in, "When I go home, suddenly I'm back with having to be in before midnight or my mother will lie awake and worry until I come home."

Another says, "How do I let them know that I don't need that much parenting anymore? I feel myself falling back into being-your-child-again, and at the same time I witness them go through the transformation into we-are-your-parents. They never see you in any other role—when you return home it's this weird time warp—as if you have never been away."

Another says about going home, "I was a guest but I was also responsible once again for all the old assignments. I had to clean up my room when they wanted me to, not when I wanted to."

Some students found they missed their parents. There is a temptation to slip back into familiar roles. "You kind of want the child role and they want it for you. It is such a contrast to the independence at school."

"I used to just want to get out of the house and be with my friends, now I'm with friends all the time and I like to spend time with my parents. When I go home it's a lot better."

Here somebody asked, "Would anyone want to go back and live at home?" A chorus of resounding "no's."

At the point of leaving home, many students find parents hanging on too hard. "They ask 'why don't you come home and visit this Easter, Christmas, or stay all summer?' I want to spend some time with my friends."

My class discussions were with students at small private residential colleges. To balance this bias I got some feedback from a class at a community college where most students live at home. Surprisingly, a slight majority of these students were very well satisfied with their arrangements. In some cases parents seem to have given the child adult status as they entered college:

"My relationship at home with my parents is good. After high school, where my grades were scrutinized by my parents, college has been totally opposite. They leave me alone about my grades. Ironically, I always end up telling them things anyway. I think our 'college' relationship was a positive step in my maturation to adulthood."

"...They basically stay out of my way. They understand that college, working, and friends is a hard way to live.... Their main complaint is that I'm not home enough, I'm never there to talk to, pick up around the house, or watch TV. I have two jobs and school, so it gets hard. All in all, I'm happy with the living arrangements at home...."

In some cases I had the impression that students who live at home are more willing to settle for a lack of *autonomy* because the arrangement is otherwise so useful to them.

"I'm not saying our relationship is perfect, 'cause by far it isn't but I can tell you the more I respect them, the better it gets. So maybe kids should respect their parents more, after all, they do know a lot more than us."

Those who reported not liking life at home had many of the same complaints as those voiced by students living away from home, only in the former case the conflicts have a greater impact on the student's life. "Living with my parents is difficult during college because they tie everything I do to my grades. Their control level is tremendous. Because they are paying for my education, everything in my life must not be private."

"They put a lot of pressure on me by trying to do family functions and continuing family togetherness. They don't understand that as we get older we want to be with friends."

These conflicts are so common, even when relations in the family have been good, that we must look for a *pervasive* cultural pattern. The problem is that for 18 years, your parents protected you, felt a tremendous responsibility for you, tried to ease your path and warn you about the pitfalls of life; and now, suddenly they have to shift gears. They have to trust the wisdom of their own child rearing, and have to trust you to survive your own mistakes. They have to restructure the whole relationship.

At the same time, in our culture, a child is expected to leave home and become a full-fledged adult during the late teens and early twenties. Unlike the situation in many other societies, children are not supposed to remain blindly obedient to their elders. There must be a "breaking free." You all sense this and try to act accordingly. It is, indeed, difficult to go from a highly structured home situation into a very unstructured college situation.

As you meet the cultural requirements of thinking for yourself, you encounter disagreements with your parents. As one student put it, "Can you love your parents and not necessarily agree with them? If you express your disagree-ment, can they hear where you are coming from such that it doesn't mean you don't love them? If I ever disagreed with my dad, it would be World War III." I asked her if she had actually tried an open disagreement. She said she had not. I urged her to try but be sure that, for her part, the disagreement wasn't part of a desire to reject him in her turn.

Breaking-away is better confronted on concrete issues of parental control: for example, when they demand that you come home by midnight or insist that you have to clean your room on time. Differences of opinion work better if you are just exploring your new ideas with your parents, rather than against them.

Where there has been real love between children and parents, the diffi-cult transition period will pass. It is always surprising to college seniors how much their parents have matured in four years. A few *filial* relationships are so good that the struggle never happens. After listening to the class discussion for some time, one young woman said, "I am really amazed to hear all this because I still live at home with my father, but we don't have any conflict. I think he has always sort of treated me as an equal. I am very comfortable in the situation."

Another said, "Even when you are 30, they'll still have the chicken soup ready. But I think college is the time to branch out. My parents and I are separat-ing, but the relationship exceeds what we had in high school."

In these healthy families, parent and child may enjoy role-reversal, which the child's new adulthood makes possible. An older student said, "My daughter graduated from medical school. We were going to her own home. We were her guests. She was making all the arrangements. What a feeling to have total role-reversal. My daughter worried about my son being late, and I thought, 'Oh, that's what I used to do'."

Unfortunately, some parent/child relationships are deeply neurotic and tense. Here the struggle to break away can be traumatic for both sides. In deal-ing with neurotic relationships, the student may be up against raw fear. When we are children parents are all powerful for us. Their nurturance is a matter of life and death. So, it may be necessary to get past this fear.

Sometimes parents pressure students about their choices of major, career, or even extra-curricular activities. "Why don't parents understand that their chil-dren have to make their own choices. I think it is because they are distant from their children. They never really see who the child is. My folks used to say, 'What-ever makes you happy.'"

Where you come up against disagreements about college majors and ca-reers, I think you must try to prevail. You cannot let yourself be put into a posi-tion of living out your parents' hopes for themselves in your own life. I would advise you to do some thorough research about your desired major, career plan, or summer job prospect. Most college campuses have an office of career plan-ning which gives vocational and aptitude tests. Take these and show the results to your parents. Thus prepared, you will have an easier time staying calm and reasonable—always the position of strength.

Never having been a parent myself, I couldn't tell you how this whole process looks from the parents' viewpoint. So I asked some wise mothers of my acquaintance for some words of wisdom.

"I always looked on college as a maturing experience. Go, have a good time, meet people, broaden your interests. If you also happen to learn something, that's nice. If it contributes to your career, that is remarkable. Actually, my son's extracurricular activity, photography, is now his career."

"I think that college is really the last significant gift you can give your kids. Education in general. One should be generous and gracious about it and grateful that they have come this far."

"This is how we have always felt about children. Parents do not own their children. Children are very special gifts—to be loved, enjoyed, nourished, educated, guided to a recognition of moral values, and to a sense of responsibility and accountability. Then follows the difficult part—a time to trust, to let go, and to hope they've done a good job. Deep inside, mothers and fathers never stop being mothers and fathers, never stop caring, but they can adjust. They can recognize maturity, and value sons and daughters as mature young men and women, capable of making good decisions."

One mother sent along the following poem saying, "For as many years as I can remember I've treasured a very faded clipping that has guided me. It's on my refrigerator right now."

Children Are Like Kites

Children are like kites.
You spend years trying to get them off the ground.
You run with them until
you're both breathless.
They crash ... they hit
the roof top ... you
patch, comfort and assure
them that some day they will fly!
They need more string, and you
keep letting it out. They tug.
There is a sadness that goes with
joy. The kite becomes more distant,
and you know it won't be long
before that beautiful creature
will snap the lifeline that binds
you together and will SOAR, as
it was meant to soar—free and
alone! Only then, do you know
that you have done your job.

From Inge Bell, *This Book Not Required* (Fort Bragg, CA: The Small Press, 1991).

 # Vocabulary

As you think about this essay, these definitions may be helpful to you:
1. **vexation**   something that is troubling, irritating
2. **maturation**   the state of having completed natural growth and development
3. **autonomy**   self-directed personal freedom
4. **pervasive**   diffused throughout every part
5. **filial**   having the relation to a child or offspring

 # Discussion Questions

1. What are some key issues between students and their parents that are discussed in this essay?
2. Why are some students comfortable living at home while attending college, whereas others are not?
3. Our society pressures young people to be independent of their families. How does this differ from other cultures?

 # Suggestions for Your Journal

Write about your relationship with your parents when you first left for college and how it was (will be?) different during your home stay over the holiday break.

   In what ways would you like your relationship with your parents to change? To stay the same?

: Loneliness

: *Barbara M. Newman and Philip R. Newman*

: Barbara and Philip Newman are the authors of many books on human development.
: They are especially well known for *Development through Life: A Psychosocial*
: *Approach,* now in its seventh edition.

: Some students may experience feelings of loneliness as they enter a new and foreign
: college environment. The authors describe loneliness as a common college experience
: and suggest that friendships can play a key role in overcoming it.

College brings new opportunities for friendship, but it also brings new experiences of isolation and loneliness. Many college students leave the comfort and familiarity of their support system at home for a new environment. Others break ties with old friends who have gone to work or entered the military right after high school. The early weeks and months of college are likely to bring deep feelings of isolation and loneliness. These feelings are intensified because students usually approach the transition to college with such positive anticipation. They often do not even consider that this change will bring any sense of *uprootedness* or loss.

Loneliness is a common experience of college life. An estimated 25 percent of the college population feel extremely lonely at some time during any given month. These feelings are likely to be most noticeable during the freshman year because of the sharp contrast between the structure of high school life and the independence expected of students in college. However, loneliness can be a theme throughout the college years. The process of becoming an individual brings with it a new appreciation for one's separateness from others. As young people discover their own uniqueness, from time to time they are bound to feel that no one else really understands them.

Your parents may also experience periods of loneliness. They miss the physical presence of a person they love. They miss the daily interactions. Now and again, they may yearn for things to be more like they were and wish to be less separate.

Loneliness can be classified into three categories: *transient,* situational, and chronic.[1] *Transient loneliness* lasts a short time and passes. College students may feel this kind of loneliness when their friends are out on dates and they are alone in the dorm. This type of loneliness may occur when a student is the only one to take a certain position in a discussion; the only black student in a class; or the only one working out in a large, empty gym.

Situational loneliness accompanies a sudden loss or a move to a new city. Students commonly experience this kind of loneliness when they first come to

[1]These categories are adapted from J. Meer, "Loneliness," *Psychology Today,* July 1985, pp. 28–33.

college, especially if they are away from home. Most of us are *disoriented* when we move to a new town. Going to college is no different. Despite the many new and wonderful facets of college life, most young people experience situational loneliness due to the loss of the supportive, familiar environment of their homes and communities.

Your parents may undergo situational loneliness because of the loss of your presence. Even though they have planned and saved for this opportunity, they may experience intense loneliness following your departure. Rather than trying to create a myth that no one is feeling lonely, parents and college students can help each other through this time by admitting their loneliness and doing their best to reduce it. Frequent telephone calls, letters, and visits home in the first few months can ease the feelings of loss.

Chronic loneliness lasts a long time and cannot be linked to a specific event or situation. Chronically lonely people may have an average number of social contacts, but these contacts are not meaningful in helping the person achieve the desired level of intimacy. Chronically lonely people often seem reluctant to make contact with others. There appears to be a strong relationship between social skills and chronic loneliness. People who have higher levels of social skill, including friendliness, communication skills, appropriate *nonverbal* behavior, and appropriate response to others, have more adequate social support and experience lower levels of loneliness.

You may not recognize that you suffer from chronic loneliness until you are away at college. While children are living at home, parents are usually able to provide the amount of social support their children need. At college, children may find it extremely difficult to replace the level of trust and closeness that were provided by family members and high school friends.

Inadequate friendship relationships may actually interfere with your academic performance as well as your physical and mental health. Substantial research evidence supports the relationship between inadequate social support and *vulnerability* to illness. People who are part of a strong social support system are more likely to resist disease and to recover quickly from illnesses when they occur. Their general outlook on life is more optimistic.

A college student's circle of friends plays a key role in keeping the young person integrated into the social environment. Friends look in on you when you are sick; they make sure you have an assignment if you miss class; they invite you to join them if they are going to a party, a special lecture, or a campus concert. Friends worry about you and remind you to take care of yourself. Friends monitor your moods and prevent you from becoming too preoccupied or too discouraged. Friends value you and support your emerging identity. They understand the importance of the questions you are raising, and they encourage you to say what's on your mind. Building and maintaining satisfying friendships are key ingredients to feeling at home and succeeding in college.

• •

 Vocabulary

As you think about this essay, these definitions may be helpful to you:
1. **uprootedness**   in psychology, a sense of being displaced
2. **transient**   passing through with only a brief stay or sojourn
3. **disoriented**   having lost a sense of time, place, or identity
4. **nonverbal**   involving minimal or no use of language
5. **vulnerability**   openness to attack or damage

 Discussion Questions

1. What factors may trigger loneliness in a college student?
2. What are the three categories of loneliness described by the authors?
3. How does transient loneliness differ from chronic loneliness?
4. Why are students with little or no social support more vulnerable to illness?
5. What is the hardest part of maintaining a friendship?

 Suggestions for Your Journal

Did you experience situational loneliness when you started college? How did it feel? Do you know students who are lonely? How can building and maintaining friendships be helpful in overcoming loneliness? How can you as a friend help another student through lonely times?

Tips on Becoming Personally Effective

Susan Jones Sears

Well known for her work in counselor education, Susan Jones Sears is a professor in the College of Education at The Ohio State University. In this essay, she offers some practical tips for becoming a competent and successful student.

• • • • • • • • • • • • • • • • • •

Whether you are a new college student or a more experienced one, you are probably impressed with the number of talented and highly skilled individuals in your classes—individuals who seem to know more than you do and who are motivated, bright, and dedicated. With increasing competition in the classroom and the workplace, individuals have begun searching for a psychological edge, an advantage to help them excel and be recognized as competent students and workers. Think about the concept of personal effectiveness—personal behaviors and skills that result in enhanced performance in college, at work, and in life. As you begin your college career and prepare for the work world, you can benefit from reflecting upon what it takes to excel.

What are the ingredients of success? During the last two decades, hundreds of books have been written with the intent of helping people improve themselves and increase their chances for success. Techniques for improving your personality, learning to communicate more effectively, and managing stress are all familiar topics to readers who avail themselves of the self-help books in their local bookstores or on the Internet. In the early 1980's, those interested in improving their performance read *Peak Performers* by Charles Garfield; in the latter 1980's and early 1990's, they read *The Seven Habits of Highly Effective People* by Stephen Covey. In the 2000's, Philip C. McGraw is the latest self-help guru.

Today, many books on coaching are generating a lot of attention and discussion. Professional athletes and actors have used the services of coaches for decades, and now ordinary individuals are hiring coaches to give them advice and offer strategies on how to improve their personal and professional lives.

If you study high achievers or personally effective individuals, you begin to see that they function at higher levels not because of a single talent but, rather, because certain factors, taken together, result in greater accomplishment. Individuals who know what they want to do in life, who have a vision, a game plan, or a purpose or goal, are more successful than those who do not. If you have a sense of purpose, you will naturally attract those who are going in the same direction. What is your purpose or goal in life? What are you trying to achieve?

Maybe you want to find a major or a career that you will enjoy and [that will] bring you fulfillment, or maybe you want to travel to learn about other cultures. Take a few minutes to think about your goal or purpose for the year.

Replacing Distractions with Energy Boosters

Petty annoyances are often small irritants, but they tend to become real hassles when they are not dealt with. They drain your energy and distract you from your quest for success. Perhaps something around the house or apartment is broken, but you can't seem to get around to repairing it. Or your roommate is a "night owl" and you are not.

Maybe one of your own bad habits is annoying you! Your notes are disorganized and scattered, and when it is time to study for a test, you procrastinate. Or maybe a friend has a habit of making fun of you or putting you down when you make even a small mistake. You have tolerated it but find yourself getting angrier each time it happens. Many of us tolerate petty annoyances and really don't realize how much they are irritating us, wearing us down, and draining our energy. Write down a list of the things you are putting up with or tolerating that are draining your energy. Now set aside a day within the next week to tackle some of these petty annoyances. Try to eliminate everything on your list that you can.

Some annoyances take time to eliminate. If you are having difficulty in a relationship and want to rebuild or repair it, you probably can't do it in a day. But at least you can begin. When you succeed in working through the annoyances that bother you the most, you should reward yourself by indulging in some favorite activity.

Simplifying Your Life

One way to attract something new in your life is to make space—get rid of the clutter, toss out old notes, clothes, and memos, and sell those old books and CDs. Ask yourself: "Have I used this in the past six months?" If your answer is no and it isn't a seasonal item, toss it. If you don't know where to start, take one part of a room at a time. Give your usable items to a local charity. Someone will appreciate what has been cluttering up your space. Getting rid of things you do not need can invigorate you and create the sensation of starting anew.

Once you have rid yourself of the clutter in your life, look at your schedule. If your schedule is packed with stuff to do, people to meet, and places to go, it may be time to simplify. People who are too busy can miss opportunities because they don't notice what is going on around them and don't have time to think. Consolidate your credit cards so you don't spend so much time paying and keeping track of bills. Turn your cell phone off. Before you say yes to a social event, make certain it is really something you want to do.

Managing Your Time Effectively

Do you attend classes, study as hard as you can, and then run to your part-time or full-time job? Do you find yourself complaining that there aren't enough hours in the day? If you feel pressured for time, perhaps you should take a week and track your time in one-hour increments. Keep a notepad in your pocket or bookbag and write down what you are doing each hour from the time you rise until you go to bed. Writing just a few words will allow you to keep track of how you are spending your time. At the end of the week, quickly calculate how much time you spend on major life activities such as attending classes, studying, talking on the phone, sleeping, watching television, listening to CDs, hanging out with your friends, e-mailing or instant messaging. Are you surprised by how you spend your time? In what areas do you think you are wasting your time? How can you reschedule your time so you will use it more effectively?

Learning to Say No

Are you overcommitted with work and social obligations? Do you find yourself participating in activities that don't really interest you? Perhaps you need to learn to say no. Women in particular are brought up in our society to please and to be liked. As a result of this kind of socialization, they find it harder to say no when asked to do favors or take on extra work. Some fear that saying no will turn off their friends, but in reality it doesn't. Often your friends and colleagues respect you more when they learn they cannot take advantage of you. Learning to say no is one way of getting control of your time and your life.

Managing Your Money Well

During the last 20 years, it has become acceptable to have debts. Your parents probably saved money before they purchased a cherished item, whereas you may find it easy to simply charge the cost to your credit card. The costs of immediate gratification (charge it now) can be high. First, the interest rate on debt is high. Second, too much debt can lead to stress that can drain your energy, making it difficult for you to be your best and attract the people and opportunities you want. Instead if you pay off the balance on your credit cards each month, you will feel lighter, more free, and in control of your life.

Building a Strong Network of Friends

Part of your success in life and work is having some close friends with whom you can laugh, love, and celebrate your and their successes. Be aware of the people around you, and get to know those who are particularly interesting. With our increased mobility, we sometimes have to create our own communities, a circle of friends with whom we feel comfortable and supported. Some create this circle of friends at college or at work, and others find opportunities to create friendships at church or in clubs. Be proactive and create your own network of friends.

Making Time for Yourself

Life can become boring if we do not have something to look forward to. Taking a walk, talking to friends, taking a hot bubble bath, or listening to your favorite music are just a few example of activities that might be pleasurable and inspiring to you. Taking time for yourself is an important way to keep balanced in today's hectic world. Think about the activities that you really look forward to doing, and then how can you change your schedule to include them in your daily life.

Identifying and Managing Stress

If you are to become truly effective, you must begin to identify the sources of stress in your life and learn to manage stress at work, school, and home. Stress can be either a positive or a negative force. It is negative when it interferes with your ability to function at your optimal level. It is positive when it enhances your performance or your effectiveness. That is the key to stress management.

What does the term *stress* really mean? According to psychologist Donald Meichenbaum, you experience stress when you appraise an event (a demand on you, a constraint, an opportunity, or a challenge) as having the potential to exceed the resources you have available. You may think it's too hard, too frightening, or too challenging. Stressors or events that can create anxiety vary greatly from individual to individual. Three classifications are:

- *external* physical stimuli, such as heat, cold, crowding, loud noises
- *interpersonal* difficulties with others
- *internal* stimuli, such as our own thoughts or feelings

Although stressors are specific to individuals to some extent, universal categories of stressors are: environmental stressors, life stress events, and daily hassles.

Environmental stressors include things such as noise, crowding, commuting time, worry about crime, traffic and pollution, economic difficulties, isolation, restricted leisure opportunities, and job insecurity. These often are a function of where you live and sometimes your socioeconomic class.

Life stress events are major occurrences that create stress and require people to change and adapt. Holmes and Rahe identified 43 life events that cause significant stress and assigned each event a weight, using what they called "life change events." Events that call for a greater amount of change and adaptation are assigned a higher number of life change units. For example, the death of a spouse is assigned a very high weight. Holmes and Rahe used their instrument, the Social Readjustment Rating Scale, to measure the amount of life stress a person was experiencing. They found that too many life stress events forced the body to adapt and change so much that those stresses weakened the immune system.

In fact, researchers have made connections between life stress events and both physical and mental illness. Evidence has shown that life stress events contribute to emotional disorders, heart disease, accidents, and other conditions. Whether individuals who experience stressful life events subsequently come ill, however, also depends on their personal vulnerability, as well as the amount of social and emotional support available to them.

Daily hassles (for instance, physical appearance, concerns about weight, too many things to do, and losing or misplacing things) are also stressors. Until the early 1980's, little research had been done on the effect of minor but more common daily hassles. Since then, researchers have paid considerable attention to studying effects of hassles on health. Hassles seem to vary depending on age and, to some extent, the circumstances in which people find themselves. Some common daily hassles for students are:

Taking tests or exams
Worrying about not meeting academic deadlines
Not knowing how to study effectively
Taking hard and demanding classes

Strategies for Managing Stress

Preventive approaches such as relaxation training are important to any stress management program. The term *relaxation training* refers to any technique whose purpose is to decrease the negative symptoms the human body experiences under stress. If individuals can be taught to relax, they should be able to produce voluntarily an alternative physiological response to offset the negative stress symptoms. For example, if a stress reaction results in increases in muscle tension, blood pressure, or heart rate, the voluntarily induced state of relaxation can reverse these increases.

Engaging in a healthy lifestyle goes a long way in managing stress. Individuals who experience the physiological effects of stress are endangering their health. If they also are practicing unhealthy habits that weaken the body's ability to resist stress, their level of stress may increase. Clearly, if you are stressed, you should practice good eating habits, use alcohol only moderately if at all, not smoke, and get regular exercise.

Accepting and Adapting to Change

Change is anything that causes us to shift from old and familiar ways or situations to ones that are new, different, and often challenging. More than a decade ago, Alvin Toffler talked about "waves of change" that are accelerating at a faster and faster pace. The rate of change in today's world is greater than any other time in our history. Global competition, almost unbelievable advances in technology, particularly communication technologies, and a knowledge and information explosion all contribute to this fast-paced change. Learning how to adapt and adjust to change is a critical skill that can be learned.

In times of rapid change, you must be able to adapt quickly. Below are several suggestions on how to adapt to change rather than ignore or resist it:

• Withhold judgment and tolerate ambiguity or uncertainty until you see the results of whatever changes you are experiencing.
• Be flexible and try new approaches.
• Stay current about changes and trends in your field and try to understand their potential impact.
• Anticipate the new skills needed in your field and acquire them.
• View change as part of a natural process of growth.
• Look to the future; don't glorify the past beyond its worth.
• Scan your environment and reassess your goals regularly.

Think about the changes that have occurred in your life in the last 18 months. How did you respond? For example, did you try to avoid change at all costs, complain about the change, reluctantly change, or see change as an opportunity and develop ways to deal with it? At times, change can create situations in which you feel you have little or no control over events going on around you. When that happens, we usually experience anxiety or stress. Although we cannot always control what is happening in life, we can control our reaction it. We can decide how to react to change so it does not overwhelm us.

The personal characteristics and skills outlined above can give you the psychological edge in school, work, and life in general. As you establish your educational and career goals, developing these habits, attitudes and skills can enhance your success in all areas of life.

Works Cited

Covey, Stephen. *The Seven Habits of Highly Effective People.* New York: Simon and Schuster, 1989.

Garfield, Charles. *Peak Performers.* New York: Avon, 1986.

Holmes, T. H., and Rahe, R. H. The Social Readjustment Rating Scale. *Journal of Psychosomatic Research, 11*(2), 213–218, 1967.

Meichenbaum, Donald. *Stress Inoculation Training.* New York: Pergamon Press, 1985.

Toffler, Alvin. *The Third Wave.* New York: William Morrow, 1980.

From Susan Jones Sears and Virginia N. Gordon, *Building Your Career—A Guide to Your Future,* 3rd edition (Upper Saddle River, NJ: Prentice Hall, 2002). Reprinted with permission of Pearson Education Inc., Upper Saddle River, NJ.

 Discussion Questions

1. What does becoming a "personally effective student" mean to you? Does being a competent college student differ from being a competent high school student? If so, how?
2. Which of the author's suggestions for improving your daily life would be the most difficult for you to accomplish? (For example, do you have trouble saying no when friends ask for a favor?)
3. What are some stressors in your life, and what can you do to alleviate them?

 Suggestions for Your Journal

Reflect on your ability to accept and adapt to change. Since you began college, what changes (for example, in your daily routine, in the classroom, in your relationship with your parents) have been the most difficult to deal with? The easiest?

What has surprised you the most about how being a college student has changed your life?

UNIT SUMMARY

The readings in this unit discussed many aspects of college life and its effect on students. Although adjusting to college may take some time, the challenge and excitement of being a student makes this experience unique and memorable.

Summary Questions

1. How do the expectations about college expressed by the readings in this unit differ from your own? How are they similar?
2. How can the college experience help you in your intellectual, personal, and career development?
3. If you were not attending college, how would your life be different? Evaluate the differences.

Suggested Writing Assignments

1. Write a brief essay on how you have changed since your first day in college. How do you expect to change by the time you earn a degree?
2. Describe one experience that you have had with taking control of your situation in life. How did you manage the change?
3. Describe one of your own college experiences that was also described by an author in this unit. Some examples are loneliness, stress, relationships with parents, and classroom experience. Compare your experience with that author's account.

Suggested Readings

Chickering, Arthur W., and Linda Reisser. *Education and Identity,* 2nd ed. San Francisco: Jossey-Bass, 1993.
Gilligan, Carol. *In a Different Voice.* Cambridge, MA: Harvard University Press, 1982.
Nist, Sherrie, and Jodi Holschuh. *College Rules.* Berkeley: Ten Speed Press, 2002.

How Can I Succeed Academically?

Academic success can be defined from many perspectives. Some measure it by grade-point average (known commonly as GPA) or by "accume," which is short for cumulative point-hour ratio. A student with a 3.5 GPA, for example, is usually considered more successful academically than a student with a 1.9. Academic success is also defined by one's accumulation of knowledge. Students who, when tested, can successfully throw back to their instructors the facts and concepts they have memorized may be considered academically successful. Still others define success by the salary and prestige of the job they are able to acquire at the end of their senior year. Some students may consider what they have genuinely learned to be the true measure of their academic success. Learning how to learn is a skill that can be used for a lifetime. Successful students will always be intensely involved in their own learning.

Regardless of how a student measures academic success, certain activities in which students engage are essential to the learning process. Among them, reading and writing are

'Tis education forms the common mind. Just as the twig is bent, the tree's inclined.

—ALEXANDER POPE

55

two of the most critical. Some first-year students find themselves ill prepared in these basic skills. Most new students who understand the value of these activities work hard to improve their reading and writing skills throughout their college years.

Some other skills closely associated with academic success are:

Communication Skills. These include being able to communicate ideas and concepts effectively in a prepared presentation or in the conversational give-and-take of a committee meeting. Such skills are important in the classroom and marketable in the workplace.

Writing Skills. Students who can express themselves well in writing have a highly marketable skill. The ability to write clear and persuasive reports, proposals, and similar important documents is essential in every work environment.

Organizational Skills. Students need to set goals and priorities and to organize their time and energy accordingly. Self-discipline plays a key role in how students balance their academic life with other personal and social demands.

Analytical Skills. Learning to think critically and logically is important to academic success. Identifying problems and solving them creatively are central to accomplishing many academic tasks.

Research Skills. Students need basic research skills to fulfill many academic assignments. Defining a problem, formulating pertinent questions, using appropriate resources to study the problem, and employing a variety of research methods to solve the problem are all part of the research process that students use constantly.

The authors in this unit would certainly agree on the importance of the five categories of skill listed above. O'Hanlon outlines the skills necessary for library and Internet research, Gold suggests punctuality, and Brown requires regularity in attendance to class. Burtchaell and Raspberry offer perspectives on selecting a college major that may surprise some readers—especially those who have been conditioned to believe that selecting a college major is roughly equivalent to making a lifelong commitment to a single job. Minnick provides some ways for thinking about elective courses, which are all the classes you take that are not stipulated as some requirement. Rich emphasizes the art of active listening in the classroom. All these readings can have a bearing on your thoughtful approach to course selection.

Major Decisions

James Tunstead Burtchaell

Father James Tunstead Burtchaell, professor emeritus of Theology at the University of Notre Dame, served as provost for many years. While holding that title, which in a university is normally the position of chief academic officer and ranks just below the president, Burtchaell lived in student residence halls and saw firsthand the student concerns that he discusses in this reading. Although many colleges strive to get students to decide on a major early, often before being admitted, Notre Dame in Burtchaell's time told students that, as first-year students, they could specify an intent but not declare a major. This essay explains why.

M ore than two out of every three undergraduates at this university change majors between the time they are accepted and the time they graduate. A good number change two or three times. Any decision that has so many students second-guessing must be tricky, and it is.

The difficulty comes from several directions. First, there are so many options that you had no opportunity to sample in high school. Everyone has some experience studying literature, mathematics, French and physics, but no high school in the country offers electrical engineering. Nor can you get a running start in microbiology or finance or metallurgy or philosophy. More than half of the disciplines we offer are new to you. So how can you have a responsibly cultivated preference early enough to select one as your principal interest here?

Another difficulty is pressure. Some students get pretty clear advice from their parents about what a sensible major would be. Most of that advice tends to have something to do with earning a living after college. And much of it is bad advice.

In the old days there were parents who threatened to cut off tuition money unless their child studied the subject they thought was right. That rarely happens today, but there is another kind of pressure that may be worse. There are few students at Notre Dame whose parents didn't make sacrifices for them to be here. And most students are backed by parents who didn't have, or weren't free to accept, the kind of education they worked hard to provide their children. The result: Most people on this campus walk around with an abiding and compelling sense of gratitude to their parents.

For every student here whose parents have told him what to study, there are a hundred whose parents never breathed a word of instruction on the matter. But most of those hundred, in the privacy of their hearts, want to make a choice that will satisfy their parents. They are drawn to major in subjects their parents can see as oriented toward a useful future. One somehow feels it would be ungrateful to receive a first-rate university education and not put it to maximum use from the start. That is a more *insidious* and damaging form of pressure precisely because there is nothing the parents can do to change it. They had nothing to do with imposing it.

In addition, high school counselors often talk to seniors in a way that is excessively career oriented. They make the student aware, even before she sets foot on a college campus, that she is going to higher studies with an eye toward an eventual profession or job. The message is that it is wasteful to spend four years without any clear idea of where all that expensive study is leading.

Students also have a tendency, especially in their early years at college, to feel crowded by competition. Most freshmen look up and down the corridor the first week they're here and feel intimidated. Everyone they encounter seems to have been a valedictorian, student council president, all-state breast-stroke champion, published poet.

I exaggerate, of course, but most people here *are* used to being at the head of the line. That is how you got here. Now you are at a place with a lot of others who were at the head of *their* lines, and there just isn't room for all of you at the top of this class. So you tend to figure that your choice of study here will have to be canny and careful if it's going to make you competitive with such bright and aggressive classmates.

After a few years you discover everyone else is as normal as you, but by then you've begun to worry that since Notre Dame accepted you it must be a second-rate institution. There are all those other more talented people out there at better places who, when they emerge, are going to have a running start on you. So your choice of what to study is fretful because you have these other, more quick-witted people to compete with.

Those are three difficulties that most of you have to cope with: the subjects are so unknown, the choice is so pressured, and the competition is so strong. Unfortunately these difficulties cause students to stumble into a few classical misunderstandings, which in turn lead them to wrong decisions about their major.

The first misunderstanding is to confuse education with training. An institution that offers you training is trying to provide you with the information and skills you need for a specific career. A law school must acquaint you with how to interview clients, how to plead before a court, and how to draw up proper legal documents. A welding academy will teach you the materials and methods of the trade. Advanced training in computing will prepare you not simply to keypunch or to program, but to create software, to understand the mysteries of central processing, and then to grasp the theoretical underpinnings of applied mathematics.

All of that is training: specific knowledge needed for specific professional or skilled work. It is not education.

Education is the opportunity, through studying a variety of subjects, to gain the information and the dexterity to use your wits and your expression. Education prepares you to *be* someone more than to *do* something. Education is what prepares you to hear more when you listen, to reach deeper when you think, to say more when you speak.

Education is quite different from training, which prepares you in advance to do the tasks that are well known in a given job. Education prepares you in advance to see beneath and beyond what is well known. The principal value that an educated person brings to her career is intelligence. What one wants of an educated person, beyond his skills, is the ability to see into problems that cannot be foreseen. A welder must know in advance all the techniques he has to use, but a banker or a physician or a teacher or a member of the city council is expected to move beyond previous experience and apply his wits to the heart of new problems.

A good university such as this one will give you quite a few skills and a broad grounding of information. But we do not exist to teach skills to under- graduates; we do that in our graduate and professional programs. The result of a college education should be a person whose mind is enlivened and whose imagination is limber. England's Robert Benchley put it in his own peculiar and wise way:

"Gentlemen: You are now about to embark upon a course of studies which will occupy you for several years. Together they form a noble adventure. But I would like to remind you of an important point. Some of you, when you go down from the University, will go into the Church, or to the Bar, or to the House of Commons, or to the Home Civil Service, to the Indian or Colonial Ser- vices, or into various professions. Some may go into the Army, some into indus- try and commerce, some may become country gentlemen. A few—I hope very few—will become teachers or *dons*.

"Let me make this clear to you. Except for the last category, nothing that you will learn in the course of your studies will be of the slightest possible use to you in after life, save only this: That if you work hard and intelligently you should be able to detect when a man is talking rot, and that in my view is the main, if not the sole, purpose of education."

People fortunate and qualified enough to receive a university education will make their living by their wits. You will be served less by what you *have* learned than by what you *can* learn.

The good thing about education is that it matters hardly at all what sub- jects you choose to study. You can be educated in any discipline, because there is no direct connection between an educational subject and a specific career. So never ask what you can *do* with your major.

This touches on the second classical misunderstanding that has led so many students astray. The choice of a major is not the choice of a career. Undergraduates are not making lifetime decisions. When they imagine they are, it can be paralyzing.

As you know, Notre Dame has delaying tactics to slow you down in the selection of a major. Before coming here most of you speculated about your eventual career, and then about what course of study you would select. You arrived here ready to declare a major, but the Freshman Year of Studies would not allow that. The most you were permitted was to designate an "intent." We wanted you to get the maximum exposure and experience here, and a year or two more of self-knowledge, so that your intellectual curiosity and interests could ripen and the decision would be more sound, more considered.

Let me say a bit about that. Some talents show themselves early in life. If you are an excellent athlete, you already have the coordination and stamina and pleasure from sports in your early teens. Nobody suddenly develops into a star athlete in her 30s. The same is true for mathematical ability. If you are good at quantitative understanding, you are already good at it in junior high school; in fact, you tend toward high achievement in math and other related subjects. You know science is your strong suit, and you come to college aware that you will study science and excel in it. Then things go wrong. Physics will begin to bore some of you. You will conceal from your parents that you signed up for a few extra theology courses, and you'll write poetry by flashlight under the covers at night. You may plug on and earn good grades, but with less and less appetite. It is *disconcerting* to develop a new range of interests when your track record of achievement and satisfaction is so definitely in another direction. But that is what happens when a new range of talent begins to mature and to rival other talents that had declared themselves earlier. No one tells you in advance that philosophical thinking matures later than mathematical thinking. The choice of a major needs to be slowed down to allow you to get confirmation of your emergent strong interests and abilities.

But even then, near the close of your sophomore year, you are only choosing a major, not a career. Still more developments and experiences will come. Fixing on a lifetime career when you are a sophomore in college is like getting engaged at 14.

What you study here may have little necessary connection with what you will do later. We give baccalaureate degrees in about 40 disciplines and in many combinations of subjects. But people graduate in philosophy and end up lawyers. They study mechanical engineering and end up as business executives. They get degrees in English and go to medical school, do art history and run the family business, choose chemistry and go into politics. They major in sociology and become priests. They finish in accountancy with their CPAs and choose to be homemakers and mothers.

Even if they emerge from a program most students would consider a direct pipeline to a specific profession—architecture, for example—they are really much more free than you would suppose. Do you know how many people with degrees in architecture practice architecture? About half. So consider yourself enhanced, rather than caught, by what you choose to study. You are not making a lifetime decision, you are making a decision for the next two or three years . . . or until you change that decision.

This is not to say that there should be no natural growth from study to career. It does imply, however, that educated people have such enormous advantage and versatility that they retain a basic freedom to do whatever they please in life. To have graduated in any discipline that Notre Dame offers in no way forecloses career possibilities. It has become increasingly the case that you will enter a career that requires or provides specific training. About 60 to 70 percent of you will go on to graduate or professional schools; others to corporate training programs. Do not suffer a failure of nerve by imagining that you are more attractive to employers if you have more advanced professional training. For then you will forfeit the unrepeatable and more valuable opportunity to get an education first.

You have talents that will be enormously attractive to employers, talents so superior that you are free to make your living by your wits, your versatility of understanding, your imagination. Don't double-think the future.

The temptation is to figure out your career and then choose the studies that lead up to it. That is exactly the wrong way round. You are not ready to choose a career, except in the most tentative and speculative way. You are barely ready to choose a major. Select what you want to study with the belief that it will lead you to the point of deciding—well, not quite your career, but what you will do after graduation. What educates you best is not what you figure will lead somewhere, but what you now believe will give you most enjoyment. Pick your major on the pleasure principle, for what you most enjoy studying will draw your mind in the liveliest way to being educated.

If you want to study medieval history, don't fret about what you can do with it. You are not at a trade school. If you want to study marketing, do it because you find marketing the most fascinating subject we offer. If you came to Notre Dame determined to become a physician but in your freshman year you couldn't stand math and you failed chemistry and you threw up over your laboratory frog, there's a message there. It's not that you are incapable of becoming a doctor, but that the kind of disciplines that govern a doctor's work do not really appeal to your appetite. If in the meantime drama has caught your eye, then make that your choice and let the future handle itself. Or, more accurately, let it help you to become more qualified to determine the future. If throughout the course of four years you progressively follow your intellectual nose into what fascinates you most, when you emerge you will be in a much wiser position to choose the threshold of the proper career than you were at the start.

In the meantime don't feel pushed to make the decision prematurely. Our curriculum is versatile enough that the decision can be reviewed and postponed and changed. I am not arguing for indecision or instability. I am merely pleading for a sense of freedom, a certain responsible recklessness about study, that too many students feel guilty about having.

Let me put it this way. Imagine you are told now that on graduation day you will die. It will be painless and gentle; you will slowly and beautifully fade, right here on the main quad, with family and roommates gathered round, the Glee Club singing under the trees, and *Father Hesburgh* giving you a potent final blessing. Knowing of your death now—realizing that whatever your major is, it can never lead you into a career but will be only for your pleasure and fascination—would it make any difference what you choose to study in the interim? If it would, then you ought to change. Ironically, what you then choose will lead you, by steady and proper pacing, into the most reliable future.

It is essential to realize that any major can lead to any career, and that the best major is the one you choose with no lookout out of the corner of your eye to where it will lead.

Once that is cleared up, the difficulties are less difficult. Yes, most of the majors possible here are subjects you cannot have studied before. So use the first and especially the second year to explore. Use the freedom the curriculum provides. Far too many men and women graduate from here and come to this regret: If they had it to do over again, or had had the nerve earlier, they would study another subject.

As for the pressure from parents whose approval you seek, remember: If you are mature enough to undertake university studies, you have to be mature enough to choose those studies. You might choose unwisely, but it should be your choice.

Parents who virtually demand what their children will study at college are misguided and, fortunately, rare. I think parents ought to have the freedom to suggest or lobby for a choice of major, but you take away your parents' freedom if you transform their cue into a command. Parents ought to be able to promote an idea without children complaining they are being forced or browbeaten. If your parents do suggest a course of study, give it serious thought, but don't pretend you owe it to them to follow their recommendation.

And don't get up a guilt if you choose another major, because you may in fact be trying to make *them* feel guilty for something they never did.

And if you feel tempted to make a curriculum choice to gain your parents' respect: don't. If you have anything to be grateful for, it is that your parents have wanted you to get the best education within your reach and theirs, precisely so that you could and would make these kinds of decisions responsibly for your own satisfaction. If they didn't want you to develop independent judgment they would have kept you home.

How can you choose your major to sidestep most of the rush-hour traffic of competition? By ignoring competition. Only about 40 percent of your fellow Americans manage to enroll in college, and only about half of those graduate. Virtually all of you at this University will complete your degree requirements. That puts you among the top fifth of all people your age. And among that 20 percent, only the most highly qualified are competitive for admission to a university like Notre Dame, which means you have educational opportunities that rank you among the top one or two percent in the country.

It makes one feel uneasy to hear such talk of exclusiveness, but these are simple facts. So when you get uneasy because everyone in the corridor seems pretty swift of mind, calm down. You are moving among classmates who have the same advantaged education you have, who have been *sieved* through highly selective admission processes. After a while they may begin to look ordinary enough, but they aren't. And you aren't. The older one gets and the more experience one accumulates, the more clear it becomes that the number of really quick-minded people is small. You wonder how the world gets by with so few. Rather than imagining yourself as part of a large, capable crowd trying to crush through a narrow doorway of opportunity, it is more realistic to understand you are advantaged to an embarrassing degree, and there aren't nearly enough of you to go around.

To select a major program of study wisely you need not figure out what other people want of you. You need to figure out what you want. And that's not easy. It requires much self-knowledge.

But that is both what education gives and what education requires. William Johnson Cory, a Cambridge man, expressed impatience when critics complained that English schools were offering an education that was not useful enough. Education was not supposed to be useful, he retorted.

"You are not engaged so much in acquiring knowledge as in making mental efforts under criticism," he continued. "A certain amount of knowledge you can indeed with average faculties acquire so as to retain; nor need you regret the hours that you spent on much that is forgotten, for the shadow of lost knowledge at least protects you from many illusions.

"But you go to a great school, not for knowledge so much as for arts and habits; for the habit of attention, for the art of expression, for the art of assuming at a moment's notice a new intellectual posture, for the art of entering quickly into another person's thoughts, for the habit of submitting to censure and refutation, for the art of indicating assent or dissent in graduated terms, for the habit of regarding minute points of accuracy, for the habit of working out what is possible in a given time, for taste, for discrimination, for mental courage and mental soberness.

"Above all, you go to a great school for self-knowledge."

There are crucial freedoms that others can neither keep from us nor give to us. We must take possession of them ourselves. The sense of freedom that leads one to follow his or her own sensible instincts into a major course of study, confident that if one does that, then—and only then—will one be ready to make other even more crucial decisions: that is the sense of freedom I urge upon you before it is too late, and even before it is too early. Go ahead.

And after you have made your choice, remember that your major is only a minor portion of your higher education. You are invited—prodded—to surround and enliven your mind with elective courses. Relish them. The instructors in your discipline believe that you can never study enough of it, and some of us would advise you to take every elective our discipline has to offer. That is because we hanker to have our students love what we love, and this tempts us to tempt you to forgo your education and begin training in our field. Instead, browse in the clover.

When I was an undergraduate in philosophy, we were directed to read only primary sources; only the great thinkers, not the secondary folks who wrote textbooks about them. Excellent. But in retrospect, the good times were the hundreds of hours when I got lost in the stacks of the library and read my fascinated way through an education that no one had planned, but was lavishly provided.

Your duty is to enjoy. Nothing you might do could be more useful.

Reprinted by permission of the author.

 Vocabulary

As you think about this essay, these definitions—and one identification—may be helpful to you:

1. **insidious**   harmful but enticing or having a gradual but cumulative effect
2. **dons**   the British educational system's equivalent of college teachers
3. **disconcerting**   unsettling or emotionally disturbing
4. **Father Hesburgh**   for more than twenty years, the legendary president of the University of Notre Dame
5. **sieved**   filtered

 Discussion Questions

1. What are the three difficulties that cause undergraduates to make wrong initial decisions about a major?
2. For Burtchaell, what distinguishes training from education? Give some examples of your own for training.
3. According to Burtchaell, what should a "good university" provide its students?
4. Based on your experience and that of your friends, is Burtchaell correct in saying that new students have insufficient information to select a major?
5. Burtchaell's final two sentences may have surprised you. Did you expect a serious teacher to draw this conclusion? How does he justify it?

 Suggestions for Your Journal

Write about how you chose your academic major. If you have not decided on a major yet, discuss why you have not done so.

What is your reaction to Burtchaell's ideas about not putting pressure on students to make a choice too soon in their first year? Do you agree that choosing a major is not necessarily choosing a career? Why?

Do you agree or disagree with Burtchaell that choosing a major should be done on the "pleasure principle"? Why?

College Major Doesn't Mean All That Much

William Raspberry

William Raspberry is a widely syndicated columnist who works with the *Washington Post* Writers Group. In this brief essay, which was first published as one of his regular columns, he stepped away from his usual commentary on the Washington scene and grew more personal as he counseled his daughter about approaching the question of what college major to select.

• • • • • • • • • • • • • • • • • •

> Soon to every *fledgling* student
> Comes the moment to decide.
> But since Angela's a freshman,
> My advice is: let it ride.

With apologies to James Russell Lowell, that is pretty much my counsel to my daughter, who is about to begin her first year in college. Soon enough, she'll have to face the sophomore necessity of choosing a major—whether or not she's decided on a career. In the meantime, I tell her, don't worry about it.

A part of the reason for my advice is the memory of my own struggle to decide on a major. I eventually had four of them, none of which related to what was to become my career. But the more important reason is my conclusion, regularly reinforced, that majors just don't matter that much. The latest reinforcement is from John Willson, a history professor at Michigan's Hillsdale College, who having heard once too often the question, "But what do I do with a history major?" has decided to do what he can to put his students at ease.

"Every sophomore has a majoring frenzy," he wrote in a campus publication. "It is typical for sophomores to say, 'I want to be an anchorman. Therefore, I will major in journalism. Where do I sign up?' They act like they have had a blow to the *solar plexus* when I say, (a) Hillsdale has no major in journalism, and (b) if we did, it would no more make you an anchorman than a major in English makes you an Englishman."

But rather than simply repeating what professionals already know, or urging colleges to dispense with the requirement for declaring a major, Willson has reduced his advice to a set of rules and principles.

The first, which college students often find incredible, is that aside from such vocational courses as engineering or computer science, any relationship between majors and careers is largely incidental. Physics majors are hardly more likely to become physicists than business majors to become *entrepreneurs*. The rule that derives from this principle: If you wanted your major to be practical, you should have gone to the General Motors Institute.

The second principle is that students (and colleges) should delay the necessity of choosing for as long as practicable. "Most students (and even more parents) have rather vague notions of what the subject of any given subject is. . . . Talk with your parents, but don't let parents, teachers, media experts, television evangelists or fraternity brothers pressure you into a majoring frenzy before you know what the major is all about." In short: All things being equal, it is best to know what you are talking about, which may even prevent majoring frenzies.

The third is a quote from the Rev. James T. Burtchaell (writing in *Notre Dame* magazine): "Pick your major on the pleasure principle, for what you most enjoy studying will draw your mind in the liveliest way to being educated." It's good advice, and not only for students at small liberal-arts colleges. A few years ago, the University of Virginia published a booklet, "Life after Liberal Arts," based on a survey of 2,000 alumni of its college of arts and sciences. The finding: 91 percent of the respondents not only believe that liberal arts prepared them for fulfilling careers but would also not hesitate to recommend liberal-arts majors to students considering those same careers. The "winning combination" derived from the Virginia survey: a liberal-arts foundation, *complemented* with career-related experience and personal initiative.

Colleges aren't assembly lines that, after four years, automatically deposit students into *lucrative* careers. What is far likelier is a series of false starts followed by the discovery of a satisfying career. In the Virginia survey, for example, only 16 percent reported being happy with their first jobs.

Willson's advice, the results of the Virginia survey, and my advice to Angela come down to the same thing: Major in getting an education.

• •

 Vocabulary

As you think about this essay, these definitions may be helpful to you:
1. **fledgling**   a bird at about the age it learns to fly; here, metaphorically, someone getting ready to start independent living
2. **solar plexus**   a *plexus* is a gathering or network of nerves, and the solar plexus is located in the abdomen; a blow to the solar plexus will cause the victim to double over in pain
3. **entrepreneurs**   people who start and maintain businesses, taking the risk for the sake of possible profit
4. **complemented**   not *complimented* or *flattered* but completed and perfected by something else
5. **lucrative**   profitable

 Discussion Questions

1. What reasons does William Raspberry give for his assertion that your choice of a major is not as important as many college students think?
2. How do you react to Raspberry's thesis that any relationship between majors and careers is "largely incidental?" Why is this perceived connection made by so many students?

 Suggestions for Your Journal

Raspberry and Burtchaell clearly agree on some important points about selecting a college major. What argument does Raspberry add to the discussion that Burtchaell does not mention? Which author do you find more persuasive? Why?

Fourteen Ways of Looking at Electives[1]

Thomas L. Minnick

Thomas L. Minnick is Special Assistant to the Vice Provost of Minority Affairs and former associate dean of University College at The Ohio State University, where he completed his bachelor's, master's, and doctoral degrees in English. He is a specialist in the English Bible and the writings of William Blake. In this essay, he encourages you to think before you schedule your electives, so they can complement your required course work by helping you to achieve some of your goals for college study.

Electives are what is left over for you to take once you deduct all your required courses.

Typically, a college degree is made up primarily of several kinds of requirements. These may include courses required of all students, no matter what degree they may have decided to seek; such university-wide requirements are often called "core" or "general education" requirements. They are likely to include some basic mathematics, one or more courses in college-level English composition, and several courses distributed among the social sciences, sciences, and humanities. Does everyone at your institution need to take some history? Then history is probably a general education or "core" requirement for your institution, whether you are working toward a bachelor's degree at a university with an extensive graduate program or toward an associate's degree at a community college.

Additionally, you are likely to have to complete some courses that everyone in your degree program needs to take. For example, students working toward a degree in engineering, no matter what area of specialization, all typically need to have at least a year of college physics, mathematics through differential equations, some basic course work in engineering graphics, mechanics, and chemistry. Similarly, business students are all required to study economics (both "micro" and "macro"), accounting, statistics, marketing, finance, and the like. Requirements shared by everyone aiming toward a specific degree are usually called "program requirements" or "degree requirements."

A third kind of required course work is that which you complete for your major. Major requirements might include an introductory survey course (or a series of them), usually taken by first- or second-year students while they learn the dimensions and variety of the major field. English majors are likely to be

[1]With apologies to Wallace Stevens. (Gentle reader, Wallace Stevens wrote a thoughtful poem entitled "Sixteen Ways of Looking at a Blackbird." You might enjoy it.)

required to take a survey of American literature and another of British literature, for example. In some colleges they may be required to have a course in
research methods for English majors. And some majors require that everyone
in the program complete a senior year "capstone" course that puts—or attempts
to put—all their previous major work into a *coherent* perspective.

Once you add up all these kinds of requirements (general education, college, and major), you are likely to find that there are still some classes you need
to take to complete your degree. At the university where I work, which follows
the quarter system and sets 196 quarter credit hours as the minimum for an undergraduate degree, the university-wide general education core and the col-
lege/program requirements usually total about 100 credits. Major programs vary
dramatically but average about 45 credit hours. Deduct 145 from 196 and you
get 41 credit hours (or eight to ten classes) that are not specified. For these,
which are "electives," our students can take just about anything they like. This
essay is about some ways you can use these extra classes to your advantage.

1. To explore possible majors. Many students enter college without
knowing what they want to study for a major. An undecided student can use
elective hours to explore several possible major programs, usually by taking the
appropriate introductory survey classes. Do you think you might like Forestry?
Sign up for a basic introduction to the field and find out through that class
whether you really have an interest and/or an aptitude for it.

2. To serve as a cushion. This use of electives is closely related to (1)
above. Suppose you started college as an engineering major and then discovered that you lack the commitment or the focus to be an engineer, so you
change programs to business. You will probably have taken some classes in your
first term (engineering graphics, for example) that are not required in your new
major. Electives allow you to move from one major to another without losing
useful credits: in this example, the engineering graphics class will still count toward graduation, and it served the purpose of helping you make a sound decision on a new major. Electives give you flexibility—within reasoned limits—to
change from one program to another without losing credits or unduly prolonging your degree work.

3. To develop a focus or cluster outside your major. Perhaps you
don't really want to be limited to a single concentration. If your college does
not provide for dual majors or minors, or if you don't want to complete *all* the
work for a second major but would like an additional focus to your degree, electives can provide the way. Imagine that you have decided to major in Elementary Education but you also have an interest in the History of Art. Using your
electives, you can build your own concentration in art history by taking the
courses in that area that attract you. In this way you may be able to select your
art history classes more freely than a formal major might allow—limiting yourself to national schools (American painting) or individual styles (contemporary
art) that you really like, while official majors may need to follow a strictly prescribed *regimen* of courses.

4. To explore your career options. Nationally, one of the most fre-quently selected electives is the career exploration course. Such courses usu-ally fall into one of two categories—fairly general in approach and scope, or quite specific. A general approach can help you assess your personal character-istics, such as your interests, abilities, values, and goals. It can also help you ex-plore educational and occupational fields that might match your personal interests and strengths. Some courses include information about techniques for writing your resume and for presenting yourself effectively in job interviews. These general career courses can teach you career decision-making strategies that will be useful throughout your life. The other, more specific type of career course is often limited to specific career opportunities in the area (or areas) related to the department teaching the class: "Careers in Agriculture" would be such a course that focuses on, and discusses in very specific detail, the career options available to people with a specific kind of education. Such a course typically provides very helpful information about specific employers who look for and hire graduates with a particular educational and career background. Career information courses—whether general or specific—can help you en-hance your understanding of who you are in relation to your academic major and related career opportunities and, in so doing, prepare you for the work world.

5. To enhance your marketability. A popular use many students make of their electives is to build a business focus—even if they are not pursuing a business degree. Suppose you are an English major who likes and knows some-thing about computers. By adding several advanced computer science courses to your English major, you become more competitive for job offers that want a liberally educated student with added skills. Your focus might take the form of several courses from a single department (a number of marketing classes, for example), or several related classes from a variety of departments (a marketing class, a course in beginning accounting, a class in business management, a course in personnel issues). A business major might like to take classes in the language and culture of a specific part of the world in order to be better pre-pared to do business with that part of the globe.

6. To develop a talent you have neglected. Are you good at singing or playing a musical instrument? Perhaps you don't want to major in that area, but it would be a shame to give up that *expertise* or let it *languish* while you com-plete your undergraduate studies. Take a class in singing, or join one of your college's choral or instrumental groups. Register for drawing or painting, or mak-ing pottery, or creating art on the computer. Sign up for a basic photography class. Electives can allow you to pursue and develop interests and talents that you do not plan to turn into a major, but that you should not neglect. Because the credit you earn with electives counts toward your graduation, you do not need to feel that courses you take just because you want to are wasted.

7. To get, or stay, fit. I am often surprised by the number of college stu-dents I talk with who participated strenuously in high school sports. Both men and women find physical exercise and competition to be challenging and exciting. Yet often, when such students get to college, they neglect their interests in being fit, largely, I think, because they equate college courses with "serious" work and sports with play. However, getting fit and staying fit are lifelong activities that help you to work and think better. They also promote a healthful lifestyle because people who have worked to keep fit as a rule avoid destructive activities like drinking alcohol to excess and smoking. If your college has a good physical education facility and offers you courses in activities you have never tried, take a few elective credits to learn and practice some of these activities—oriental martial arts, for example, or caving, or whitewater rafting, or working out on the high ropes. And all these physical activities can be great for helping to cope with the stress of college work.

  8. To develop skills in leisure time activities. Once you begin your career, your work will take up much of your life, but it will always be important for you to make time for enriching activities—especially when you are away from the stimulus of a learning environment. Develop the habit of reserving time for thoughtful entertainment. Electives may provide just the opportunity you need to learn more about theater, fine art, music, and similar interests. Do you like jazz? Check your school's course catalogue to see if there are classes in American music, or nonwestern music, that might help you to better understand the origins and history of jazz. Do you like attending plays? Take an introductory theater course, or take an acting class and try out your talents in a learning setting, or sign up to help build scenery and earn college credit while learning more about the technical details of putting on a performance.

  9. To learn to help others. Most universities provide courses, often for modest amounts of credit, in such helpful skills as first aid and cardiopulmonary resuscitation (commonly abbreviated to "CPR"). These skills can help you in getting summer work. More important, knowing how to help others in an emergency can actually save a life—maybe even your own. Less dramatic but also very helpful are opportunities to provide tutoring and similar assistance to others at your university or in your neighborhood. Interested? Ask your adviser if there is a program where you can tutor underprivileged kids or read a textbook for a blind student or help in adaptive physical education for handicapped students. These experiences can teach you a great deal about yourself and may provide some of the greatest personal rewards of your college experience.

  10. To learn life-skills that will be useful later. For example, many business schools provide a "service course" (so named because they teach it as a service to students from outside their own college) about basic financial matters, like establishing credit, managing your income, buying a home, planning for financial independence, selecting basic insurance, and the like. Courses in family financial planning for nonbusiness majors are likely to accentuate the practical and introduce theory only when absolutely necessary. Many other departments offer the chance to learn material that will have lifelong practical value. Basic courses in public speaking and communicating effectively in small groups apply to almost every later career; go to the Communications Department to find them. Most sociology departments offer a class in the varieties of modern marriage, or the sociology of the family—with obvious utility for later experience.

11. To learn to understand and appreciate different cultures. Studying other cultures can help you prepare for working with people from those cultures in your life after college. Most of your life will be spent in the 21st century, and experts predict that there will be *no* majority culture in America by that time. Many American cities in the south and west—Dallas, Los Angeles, Miami—already have no dominant majority group, only larger or smaller minorities. Even if you plan to live in a largely *homogeneous* small town, chances are you will be doing business with, or your children will need to do business with, the larger multicultural world. If you find that a little frightening, take a class in dealing with other cultures and you may find it exciting instead. Check with the appropriate language departments, and you are likely to find some classes taught in English that will help you understand the patterns and values of cultures different from your own.

12. To learn study and time management skills. Most two- and four-year colleges now provide organized help for students who need better study habits. This need is not restricted to students who did less than well in high school. Often, good students could earn better than average grades in high school with only modest investments of study time—and have consequently developed weak study habits that need to improve in the face of more difficult, more rapid college instruction. Would you like to read with greater comprehension? Could you manage your time better than you do? Check with your adviser for information about classes that teach effective study skills, time management, and related learning skills. Even if these are offered *without* credit, and so are not technically "elective hours," consider them carefully, since they can greatly improve the quality of your work as a student.

13. To develop leadership skills. Usually students turn to their extracurricular experiences (student government, interest clubs, other campus associations) for training in leadership. But there is a significant body of writings about various leadership qualities and styles, and your institution is likely to offer at least one credit-bearing class in leadership. Such courses are often taught as "laboratory courses"—that is, you get practical training in a hands-on way. If you are aiming toward a professional career in a management position, you ought to get some experience in leadership, and such a course may be your best route toward it.

14. To take some courses just because you will enjoy them. In the best of all possible worlds, every class you take would be one that you love to attend, and I hope that many of your required courses—in general education, in classes that relate to your degree program, and certainly in your major—fit this description. But in the real world we are bound to spend our time in, you may find yourself required to take some classes you enroll in only because they are required. If you anticipate that such a course is coming up next term, you may successfully balance it with an elective class that you take just because you want to take it: perhaps you've already had the instructor, and you really enjoyed his or her previous course, or perhaps you've always had a hobby of reading about a specific area, so taking a course in it as an elective would help round out your knowledge of that field.

How can you select classes for Use Number 14? I encourage my advisees to imagine that they have just won the state lottery (tonight at $35 million!) and have spent a chunk of it having fun—traveling the world, buying your parents a mansion and each of your friends an expensive car. Eventually, you tire of doing nothing, however nicely you can now afford to do it, and you realize the permanent attraction of learning. In such a case, what courses would you take? Assuming you do not financially *need* a degree, you could just take the classes you want. If you were free in this way, what classes would you sign up for? Make a list of them, then sign up for them as electives!

Reprinted by permission of the author.   •

 Vocabulary

As you think about this essay, these definitions may be helpful to you:
1. **coherent**   consistent
2. **regimen**   a systematic plan
3. **expertise**   the skill of an expert
4. **languish**   to be or become weak or enervated
5. **homogeneous**   of the same or similar kind or nature

 Discussion Questions

1. How are electives defined in this reading? How do they fit into the general structure of degree requirements?
2. What kind of electives can enhance your chances of finding a satisfying career?
3. Through what kind of electives can you acquire skills and knowledge that may be useful for your future leisure-time activities?
4. Although taking extra courses in your major is not listed as a way to use elective hours, would this be a good way to increase your mastery of the subject? Why or why not?
5. How can you expand your understanding and appreciation of other cultures through electives? Why is this a particularly good use of electives today?

 Suggestions for Your Journal

What has been your impression of the function of electives in the curriculum? Which of the 14 reasons for selecting electives appeal to you the most? Why? Look at the list of courses in your college's catalogue. If you could select any courses to take just for fun (and not worry about a grade), which would you choose? Why? What does this tell you about your choice of major?

The Right Stuff: Research Strategies for the Internet Age

Nancy O'Hanlon

Nancy O'Hanlon is an associate professor of University Libraries at The Ohio State University, where she has taught library research skills and recently developed online courses in using the Internet and other technological tools for beginning and advanced researchers. In the following reading she explains why students need to develop good research strategies, especially given that information defines the age. Books, she reminds us, will also always be an important tool for any research undertaking.

● ● ● ● ● ● ● ● ● ● ● ● ● ● ● ●

Tom Wolfe describes the unique qualities that enabled the first U.S. astronauts to meet unknown challenges as "the right stuff." For these explorers, "the right stuff" was not simply courage, but a unique combination of daring, skill, experience and a persistent determination to succeed:

> ...the ability to go up in a hurtling piece of machinery and put his hide on the line and then have the moxie, the reflexes, the experience, the coolness, to pull it back in the last yawning moment—and then to go up again the next day, and the next day, and every next day....A career in flying was like climbing one of those ancient Babylonian pyramids made up of a dizzy progression of steps and ledges, a *ziggurat*, a pyramid extraordinarily high and steep; and the idea was to prove at every foot of the way up that pyramid that you were one of the elected and anointed ones who had the right stuff and could move higher and higher....
> (Wolfe 24)

Research today challenges us to navigate effectively through Internet space. At one time, knowledge of the library and skill at using printed resources were sufficient preparation for finding useful information. Today, the Internet, particularly the World Wide Web, is the vehicle for most research. The sheer volume of information available through this medium is staggering, like the Babylonian pyramid in Wolfe's vision. To be a successful researcher also requires "the right stuff"—imagination and flexibility, well-developed searching skills, persistence and the ability to evaluate information coming from diverse sources.

Why is it important to learn research skills? During college, students are expected to find information in order to answer academic research questions, understand important societal issues and analyze complex problems. Information supplied by teachers and textbooks is no longer the sole basis for learning. College students are exposed to a wider range of information and must make judgments about the relevance and credibility of sources. In *The Craft of Research*, Booth, Colomb and Williams state that, "Those who can neither do reliable research nor reliably report the research of others will find themselves on the sidelines of a world that increasingly lives on information" (Booth 6). They also contend that "We are inundated with information, most of it packaged to suit someone else's commercial or political self-interest. More than ever, society needs people with critical minds, people who can look at research, ask their own questions, and find their own answers" (Booth 3).

Too Much Information?

How much information is available to researchers in the Internet age? Consider the following estimates provided by a recent study published online by the University of California, Berkeley:

- The world produces between 1 and 2 exabytes of unique information in all formats (print, digital, broadcast) each year. An exabyte is a billion *gigabytes*. If stored on floppy disks, the stack would be 2 million miles high.
- Digital information comprises the largest amount of this total. The Internet is the youngest and fastest growing medium today. In 2000, the World Wide Web consisted of roughly 2.5 billion static, publicly available Web pages and is growing at a rate of 100 percent per year.
- Another group of Web pages is dynamically generated and stored in Web-accessible databases. This "deep Web" is estimated to be 400 to 550 times larger than the static "surface" Web.
- Taking all kinds of Web information into account, there are 550 billion Web-connected documents, and 95 percent of this information is publicly accessible. 7.3 million new pages are added to the Web per day. (Lyman, Executive Summary)

Much of this Web-accessible information is not available in any other format. For example, *NameBase: A Cumulative Index of Books and Clippings* <http://www.namebase.org> is a database containing information about people, groups and corporations who have been influential in politics, the military, intelligence, crime and the media since World War II. These names have been drawn from various books, articles and government documents recovered using the Freedom of Information Act. Because of the way it is constructed, this database allows users to find other names that appear on the same pages and thus uncover potential relationships or connections between individuals and groups. *NameBase* is a unique part of the "deep Web" that could be useful both to investigative journalists and to students.

How can you locate useful research tools like *NameBase* among billions of Web sites? Some rules of the road for effective searching of the Web information space are described in the next section of this essay.

Smart Search Techniques

In the years since 1994, when the World Wide Web was invented, a number of powerful search tools have become available to help Web users locate information hiding within this mass of billions of documents. These tools fall into two basic categories: Web directories and Web indexes (or search engines). Success hinges on choosing the right tool as well as using it effectively.

Web directories are lists of sites, along with brief descriptions of their content, selected and compiled by knowledgeable editors. Directories can be browsed by topic and are good starting points for most Internet research because they offer quick access to the best known and most useful sites.

For example, the *Internet Movie Database* <http://www.imdb.com> is widely recognized as an excellent site for finding information on film casts, credits, plots and characters. It is relatively easy to identify using a Web directory like the *Britannica.com Internet Guide* <http://www.britannica.com>, which assigns one to five star ratings to sites in each of its topical categories.

If your information need is not met by sources listed in Web directories, you can search one of several large Web indexes to locate relevant documents. Web indexes are created by software programs called "spiders" or "robots" because they work automatically, crawling from one Web page to any others that are linked to it, harvesting information. The spiders collect every word on each Web page and store them in a huge index or list. When you enter a search, this index is what your search words are matched against.

The companies that own these search engines report that most people enter only one or two search words. When you consider the size of these Web indexes (millions of documents, with thousands of words in each document), this search strategy (or lack thereof) seems doomed to failure. You must use more than one or two search terms in Web indexes in order to narrow down search results and make them more relevant to your specific research question.

Search engines are quite literal and don't deal well with words that have multiple meanings. Using a variety of relevant search words can help with this problem as well. For example, a search for the word "spider" might retrieve this essay, since that word is used several times. [But] if you were looking for information about the insect, rather than the Web software program called a spider, you could get better results by including other search words that also describe what you want (such as "insect" or "arachnid").

Three other techniques will help to improve your chance of success when searching in large Web indexes. First, learn to use search qualifiers in order to specify the importance of your search terms and indicate any relationship between them. For example:

- To require that all of your search terms are included in each document found, you may put the plus sign (+) before each term.
  Example: +spider +arachnid +tarantula
- Use the minus sign (−) before each word that should be eliminated from your results.
  Example: +spider −Web −robot
- Use quotation marks to indicate when search words should be treated as a phrase.
  Example: "brown recluse spider"

It is also important to develop intelligent limiting strategies. In many search engines, it is possible to limit or screen search results by different variables, such as type of site (for example, government, military, educational, or commercial). This technique can be especially fruitful when you want to find varying perspectives. For example, you could limit a search for information on campaign finance reform to government Web sites, in order to learn the viewpoints of elected officials on this topic.

Finally, use specialized search tools, ones that focus on a particular topical area, whenever possible. By using specialized resources, like *FindLaw* <http://www.findlaw.com> for legal topics or *Achoo* <http://www.achoo.com> for health-related research, you are searching only the portion of Web space that is relevant for your research topic and are thus more likely to find good results.

Evaluating Information Quality

When we use the phrase "good results" in this context, we really mean search results that appear to be useful based on a quick look at the Web page. Determining the quality of information found on the Web actually takes more effort and some special techniques.

It is relatively easy and inexpensive to "publish" information on the Internet. On one hand, this open environment often permits you to see more sides of a topic than you might when relying only on printed sources. For example, when doing research on sweatshop labor in developing countries, you may be able to locate first person accounts and discussions of working conditions in overseas factories, reports of watchdog groups and other kinds of information sources that are difficult or impossible to find in print.

At the same time, because there is no real filtering mechanism to check accuracy, one cannot accept at face value the information found on the Web. In *Evaluating Internet Research Sources,* Robert Harris notes that on the Internet, information exists on a continuum of reliability and quality:

> Information is everywhere on the Internet, existing in large quantities and continuously being created and revised. This information exists in a large variety of kinds (facts, opinions, stories, interpretations, statistics) and is created for many purposes (to inform, to persuade, to sell, to present a viewpoint, and to create or change an attitude or belief). For each of these various kinds of purposes, information exists on many levels of quality or reliability. It ranges from very good to very bad and includes every shade in between. (Harris, Introduction)

Harris further notes that when evaluating information sources, there is no single perfect indicator of quality. You must make inferences from a collection of clues. Here are three important variables to consider as you review and evaluate sources:

Purpose: Consider both the purpose of the source as well as the purpose of your research when determining which Web sources to use. Sites published by advocacy groups (such as the Sierra Club or the American Civil Liberties Union) may include fact sheets, position papers and findings from scientific research studies. These groups may present evidence to support their cause but ignore contrary findings. If you are attempting to understand an organization's mission or find evidence that is representative of a particular viewpoint, advocacy organization Web sites can be quite useful. Look elsewhere for a balanced treatment of controversial issues.

Authority: The most credible information is provided by writers who have education, training or life experience in a field relevant to the information. You can read the jacket blurb to find out more about the author and the scope of a printed book. On the Web, look for an "About Us" link to find brief information about site authors and their credentials.

For example, the *nationalissues.com* Web site <http://www.nationalissues.com> has an "About Us" page that provides the names and educational/employment backgrounds of the principal staff as well as a statement about this site's intent to provide a balanced viewpoint on issues such as gun control, school reform, and taxes. The authors appear to be individuals with substantial experience in public policy research, government and journalism.

But inquiring minds may want to check credentials or learn more than Web site authors tell us about themselves. If the author is an organization rather than an individual, what is their reputation? You have access to the tools that will help you to locate this kind of information. Search in a Web index to find other documents that the site authors may have published. Use your college library's catalog and online reference databases (of newspaper, magazine and journal articles) to locate works in print written by or about individuals and organizations.

Content: When evaluating the content provided by a Web site, there are a number of questions to consider. These are the same questions that one would ask when evaluating the content of any information source.

- First, does the information appear to be accurate? Factual information may be checked in other sources.
- Is there an attempt by the author to be objective? Opposing viewpoints should be presented in an accurate manner. Harris notes that "there is no such thing as pure objectivity, but a good writer should be able to control his or her biases." Does the author use a calm, reasoned tone or resort to inflammatory language? Does the site author have a vested interest in the topic, one where "the messenger will gain financially if you believe the message ..."? (Harris, Objectivity)
- Finally, does the author cite evidence to support claims and then document (provide references to) these sources, so that they are easily available for further research? Harris recommends that you "triangulate" an important information source, finding at least two other sources that support it. References supplied by an author can help in this process, but you should look for other sources as well.

A World Beyond the Web

Does all important information live on the World Wide Web, somewhere among the exabtyes? In a word, no. Despite its size and scope, not everything useful for research is on the Web. There are numerous holes in this fabric—many important printed books and articles will never be available online, because their conversion to digital format is not cost-effective.

For example, when studying about focus group interviews for a marketing or sociology class, you should read *The Focused Interview*, the seminal work on this subject written by Robert K. Merton, an eminent sociologist who invented the technique. This book was first published in 1956 and a second edition appeared in 1990. Neither work is Web-accessible.

Although it is important to learn how to search effectively on the Web and to evaluate the information found there, it is equally important to understand that there are projects for which Web research will not be sufficient. The college library will continue to be important to successful research, despite the phenomenal growth of online information. It is the place where students can expect to find the most important or influential works on many subjects as well as personal assistance and advice about research problems from librarians. Having "the right stuff" for research in the Internet age involves the willingness to explore all spaces where information and knowledge abide, not just the most obvious ones. Booth states that by learning and practicing the craft of research, you

> …join the oldest and most esteemed of human conversations—the conversation conducted by Aristotle, Marie Curie, Booker T. Washington, Albert Einstein … all those who by contributing to human knowledge have freed us from ignorance and misunderstanding. They and countless others once stood where
> you now stand. Our world today is different because of their research. It is no exaggeration to say that, done well, yours will change the world tomorrow.
> (Booth 7)

Works Cited

Booth, Wayne C., Gregory C. Colomb and Joseph M. Williams. *The Craft of Research.* Chicago: University of Chicago Press, 1995.

Harris, Robert. *Evaluating Internet Research Sources.* Version Date: November 17, 1997. 30 October 2000 <http://www.vanguard. edu/rharris/evalu8it.htm>.

Lyman, Peter and Hal R. Varian. *How Much Information?* University of California, Berkeley: School of Information Management and Systems. 30 October 2000 <http://www.sims.berkeley.edu/how-much-info/>.

Wolfe, Tom. *The Right Stuff.* New York: Farrar, Straus, Giroux, 1979.

• •

 Vocabulary

As you think about this essay, these definitions may be helpful to you:
1. **ziggurat**   a form of early temple with the general shape of a pyramid but with recessed tiers that appear as huge stairs or ledges around the structure

2. **gigabyte** a unit of computer information. The basic unit is a binomial bit (that is, its value must be either 0 or 1). Eight bits make a byte; 1,048,576 bytes make a megabyte; and 1,024 megabytes make a gigabyte.
3. **inundated** flooded; overwhelmed

 Discussion Questions

1. What is the difference between a Web index and a Web directory?
2. What does O'Hanlon mean when she talks about a "search strategy"?
3. Explain the use of these signs in searching for information on the Web: +, -, and " ".
4. What kind of questions should you ask when evaluating a Web site? Give some examples that O'Hanlon does *not* provide for evaluating a Web site with respect to its purpose, authority, and content.
5. O'Hanlon says that we still need to consult books for much of our information. Is she right? Explain your answer.

 Suggestions for Your Journal

Sometimes a student's first experience in a college library can be overwhelming. What were your impressions the first time you walked into the main library at your college? Do you feel more comfortable doing research on the Web or with traditional book searches? Why? What library skills are you lacking? Where can you get help to improve these skills?

Please! It's Only Seven Minutes Late, Professor

Joel J. Gold

This essay describes Professor Joel J. Gold's "solution" to overdue student papers. However, after recounting a student's experience with a late paper to his classes, he was the recipient of one class's payback.

• • • • • • • • • • • • • • • • • •

Toward the bottom of the large *pseudo*-wooden door of my faculty office is a small hand-lettered sign that reads: PAPER SHREDDER. An arrow points to the space under the door where students are always sliding things, such as late papers and requests for letters of reference. My colleagues see the sign and make little jokes, but most of them don't really know the story behind it.

It began simply enough a few years back, when I was telling a class about the next essay. Allowing myself to be jollied away from the usual deadline of class time on Thursday, I told them the papers could be submitted by 5 P.M. Friday, but no later. At 5 o'clock, I would leave and turn on the paper shredder, so that anything slipped under the door later would be automatically shredded.

Now it should be obvious that in these *straitened* times no garden-variety English professor is going to have a paper shredder at his disposal. They all grinned back at me, and I figured we understood each other.

By 4:50 on Friday, all but three papers had been turned in. In a few minutes I heard someone running down the hall, and a young man thrust his paper at me. "Plenty of time," I said. He looked almost disappointed that he was not the last. At 4:57 the next-to-last paper arrived. "Am I the last one?" the young woman wanted to know. Again disappointment.

Well, now it was 5 o'clock, and one paper was still out. It was possible that it would not arrive, but the student was one of my conscientious overachievers. She was probably triple-checking her footnotes. I decided to wait.

I shut my door. I turned out my light. Then I pulled a chair up behind the closed door, gathered a couple of sheets of old ditto paper in my hand, and sat down to wait. At seven minutes past, I heard footsteps hurrying toward my office. Whoever it was stopped right outside. And panted for a few seconds. Then the paper began to come in under the door. There in the dark, I was ready.

With exactly the degree of pull you get when you try to make change for a dollar in one of those airport change machines, I tugged slightly and evenly at the proffered paper. For a moment, the person on the other side gripped the paper more tightly. Then, probably surprised at herself, she let go. Her paper was mine.

I took the ditto paper I had been holding all this time and began as noisily as I could to tear it into bits and pieces. There was dead silence on the other side of the door. Then I said aloud. "Chomp, chomp, CHOMP." Audible gasp outside.

"Please!" she said. "It's only seven minutes late." The thought of what it might look like outside that door to a passerby got me giggling. (I know, I know. It was unworthy of me. But I pictured a stricken young woman, talking to the door: "Please, door, it's only seven minutes late.") Perhaps the muffled giggling or the implication of the "Chomp, chomp, CHOMP" had just registered, but I heard the closest thing to a "Humph!" I have heard in real life before she stalked off down the hall. I suppressed my giggling, collected my papers and my *composure,* and went home.

She wasn't in class the next time it met, and I told the story—without names, of course. The class loved it, "Chomp, chomp, CHOMP!" they kept repeating throughout the hour.

I told the story again the following semester and the one after that—you can get a lot of mileage out of a good story. Students began to ask me about the paper shredder, and that's when I decided on the sign for the bottom of the door.

For a couple of semesters it was Our Joke. But you know how it is—sooner or later the old retired gunslinger is going to have to draw one more time. One of my students actually had the nerve to say, "You're always telling us about what you did to other classes, but you don't ever *do* anything about it." Now it was my turn for a "Humph!"

So amid the groaning about the deadlines for papers in my course, "The Comic Spirit," was born the idea for One More Twist. Essays were due Friday by 5 P.M. "And then the paper shredder," they chortled. "And then the paper shredder," I said.

When 5 P.M. came, and six papers were still missing, I gathered up what I had, turned out the lights, and went home. That weekend I spent much of my spare time tearing paper—all kinds of paper—into tiny bits and dropping them into a brown paper sack.

On class day, I secreted my nearly full shopping sack inside a large book bag and went upstairs. I *surreptitiously* pulled it out and hid it in my reading stand, planning to *discourse* on the papers at the end of the period.

It worked out even better. Halfway through the period, as I was shifting from *Northanger Abbey* to *Alice in Wonderland,* one of my anxious worrywarts raised his hand. "When," he wanted to know, "will you be giving back the papers?"

"I'm glad you asked me that," I said, quite sincerely. The students were now all waiting for the answer, not paying much attention to my hands, which were reaching in behind the reading stand to move the sack into position.

"Those of you who turned your essays in by 5 o'clock last Friday will get them back at the end of next week." A slight groan: They had hoped it would be sooner. They always do. "For the rest, those who slid them under the door some time after 5 P.M.—and I'm afraid I don't know how many of you there actually were . . ." By now, they were hanging on every word. The sack was in ready position. "But those of you who turned your paper in late (I had lifted the sack high above the desk) should come up after class (I turned the sack upside down and thousands—thousands—of little shreds of paper were fluttering down over the reading stand, the desk, the floor) and identify your papers. If you can."

There was an explosion of laughter, stamping feet, pandemonium, as the shower of confetti continued for several seconds. They could not believe that a university professor would do anything so idiotic.

"Now," I said, in my best professional rhythms, "let us consider the scene in which Alice finds the caterpillar sitting on a mushroom."

At the end of the period, while I tried to get as many of the tiny bits of paper into the wastebasket as I could, I saw a few of my students in the doorway, pointing at the debris. They were apparently explaining to friends and passersby what had just happened in the classroom. And I don't think they were discussing the Mad Hatter or the March Hare. At least not directly.

I knew that somewhere down the road the old gunslinger would probably have to draw one last time, but I reckoned I was safe for a couple more semesters.

I didn't have quite that much time.

Given everything else that had gone on in my honors satire class, I might have known they would be the ones. I had, of course, recounted to them the story of the paper shredder.

The day I realized just how closely they had been listening was the day their papers were due. As I unlocked my office door, I saw on the floor a few hundred strips of shredded paper. Without quite understanding what had happened, I gathered up the scraps and carried them to my desk. There, I found that the segments could be fitted together and deciphered. I appeared to be in possession of 10 or 11 (it was a little hard to tell) essays on "...andide and Saint Joan," "The Innocents in *Volpone* and *Can* . . . ," and "Satiri . . . *Travels*." Page numbers helped me piece parts of essays together. Then I realized that the scraps were all on copier paper. On a hunch, I went to see the departmental secretaries. Grinning widely, they handed me a large envelope filled with the originals.

Those wags in the honors class had copied their essays, shredded the copies, slid them under my door, and given the originals to the secretaries to whom, obviously, they had explained the whole scam.

And up on Boot Hill, the old gunslinger's tombstone reads: Those Who Live by the Shredder, Die by the Shredder.

Reprinted by permission of the author.

 Vocabulary

As you think about this essay, these definitions may be helpful to you:
1. **pseudo**   false
2. **straitened**   hard up, short of money
3. **composure**   calmness of mind, bearing, or appearance
4. **surreptitiously**   secretively, as if afraid of being caught
5. **discourse**   verbal exchange of ideas

 Discussion Questions

1. What happened to the student who turned in her paper seven minutes late?
2. How did Gold get even with the class that began to doubt his story about the paper shredder? What was their reaction?
3. How did one class "get even" with the author? How did Gold react to their prank?
4. What policies do your professors have about late work? Should there be a campus-wide policy on this issue? Why or why not?

 Suggestions for Your Journal

Have you ever turned in a late assignment? What was the result? What do you think is a fair reaction to students who turn in papers late? How would you react to Gold's policy if you were in his class?

Under what circumstances do you think it is acceptable for you to turn in a paper late? If you turn your assignments in on time and others turn in theirs late without penalty, have you been treated fairly? Why?

Why I Don't Let Students Cut My Classes

William R. Brown

William R. Brown is professor of English at the Philadelphia College of Textiles and Science. In this essay, he presents his opinions on why students cut classes and describes how he arrived at his no-cut policy in his course. The positive results from enforcing his policy are also described.

Last year I announced to my classes my new policy on absences: None would be allowed, except for illness or personal emergency. Even though this violated the statement on cuts in the student handbook, which allows freshmen cuts each term up to twice the number of class meetings per week and imposes no limit for upperclassmen, my students didn't fuss. They didn't fuss even after they discovered, when I telephoned or sent warning notices through the mail to students who had missed classes, that I meant business.

Part of their acceptance of the policy may have resulted from the career orientation of our college, but I don't think that was the main reason. After I explained the policy, most seemed to recognize that it promoted their own academic interests. It was also a requirement that virtually all of them would be obliged to observe—and would expect others to observe—throughout their working lives. It had to be Woody Allen who said that a major part of making it in life is simply showing up.

I told my classes about recent research, by Howard Schuman and others, indicating that academic success is more closely tied to class attendance than to the amount of time spent studying. I shared my sense of disappointment and personal *affront* when I carefully prepare for a class and a substantial number of students do not attend. I think they got the message that the policy is not arbitrary—that I care about their learning and expect them to care about my professional effort.

I don't claim to have controlled all the variables, but after I instituted the no-cut rule, student performance in my classes improved markedly, not so much in the top rank as at the bottom. In fact, the bottom rank almost disappeared, moving up and swelling the middle range to such an extent that I have reassessed my evaluation methods to differentiate among levels of performance in that range. The implications of so dramatic an improvement are surely worth pondering.

Additional benefits of the policy have been those one would expect to result from a full classroom. Student morale is noticeably higher, as is mine. Discussions are livelier, assignments are generally turned in on time, and very few students miss quizzes.

The mechanics of maintaining the policy kept me a little busier than usual, especially at first, but the results would have justified a lot more effort. I called or mailed notes to several students about their cuts, some more than once. I eventually advised a few with *invincibly* poor attendance to drop my course when it seemed that an unhappy outcome was likely. They did.

No doubt this kind of shepherding is easier in a small college. But it can work almost anyplace where a teacher cares enough about the educational stakes to make it work. The crucial element is caring.

At the first faculty meeting of the year, I confessed what I was doing. After all, I was defying college policy. I told my colleagues—at least those not cutting the meeting—that it rankled me when I had carefully prepared a class and a fifth, a quarter, or a third of the students didn't show. I thought my classes were good, and I *knew* Faulkner, Austen, and Tolstoy were good. What had been lacking in my classes, I said, was a significant proportion of the students. I told my colleagues that I believed my problem was not unique but was true of college classes everywhere, and that I was doing something about it.

Although no one seemed to attach much importance to my ignoring college policy, few of my colleagues gave me active support. Some were agreed that a 25 percent absence rate in a college class was not alarming. Others felt that college students must take responsibility for their studies, and that we should not feel liable for their losses from cut classes. One implied that if students could bag a lot of classes and still pass the course, it reflected badly on the teacher.

If professors have enough drawing power, another said, students will attend their classes. (How do you *parry* that?) Still another pointed out that if the professor covers enough material, there will be no time to waste taking the roll. In a large lecture, someone said, who knows who is there and who isn't? After the meeting, one *wag* told me I should consider using the acronym PAP for my "professional attendance policy," but congratulated me on at least evoking an interesting discussion in a faculty meeting, something rare indeed. It was easy to conclude that most of them preferred not to see a problem—at least their problem—in spotty class attendance.

Why do students cut so frequently? I can cite the immediate causes, but I first want to note the enabling circumstance: They cut because they are allowed to. They cut because of the climate of acceptance that comes from our belief that responsibility can be developed only when one is free, free even to act against personal best interests. That this is a misapplied belief in this case can be easily demonstrated. When substantial numbers of students do not attend, classroom learning is depreciated, student and teacher morale suffer, and academic standards are compromised. Students who miss classes unnecessarily are hurting more than themselves. With our *complicity*, they are undermining what colleges and universities are all about.

Students cut for two general reasons. They have things to do that appear more important than the class, or they wish to avoid what they fear will be painful consequences if they attend. In regard to the first, nursing an illness or attending family weddings or funerals are good excuses for missing a class. But other excuses—the demands of outside jobs, social engagements (including recovering from the night before), completing assignments for other courses—are, at best, questionable.

The other general reason is more disturbing and perhaps less well recognized. A few years ago, I asked several classes what they most disliked about the way courses were taught, and the answer was plain—anything that produced sustained tension or anxiety. I believe cutting is often a result of that aversion. The response of students to feelings of personal inadequacy, fear of humiliation, or a threatening professorial personality or teaching style is often simply to avoid class. This response feeds on itself, as frequent absences make attending even more threatening.

But what accounts for frequent cutting where the teacher tries to make the material interesting, knows the students by name, and approaches them with respect, help, and affability? I accept that question as unanswerable. I simply tell my students: Attend my classes regularly or drop the course. That's the rule.

Reprinted by permission of the author.

Vocabulary

As you think about this essay, these definitions may be helpful to you:
1. **affront**   an insult
2. **invincibly**   incapable of being overcome or subdued
3. **parry**   to evade, to shove aside
4. **wag**   joker, smart-aleck
5. **complicity**   association with or participation in

Discussion Questions

1. What, according to Brown, does research indicate about academic success as related to class attendance?
2. What happened after the author instituted his no-cut rule?
3. What benefits did he see after enforcing the policy?
4. What reaction did he get from his colleagues?
5. Why, according to Brown, do students cut classes?

Suggestions for Your Journal

Have you ever cut a class? If so, what were the consequences? If you put yourself in the place of your instructor, how would you be affected by students cutting your class? Do you think students appreciate a teacher who cares enough about them to institute such a policy? For what reasons would you cut a class? Can you answer Professor Brown's "unanswerable" question about why some students cut classes, even when all the positive aspects of the course are in place?

Passive Versus Active Studying

Jason Rich

Jason Rich is the best-selling author of more than 25 books and is an award-winning radio and television producer. This reading is about studying, a subject many new college students may think they have already mastered. After all, they were successful in high school using study techniques that were adequate to their needs for many years. Because college work can provide a much greater degree of challenge, both in quantity and difficulty, Rich recommends a specific attitude and approach to studying.

• • • • • • • • • • • • • • • • • •

Let's face it, college is about meeting new people, experiencing new things, being on your own for the first time, and learning. When you get right down to it, college is also about attending classes, reading textbooks, writing papers, and doing lots of studying. Knowing how to manage your time and studying correctly will not only provide you with plenty of extra hours per week that you can spend doing fun things but also help to ensure that you earn the best possible grades.

It's all too easy to become so caught up in the details that you lose sight of what you are studying and why. Without a sense of this big picture, you can easily feel unfocused. However, if you maintain a clear sense of what you are doing and why, you are more likely to remain on track. Throughout your studies, as you become *immersed* in the details of various subjects and tasks, make certain that you step back every so often to appreciate that big picture. Try to see how each task you go about fits into the whole. If you see how each task contributes something of use to you personally, you'll remain much more focused on your work and you'll find your studies more fulfilling.

Although they don't realize it, many students approach studying as a *passive* activity. They think that as long as they look at their notes and read their textbooks they are covering the material adequately. Studying, in this sense, is not much different from watching television: You simply look, listen and somehow "take it all in." But you probably are never going to have an exam on a particular television show.

The material you study in school is different; you will be tested on it and need to recall information in great detail. Moreover, you will often need to take information you've learned and apply it to other areas. Sitting back and "taking it all in" is therefore not going to work in this case.

Rather than approaching studying in this passive manner, you should emphasize the importance of active study. Instead of merely looking at and listening to new material, you need to think about it and make it a part of your general knowledge. As a result, you are better able to remember the information for exams and also to apply it to other situations.

In a general sense, you need to establish yourself as an active student from the start. That means acknowledging that your education involves work—hard work. Even though you might be sitting at a desk or lying on the couch reading over notes, your mind must remain hard at work. As soon as you slip into a passive *mode*, the material before you will be lost and you might as well be watching television.

The point of taking notes is not to have a copy of what the teacher has told you. If that were the case, why would there be lectures at all? Wouldn't it just be easier to read it in a book? The fact is that live communication is very powerful and very effective. For example, if you were to try to have a telephone conversation with someone who spoke a language foreign to you, it would be impossible for you to understand what was being said (unless, of course, you happen to speak that language yourself). However, if you were to try to have the conversation in person, you'd probably understand something. You'd be able to read body language, watch gestures, and pay attention to facial expressions, which provide information about what is being communicated. In turn, the speaker would see from your expression what you did and did not understand and adopt other techniques to try to communicate.

By attending live lectures, you can gain a deeper understanding of the material being presented. As in a conversation with someone who is speaking a foreign language, you'll receive additional information through body language, expression, and tone of voice. Also, simply by being present and listening attentively, you'll pick up more of the material than you would by merely reading. Live performance, after all, is generally more compelling and likely to hold your interest; that's why people pay so much for concert and theater tickets.

Learning to Listen

Taking effective notes doesn't start when you begin writing; it begins with being an effective listener. We take it for granted that we all know how to listen; that listening is a natural skill requiring no work at all. The truth is, listening is a difficult task and very few people know how to do it well. Have you ever been in the midst of a conversation with someone, nodding your head in agreement, and suddenly found yourself unable to respond to a question they have just asked? Although you may have heard them, you weren't listening to them.

Why is listening so difficult? One reason is that we confuse hearing with listening. Hearing is passive; it means some sound has *reverberated* in your ear, whether or not you want it to, and there's been a noise. Listening, on the other hand, is an active process. It implies that you must do something to accomplish it. It takes action and, often, work to listen well. For example, let's say you are sitting on a crowded train talking with a friend. You hear the noise of the train, the chatter of passengers around you, the boom box being blasted by a teenager, and somewhere in all that, you even hear your friend. But to understand what your friend is telling you, you need to distinguish her words from all the background noise. The same principle applies to classroom lectures. There may not be the same amount of noise in a lecture room as on a crowded train, but you still have to work hard to listen to the professor's words.

Following are strategies for effective listening. They can help with your note taking as well as with any interpersonal encounters, from conversations to job interviews. Develop good listening skills now and they'll last a lifetime and continue to bring you success. People respect someone who listens carefully. More important, those who listen are certain to catch important information that others don't.

Strategies for Effective Listening

1. *Make the effort.* The first step to effective listening is to realize that listening takes effort. It won't happen on its own and it's not something that is going to take place naturally just by your being there. As you go into situations where it's important for you to listen, be an active listener and determined to listen carefully. Concentrate. It may be difficult at first, but in time you'll get better.

2. *Pay attention to the speaker.* It is very difficult to listen to someone if you are not giving all your attention to that person. Ideally, you should look at the person's face the entire time she is speaking. However, in a lecture this is not always possible because you also need to look at your notes from time to time. Try, if you can, to write while keeping your eye on the professor. This may make your notes more messy than usual but, in time, you'll get more *adept* at writing without looking at the page. If you can't write and look at the professor at the same time, make certain to look up from your notes frequently. This will insure that you are maintaining a direct line of communication with her. If the professor is explaining a difficult concept, you are much better off looking at her and not writing. This way you can concentrate on listening and understanding. After the professor is finished, jot down a few notes or phrases to help you remember what was said.

3. *Minimize distraction.* To maintain that direct line of communication between you and the speaker, it is important to minimize all outside distractions. Different things can be distracting. Perhaps there is someone very attractive whom you always sit near in class and who occupies more of your attention than the professor. Maybe a friend you sit with can't resist chatting during the lecture. Even something as tame as chewing gum or a grumbling stomach can begin to sound like a major earthquake when you are trying to pay attention to something else. Choose your seat carefully and come to class well fed and prepared to listen.

   You might also decide to sit closer to the professor if it helps you concentrate better. Sitting in the first few rows is not absolutely crucial; in fact, some people feel very uncomfortable being that close to the professor. However, if you are having trouble hearing or concentrating try sitting in the first or second row. You might be surprised at how much more of the lecture you catch.

4. *Watch for lapses.* Become more attuned to the current situation when your mind is drifting to other subjects or your eyes are wandering out of the window. When this happens, focus your attention back on the speaker immedi-

ately. Be aware that everyone is prone to lapses in attention, and that if you can recognize when your mind wanders, you will begin to correct yourself much faster and not miss as much.

5. *Work at it.* Listening, like any skill, improves as you work at it. As you try to concentrate in different situations, you'll find you get more proficient.

6. *Watch for clues from the speaker.* Listening effectively means more than paying attention to the words of the speaker. People convey a great deal of information through the way they speak as well as what they say. Get in the habit of concentrating on additional signals from a speaker besides spoken words. Pay attention to the speaker's tone of voice, the volume of their speech, pauses, hand gestures, and body language—these signals can enhance your understanding of the speaker's words. Additionally, by being alert to these elements in addition to spoken words, you have more to occupy your attention, insuring that you remain actively engaged in the lecture, conversation, or discussion.

Finally, always remember to keep sight of the big picture; remember why you are in school and what you hope to gain. Set short-term and long-term goals for yourself. Be an active student, not a passive one. And think of studying as communicating—with teachers, texts, fellow students, and yourself.

• •

 # Vocabulary

As you think about this essay, these definitions may be helpful to you:

1. **immersed**   engrossed
2. **passive**   tending not to take an active or dominant part
3. **mode**   a customary or preferred way of doing something
4. **reverberated**   echoed; reflected
5. **adept**   proficient

 # Discussion Questions

1. What does the author mean when he says you need a "sense of the big picture" when studying in college? How does he suggest you do this?
2. How would you describe passive studying versus active studying? What are some specific steps you can take to be more active?
3. Of the strategies for effective listening that the author lists, which ones are most relevant to you? Why?

 Suggestions for Your Journal

Describe a class situation where you have experienced many of the ideas outlined in this reading. What techniques did you use to listen, stay alert, take notes,
or remember the important concepts in the material? How can you improve the
way you listen in class? In what specific areas do you need to improve?

UNIT SUMMARY

The writers in this unit offer many perspectives on how to be a successful student. One defining purpose of college is to learn about our intellectual and cultural heritage. To be intensely involved in learning requires great concentration and many skills. The readings in this unit have offered many suggestions for accomplishing this.

Summary Questions

1. How do the readings in this unit suggest you can become a successful student?
2. What tasks or strategies described in the readings could you adopt to improve your own attitudes or behaviors toward your academic work?
3. What skills do you hope to acquire in college to help you in your future work and in living in general?

Suggested Writing Assignments

1. Write a brief essay describing the qualities of a successful student and why you selected those qualities.
2. Select one reading in this unit and write about your personal experience with the academic concern it describes.
3. Several authors in this unit write about various approaches to learning. Describe how your own approach to learning is the same as or different from the ones they describe.

Suggested Readings

Arthur, John. *A Concise Guide to College Success: Carpe Diem.* Upper Saddle River, NJ: Prentice Hall, 2003.

Lawrence, Gordon. *People Types and Tiger Stripes.* Gainesville, FL: Center for the Application of Psychological Types, 1982.

Pauk, W. *How to Study in College,* 4th ed. Boston: Houghton Mifflin, 1989.

Robson, James B. *Beginning College 101: How to Achieve Real Success in College.* South Plainfield, NJ: College and Future Company, 2001.

Uchida, Donna, with Marvin Cetron and Floretta McKenzie. *Preparing Students for the 21st Century.* Arlington, VA: American Association of School Administrators, 1996.

How Should I Expect to Learn?

T he act of learning is so ingrained in our everyday life that we usually take it for granted. However, as psychologists who study learning professionally can demonstrate, learning is a complex process that operates differently for many people. Learning can be defined in many ways. It is not only the acquisition of knowledge and skills by instruction or study; it is also an accumulation through experience. Although students enter college after years of "learning," many find that college learning offers new and exciting challenges.

A great deal of research on how people learn has provided important insights and tools to enhance our understanding of the process. David Kolb, a business professor, has suggested that the demands of different academic disciplines require students to use different learning styles or approaches. Howard Gardner takes a multifaceted view when he discusses seven "intelligences," which he describes in terms of a set of abilities, talents, and mental skills (see pp. 99–100). Daniel Goleman writes about

I am not young enough to know everything.

—James M. Barrie

"emotional intelligence," which includes both personal competence and social competence. Goleman suggests that emotional intelligence will be especially important in the future workplace where emotional competencies will be increasingly essential for excellence in every job.

Many researchers believe there is a relationship between the knowledge that exists in the mind and the situations in which it was acquired and used. Successful learning also depends on the individual's past experiences and attitudes toward the learning process. Perhaps the most important factor in successful learning, however, is the motivation or desire to learn.

This unit offers many perspectives about learning. James reviews some newer ideas about intelligence. Siebert and Gilpin provide insights into students' varied approaches to learning. They point out that the learning circumstance or situation for one person may require a different approach than for another. Service learning is not a new notion, but is being implemented in new ways in many colleges today. Luscher provides an overview of this experiential form of learning. Distance learning—as described by Governati, Steele, and Carey—is increasingly being viewed by some as the learning mode of the future. To complete this unit, Schank presents some profound ideas about how we will learn 50 years from now.

Understanding Who Is Smart

Jennifer James

Jennifer James is an urban cultural anthropologist and a highly regarded business speaker. A university professor for 14 years, she is the author of six books and has written a weekly newspaper column. In this essay James writes about a new vision of intelligence and how "system thinking" can help us understand change.

· · · · · · · · · · · · · · · · · ·

The debate over intelligence is a debate over higher standards. Over the past forty years, researchers of all kinds have uncovered the weaknesses of our tests and shown new respect for a broader-based definition of intelligence that reflects more than traditional fact retention and computation skills. Educators, in particular, are looking for a battery of tests that is more predictive of real-world success. The designers of a school testing program in California, for example, put a premium on the skills required for "reasonably deciding what to think and do." Among other things, students had to be able to determine the relevance of information, distinguish between fact and opinion, identify unstated assumptions, detect bias or propaganda, come up with reasonable alternatives or solutions, and predict possible consequences. Intelligence is the ability to make adaptive responses in new as well as old situations.

At Harvard, philosopher Nelson Goodman wanted to understand why some people were "creative" and others were not. In his work, Goodman expanded the concept of intelligence from "How smart is he or she?" to "How is he or she smart?" Motivation and interest in the task at hand—along with traits such as concentration, intention, purpose, drive and tenacity—emerged as important influences.

Howard Gardner, a psychologist who helped to conduct this research, thought of intelligence as the ability to solve problems or create products. He devised the following list of eight primary forms of intelligence (to which I have added one of my own):

1. **Verbal/linguistic intelligence.** This form of intelligence is revealed by a sensitivity to the meaning and order of words and the ability to make varied use of the language. Impromptu speaking, story-telling, humor, and joking are natural abilities associated with verbal/linguistic intelligence. So, too, is persuading someone to follow a course of action, or explaining, or teaching. Will Rogers had this form of intelligence. Good journalists also have it.

2. **Logical/mathematical intelligence.** This form of intelligence is easiest to standardize and measure. We usually refer to it as analytical or scientific thinking, and we see it in scientists, computer programmers, accountants, lawyers, bankers, and, of course, mathematicians, people who are problem

solvers and *consummate* game players. They work with abstract symbols and are able to see connections between pieces of information that others might miss. Einstein is one of the best examples of someone with this form of intelligence.

3. **Visual/*spatial* intelligence.** Persons with this form of intelligence are especially deft at *conjuring* up mental images and creating graphic representations. They are able to think in three-dimensional terms, to re-create the visual world. Picasso, whose paintings challenged our view of reality, was especially gifted at visualizing objects from different perspectives and angles. Besides painters and sculptors, this form of intelligence is found in designers and architects.

4. **Body/kinesthetic intelligence.** This form of intelligence makes possible the connections between mind and body that are necessary to succeed in activities such as dance, mime, sports, martial arts, and drama. Martha Graham and Michael Jordan delighted audiences with their explosive and sensitive uses of the body. Because they know how we move, inventors with this form of intelligence understand how to turn function into form. They intuitively feel what is possible in labor-saving devices and processes.

5. **Musical/rhythmic intelligence.** A person with this form of intelligence hears musical patterns and rhythms naturally and can reproduce them. It is an especially desirable form of intelligence because music has the capacity to alter our consciousness, reduce stress, and enhance brain function. For example, students who had just listened to Mozart scored higher on standard IQ tests than those who had spent the same period of time in meditation or silence. Researchers believe that the patterns in musical themes somehow prime the same neural network that the brain employs for complex visual-spatial tasks.

6. **Interpersonal intelligence.** Managers, counselors, therapists, politicians, mediators, and human relations specialists display this form of intelligence. It is a must for workplace tasks such as negotiation and providing feedback or evaluation. Individuals with this form of intelligence have strong intuitive skills. They are especially able to read the moods, temperaments, motivations, and intentions of others. Abraham Lincoln, Mohandas Gandhi, and Martin Luther King, Jr., used interpersonal intelligence to change the world.

7. **Intrapersonal intelligence.** Sigmund Freud and Carl Jung demonstrated this form of intelligence, the ability to understand and articulate the inner workings of character and personality. The highest order of thinking and reasoning is present in a person who has intrapersonal intelligence. We often call it wisdom. He or she can see the larger picture and is open to the lure of the future. Within an organization, this ability is invaluable.

8. **Spiritual intelligence.** This form of intelligence is tentative; Gardner has yet to decide whether moral or spiritual intelligence qualifies for his list. It can be considered an *amalgam* of interpersonal and intrapersonal awareness with a "value" component added.

9. **Practical intelligence.** Gardner doesn't list this form of intelligence, but I do. It is the skill that enables some people to take a computer or clock apart

and put it back together. I also think of practical intelligence as organizational intelligence or common sense, the ability to solve all sorts of daily problems without quite knowing how the solutions were reached. People with common sense may or may not test well, but they have a clear understanding of cause and effect. They use intelligence in combination with that understanding.

QUALITIES OF MIND

Rate yourself on each of these forms of intelligence. What are your strengths and weaknesses? How are they reflected in the kind of work you do and your relationships with others?

	Low				Moderate				High	
	1	2	3	4	5	6	7	8	9	10

1. Verbal/linguistic
2. Logical/mathematical
3. Visual/spatial
4. Body/kinesthetic
5. Musical/rhythmic
6. Interpersonal
7. Intrapersonal
8. Spiritual
9. Practical

Don't let this list intimidate you. There is increasingly strong evidence that intelligence can be taught, despite ongoing arguments about genetic predetermination. Also, the levels of each of these forms of intelligence can vary from one person to the next. Albert Einstein had a high degree of logical and spatial intelligence, but his lack of personal skills was legendary. He left those details to others.

Regardless of the forms of our intelligence, we also need to know how we think. Researcher Gail Browning studies approaches to problem solving. She identifies four "styles" that people use to process information: analytical, conceptual, structural, and social. She concludes that most of us use more than one of them, depending on the problem before us. Her work helps us visualize thought processes, something that makes communication and negotiation easier. When forming a creative and productive team for problem solving or futuring consider combining different thinking styles.

Analytical thinkers are the most logical. They must have facts, figures, directions and reasons to approach problem solving. They want to design a system. They see themselves as straightforward, clear and purposeful. In a team meeting they ask, "Is this feasible?"

Conceptual thinkers accept information in almost any form. They enjoy a challenge and often plunge into the problem-solving process before considering what direction to take. They want to paint a picture. They don't mind mistakes. They usually suggest, "Let's look at this problem in a different way."

Structural thinkers draw comparisons and look for systematic links to determine the source of a problem. They prefer creating flow charts. They organize the components of the problem and the possible solutions and ask, "How does this apply to our situation?"

Social thinkers are the facilitators of group process. They talk to everyone; they weigh all the solutions equally; they may identify the best solution but not know how they reached it. In a team situation they ask, "What do you think of this idea?"

Review these four styles and combine them with the nine forms of intelligence outlined. Try to identify yourself and imagine how different problems or situations engage different aspects of your intelligence or thinking style. Create a perfect team for a problem you are currently trying to solve. What ideal set of minds would potentially be the most intelligent and the best at processing?

British researcher Edward De Bono, in a series of books on intelligence, believes he has the answer. He adds the term lateral thinking to this mix. He sees it as the most productive thinking process because it is easily taught and allows everyone in a group, regardless of their intelligence frame or thinking style, to operate with the same broad set of thinking tools.

Lateral thinking is similar to what others currently call critical or system thinking. It enables us to view a problem from all sides and understand all the alternatives before devising a solution. It requires us to abandon certainty and security, at least for the moment. De Bono's most useful exercise in lateral thinking is called PMI, an acronym for Plus, Minus, and Interesting. Participants are divided into small groups and are asked to evaluate what is good (plus), what is bad (minus), and what is interesting about an idea. In a session with a group of auto manufacturers, for example, De Bono posed the suggestion that all cars should be painted yellow. . . .

[Table 1 on page 103 shows] how the group reacted.

Exercises in lateral thinking work best if each category (good, bad, and interesting) is considered separately and in order when pondering an idea or a problem rather than brainstorming them in the random fashion preferred by conceptual thinkers. Such exercises can be particularly useful when you are floating some new idea or looking for a solution to some problem. They help people focus their perceptions and articulate their reactions and responses. *Common Ground,* a PBS series designed to bring opposing sides together on several controversial issues, used lateral thinking with powerful results. Participants were able to put aside rhetoric and emotion and find they had far more in common than they realized. . . .

We are all, to one degree or another, system thinkers. (I prefer the term system thinking to De Bono's lateral thinking because we are looking at the whole to understand the parts.) We must also combine disparate parts into coherent wholes to put together the puzzles and solve the problems of daily life. A system

Table 1

Good (Plus)	Bad (Minus)	Interesting
Easier to see on the roads.	Boring.	Interesting to see if shades of yellow arose.
Easier to see at night.	Difficult to recognize your own car.	Interesting to see if people appreciated the safety factor.
No problem in deciding which color you want.	Very difficult to find your car in a parking lot.	Interesting to see whether attitudes toward cars changed.
No waiting to get the color you want.	Easier to steal cars.	Interesting to see if trim acquired a different color.
Easier for the manufacturer.	The abundance of yellow might tire the eyes.	Interesting to see if this were enforceable.
The dealer would need less stock.	Car chases would be difficult for the police.	Interesting to see who would support the suggestion.
It might take the "macho" element out of car ownership.	Accident witnesses would have a harder time.	
Cars would tend to become transport items.	Restriction of your freedom to choose.	
In minor collisions the paint rubbed off onto your car would be the same color.		

thinker believes in cooperation and knows that pooling or combining ideas, skills, and experience improves innovation, efficiency, and performance. I think of system thinking as broadscope intelligence and very much like *synergy*, a buzz-word in business in the 1990s. Companies that practiced synergy did so by buying or developing related businesses or by welding their existing units into a more coherent whole.

Social scientists used system thinking in the 1970s when they began working together to examine the "culture of poverty" as a whole. Edward Deming used it to fine-tune quality processes. The earliest ideas about man and environment as a whole organism represented system thinking. The interrelationship of mind and body in the healing process is another example. When we think about parts of a system, separate from the whole, we cut ourselves off from important information.

System thinking can bridge the gap that sometimes exists between reality and our perception of reality. For example, unproductive workers, falling orders, and sagging profits are indicators of serious problems in any business. Our usual way of thinking may cause us to look at each in isolation. But system thinking helps us understand that all parts of a business or a process are connected, and that when one part is challenged, all the others are as well. We may look for productivity problems on the production line and create new incentives if salespeople are not doing well, but the real "cause" of our problems may be hidden in the system that underlies the entire enterprise. System thinking accepts the inter-relatedness of all things. System thinking is usually the best way to find out what is going on.

System thinking can help all of us understand the zigzags of change. It enables us to see the big picture. From that vantage point we can more easily perceive the changing realities of our work and lives and solve problems. Here are some of the basic characteristics of a system thinker:

- You are physically and intellectually alert.
- You are always wondering how things can be improved.
- You are able to resolve conflict by agreeing to disagree on some points and moving the discussion forward.
- You do not demand perfection from yourself or others.
- You are imaginative and creative.
- You are empathetic and compassionate.
- You are comfortable with chaos.
- You are a nonconformist in one way or another.
- You have a sense of humor.

The future challenges us to question our own minds and how we think, to reexamine our assumptions and see how they connect to the changing realities of our world. Thinking must become a more fluid process; I call it "water logic" because the future will require the development of a fluid, more adaptive level of reaction and response. As humanity evolves, creating ever more complex patterns, the ability to understand, synthesize, and adapt to those patterns will become basic intelligence.

• •

 # Vocabulary

As you think about this essay, these definitions may be helpful to you:
1. **consummate**　extremely skilled and accomplished
2. **spatial**　relating to three-dimensional space

3. **conjuring**   imagining
4. **amalgam**   combination of different elements
5. **synergy**   combined action or operation

 Discussion Questions

1. In her first paragraph, Jennifer James provides her own definition of intelligence. What is it?
2. What traits seem to be important in Nelson Goodman's expanded concept of intelligence?
3. Why are Howard Gardner's eight basic forms of intelligence important in broadening our concept of intelligence? Is the form that James adds to Gardner's list different from the others? How?
4. Do you agree with the author's addition of "practical intelligence"? Why?
5. What is "lateral thinking"? How can it be used in problem solving?
6. What are the characteristics of "system thinking," according to the author? How can system thinking be used to analyze problem areas?

 Suggestions for Your Journal

What does being intelligent mean to you? On which of the eight forms of intelligence do you rate yourself highest? Lowest? Which do you think are most important for being successful in college? In the real world? Are you intelligent in some ways that Gardner or James have *not* described?

Learning Styles: They Can Help or Hinder

Al Siebert and Bernadine Gilpin

Al Siebert is a psychologist with more than 20 years of teaching experience in adult education. Bernadine Gilpin started college at age 35 after rearing five children. She has more than 15 years' experience as a teacher, administrator, and counselor.

Siebert and Gilpin believe that understanding how one learns best can help make studying and learning easier. This essay points out how mismatches between teaching and learning styles may cause difficulties and makes suggestions for recognizing and overcoming this common problem.

R esearchers wanting to understand all aspects of success in college asked: "Why do some students do well with one instructor but not another?" Their research uncovered a simple truth about academic life: The way some people teach does not always match up with the way other people learn.

Other research looked at why students show wide differences in the time of day and the circumstances best for learning. This research identified an important truth about studying and learning: The learning circumstances best for one person may not be good for another.

Research findings and experience have identified the following important differences in how people learn.

Auditory Versus Visual Styles

Have you ever noticed that someone can read a note you've left him, but the message doesn't get through to his brain? Or that you can tell a person something, but it doesn't register unless you write it down for her? That's because people differ in how information gets into their conscious mind.

Some people learn best by listening. Information doesn't stick well unless they hear it. Other people learn best by reading. They must see something before they believe it and remember it. Some people learn best by doing. What is your natural style?

Do you remember best what is said to you or what you read?

Do you prefer television or newspapers as your source of news?

Would you rather hear an expert talk on a subject or read what the expert has written?

When you purchase new equipment, do you read the instruction manual carefully or do you rarely read manuals?

Is reading the college catalog your main way of learning about your program and classes, or do you merely skim the catalog and go see an advisor who tells you everything you need to know?

Based on your answers to these questions, which learning style do you prefer, auditory or visual?

Everyone learns both ways, of course. It is not an either/or situation. Yet the differences between people are sometimes extreme enough to cause problems. If you have a visual learning style, you operate mainly on the basis of what you read. You may have difficulty with an instructor who believes that telling people what and how to learn is sufficient.

Auditory Learning Style

If you have an auditory style, you will probably do well with an instructor who says everything to learn and do. You may have difficulty with a visually oriented instructor. Such an instructor hands out a written statement about what to do to pass the course without discussing it and assigns textbook material and outside readings that are never discussed in class.

The solution, if you have an auditory style in a class taught by a visually oriented instructor, is to:

1. Find classmates who will tell you what they learned from the textbook readings.
2. Dictate the main points from the reading assignments and handouts onto cassette tapes and then listen to the tapes.
3. Consciously work at improving your ability to acquire information visually. (Note: For professional help, go to the reading improvement center or the office of disability services at your college.)

Visual Learning Style

If you learn best visually, you may be in trouble with an instructor who doesn't use handouts, emphasizes class discussion, and doesn't write much on the blackboard. The solution with a verbally oriented instructor is to:

1. Take good notes on what the instructor and your classmates say. After class fill in sentences and compare notes with other students.
2. Ask the instructor for suggested articles or books that will let you read the information you need to understand better.
3. Consciously work at listening and remembering what the instructor says. TIP: One woman wrote to us saying that she types her lecture notes immediately after each class.
4. If you are confused about a point, ask the instructor to tell you again and write down what you hear.

External Versus Internal Learning Styles

Psychologists have done extensive research on a significant personality variable. It is called the "external and internal *locus of control.*"

Externally oriented students believe information when it comes from an authority or expert. Information or suggestions from other sources aren't trusted as accurate.

If you prefer to get the guidance from expert sources and your instructor enjoys being an expert, then you have a good match. The more you need an instructor who tells the class exactly what to learn, the better you will do with this type of instructor. If you need clear guidelines from instructors but take a course from someone who provides little direction, you may flounder. You may be sitting in class waiting for the instructor to tell you what the answer to a problem is, only to have him or her ask the class, "What do you think?" After the class talks for a while, the instructor may refuse to say what the right answer is. He or she might say, "You may be right," or "There is some truth to that."

Some students react negatively to classes in which the instructor encourages discussion and encourages students to develop their own views and answers. These students protest, "I didn't pay good money to sit and listen to a bunch of uninformed people express their opinions. I can get that in the coffee shop." This attitude is legitimate. It is also narrow-minded.

The word *education* means to "draw out of." It does not mean "shovel into." A good education teaches you to think for yourself. It teaches you to ask good questions and then how to find the answers on your own. A good education does not give you a diploma for learning how to seek out an expert for any question you have. It teaches you how to both listen to authorities and come to your own conclusions.

Self-motivated, internally oriented students appreciate an instructor who allows them freedom to follow their own paths. Such students get upset with instructors who tell them exactly what they must learn, and in what way. For them, too much course structure is *abrasive*. They feel handicapped more than helped. Such reactions are legitimate and narrow-minded.

In every field of study, certain basics must be mastered. There are basic terms and concepts that must be understood. There are some techniques fundamental to the mastery of the subject even though the reasons why may not be given.

Being Both Internal and External in Learning
Students who get the most out of school are able to follow the tightly controlled steps used by some teachers and, at the same time, organize their own learning experiences when in a class taught by someone who gives few guidelines. Can you learn to do both?

Differences in Temperament
Isabel Myers and her mother Katharine Briggs developed a test to measure four dimensions of *temperament* identified by psychotherapist Carl Jung. Myers-Briggs tests are probably the most popular personality tests in the country because many people benefit from seeing how differences in temperament explain misunderstandings between people.

This means that differences in *how* you and an instructor think are more important than differences in *what* you think. Here's how the four temperaments influence your learning style.

Extroversion Versus Introversion

Instructors and students vary widely in how friendly they want to be and how much emotional distance they need to have. A friendly, *extroverted* instructor enjoys after-class contact with students. He or she will ask students to coffee or out for pizza. If you are similarly friendly, you will have a great year.

If you are a more *introverted* person, however, you may suffer from too much personal attention and closeness. You would much rather have a quiet, tactful instructor who respects your need to be left alone. Such an instructor understands how embarrassing it is to be called on to talk in class or to be openly praised for getting a high score on an exam.

On the other hand, if you are an extroverted person with a more introverted instructor, you may find it puzzling to have him or her pulling away from you after class. After all, what are instructors for if not to be available for students? Yet your desire to be friendly may cause the instructor to stare at you and make excuses to get away. After that, you may feel avoided.

When it comes to studying, the introverted person needs a private, quiet place where everyone stays away. The extroverted person likes to study in the kitchen, in a student lounge, or with classmates. Don't hesitate to tell friends, relatives, and classmates with temperaments different from yours what you need.

Thinking Versus Feeling

Descriptions of this dimension of temperament match up closely with left-brain/right-brain research findings. The left brain is where the speech center develops in most humans. The left brain is where you remember words, use logic, and think analytically. It gives you your ability to think rationally and unemotionally. The left brain thinks in a linear fashion. It is time oriented.

The right brain carries your memory for music. You think visually, emotionally, and irrationally in the right brain. It is the source of creativity and intuition. Right-brain thinking follows emotional logic. Using it, you can visualize and think in patterns jumping from one spot in a pattern to another without apparent logic or reason.

If you tend to be left-brained, you will be well matched to an instructor who gives you thorough, unemotional listings of facts, data, analytic explorations, hypotheses, logic, evidence, numbers, definition of terms, and rational conclusions.

If you tend to be left-brained and get an instructor who teaches in a right-brained way, you may find the course to be a bewildering experience. You may experience the instructor as weird, too emotional, disorganized, and a bit nutty.

If you tend to be right-brained with a left-brained teacher, the course will be painful for you. You'll feel like a thirsty person handed a glass of water only to find it is filled with sand.

To resolve personality conflicts such as these, avoid indulging in the attitude, "If only other people would change, my world would be a better place for me." When you have a mismatch, you can try to find someone (perhaps even the instructor) who will translate the material into a form you understand better. More important, however, make an effort to gain more use of your other brain.

The situation may not be easy at first, but it does give you a chance to add another dimension to yourself. And isn't this why you're in school?

You do not have to give up your more natural and preferred way of thinking, feeling, and talking. What you can do is add more to what you already have.

Sensation Versus Intuition

Sensation-oriented people like to be sensible. They are guided by experience. Intuitive people like fantasy. They are creative dreamers. According to David Keirsey and Marilyn Bates, authors of *Please Understand Me*, differences on this dimension cause the widest gulf between people.

The sensation-oriented student is practical, wanting facts and evidence. An intuitive instructor can fill the lecture hour with hypothetical explanations, theories, concepts, and a long list of views held by others.

A sensation-oriented instructor gives practical instructions on what to do. An intuitive student wants to know what the underlying theories and concepts are, and asks "but what if?"

What to do about this sort of conflict? Stretch your understanding. Ask for what you need. Try to minimize the judging dimension of the next pair of traits.

Judging Versus Perceiving

If you remember Archie Bunker from the television series "All in the Family," you have seen an excellent example of the judging temperament. Such people make up their minds quickly. They judge others and situations as good or bad, right or wrong.

The perceiving style is to observe without judgment. Such people can watch world events, movies, and sports events without taking sides or having an opinion.

A judgmental style instructor believes the purpose for being in college is to work hard to become qualified for an occupation where hard work will get you ahead. The instructor works hard, expects the same from every student, and privately judges students as good ones or bad ones.

A perceiving instructor looks for ways to make learning fun, tries to minimize office work, and sees all students as learners. This instructor is frustrating for a judging style student who wants serious homework and wants to know how he or she compares to the other students.

Practical Suggestions

What do you do when a teacher is less than ideal? Do you get distressed? Complain?

By now we hope you have realized that finding a really good match between yourself and an instructor does not happen all the time. In fact, if you are an experienced victim, then the college will provide you with many chances to be upset, complain to classmates, and criticize instructors you judge to be imperfect.

As an alternative to being a victim, we have the following suggestions:

1. Before registration ask around to find out about various instructors. If you have a choice between instructors, you'll know which one to choose.
2. Try to get as much out of every course as you can, regardless of who your instructor is or how much the teaching style does not fit your preferred learning style. Be open to try a new way of learning.
3. When you have difficulty understanding what is happening in a course, make an appointment to talk with the instructor. Be prepared to ask for what you want.
4. If you still have problems, go to the office or center that teaches studying and reading skills. The specialists there can be very helpful.

Learn to Appreciate Human Differences

When you experience conflicts with others at school, at work, or in your family, question your attitudes about what other people should be like. If you experience an irritating difference, use that as an opportunity to learn more about human nature. You might as well, because you won't change other people by criticizing them!

We humans are all born with different temperaments and different ways of functioning in life. That is simply the way things work.

Do You Know Where and When?

Several final suggestions: If you grew up in a large family you may study best in a noisy place with lots of people around. Experiment with locations to see what works best for you.

Time of day is another learning style difference. If you are a morning person, get up and study for an hour before others get up. Leave chores for evening when your brain is disengaging. If you are an evening person go ahead and study until one or two in the morning.

The better you know yourself, the more skillfully you will manage your learning style and the easier it will be to succeed in college!

From *The Adult Student's Guide to Survival and Success: Time for College* by Al Siebert and Bernadine Gilpin. Copyright © 1992, Practical Psychology Press. Reprinted by permission.

• •

 Vocabulary

As you think about this essay, these definitions may be helpful to you:
1. **locus of control**   center of self-control, either by internal or external influences

2. **abrasive**   causing irritation
3. **temperament**   characteristic or habitual inclination
4. **extroverted**   being predominantly influenced by what is outside of the self
5. **introverted**   being wholly or predominantly concerned with one's own mental life

 Discussion Questions

1. What is a learning style?
2. What is the difference between the auditory and visual style of learning?
3. How does temperament affect your approaches to learning?
4. What aspects of learning does the left brain control? What aspects does the right brain control?
5. What four temperaments can influence your learning style? Describe them and how they affect the way you learn.

 Suggestions for Your Journal

Analyze how you learn best. Are you more visual or auditory? Have you ever experienced a class in which the instructor's teaching style did not work with your best learning style? What happened?

Do you think a student who does not learn well with a certain teacher's style should switch instructors or learn to adapt? What suggestions given by the authors for learning more effectively pertain to you?

Service Learning: Education Through Experience

Keith F. Luscher

Keith F. Luscher is currently a media consultant for Goettler Associates, a fundraising consulting firm serving nonprofit organizations nationwide. A writer and speaker, Mr. Luscher is also a frequent contributor to collegerecruiter.com.

• • • • • • • • • • • • • • •

From the time he was a child, Jeremie Maehr had a keen interest in the environment. "When I was very young growing up in New Jersey," Jeremie recalls, "the water in our neighborhood was contaminated by harmful, toxic waste dumping."

Experiences tied to this event enlightened Jeremie as to how information—its presence or lack thereof—influenced how people reacted to various crises. As a result, during his freshman year at Case Western University, Jeremie became involved with the university's Center for the Environment, building community awareness of environmental issues in Cleveland neighborhoods. Jeremie also joined the CWRU's Office of Student Community Service and AmeriCorps to continue addressing local environmental needs. Jeremie organized fellow student volunteers to collect and analyze soil samples, and to conduct educational programs for inner-city children.

Of Service Learning, Jeremie says, "It provides a perspective on your work which you don't get from the classroom alone. I remember during my senior year, I was working with a team of other students on a community-based, *watershed,* Service Learning program. As we were taking measurements and making calculations, which would then be passed on for use by engineers, I will never forget what a fellow student told me. She said, 'Even though I have done all the chemical analysis, I'm still worried about the accuracy of the results.'

"The point was, our work wasn't a lab experiment, it was real. Lives were going to be affected by what we did, and how well we did it."

Jeremie's advice to other students: "Service Learning allows you to really see the differences you can make, and to reflect on those experiences with others. You make friends, build relationships with people, many of whom will really work to help you when you need it. But to build trust, you must always be honest. Ask questions. If you don't have answers, admit it. And be open to other people's opinions, even if they contradict your own. I guess I can be an example of how Service Learning can lead directly to career opportunities since I was working at my current job as an intern before I even graduated."

Many colleges and universities across the nation are beginning to recognize the value of Service Learning, which is why they are now incorporating it into their academic curriculums. Service Learning is a growing philosophy and practice which recognizes the important role that public and community service can play in education. In simple terms, Service Learning, through first-hand experience, shows students how their talents and efforts can be applied to improve other people's lives and better their communities. This experience also helps students develop values that stress social responsibility.

Service Learning can be implemented in a variety of ways. Sometimes it is through supplementary activity within a classroom-based course. Sometimes it is a course itself. Often a student will earn some academic credit for a specified number of hours served every week.

How does Service Learning differ from ordinary internships or voluntary action? In the many academic volumes and articles that have been written on Service Learning over the years, you may see dozens of different answers to this question. But actually, Service Learning does not "differ" from regular internships or volunteerism. It is more of an *extension* of both, taking the best points of each, combining them and filling in the gaps. Thus, through Service Learning, you can have the best of both worlds.

Like an internship, Service Learning allows a student to perform work that relates specifically to his or her intended vocation, thereby enhancing that student's professional skills. Service Learning programs, like some internships, often give course credit, and they usually provide students with the advice of a professional in the field.

Like a volunteer program, the Service Learning experience turns the whole world into a classroom. Service learners often *see* the value and difference their efforts play in other people's lives and in the community. As with volunteering, students in Service Learning programs will also develop skills that employers seek out universally.

Praxis is an academic term which describes the relationship between action and theory in the learning experience. Because it is important not just to take action, but to contemplate that action and the results, many Service Learning programs include a time of reflection in which you can both share your experiences with fellow teachers and students, and hear about their experiences in return.

Thus, a student, upon learning a theory, has the chance to apply that knowledge through action. Afterward, the student returns to the classroom where he or she may reflect on and dissect that experience, and then use it to develop even more refined theories. Those theories are then shared with the rest of the class.

For the students who participate in praxis, their time of reflection will not necessarily require them to revise theory taught only in the classroom. Rather, by reviewing and sharing their service experiences for themselves and for their colleagues, the students gain a deeper insight into how their service affects them as well as the community.

Most of all, Service Learning programs are specifically designed to benefit the student and the community. Instructors will often go out to the community and determine what needs exist that their students can fulfill in a mutually beneficial way, and then develop a specific program from there.

Among the universities and colleges now using the Service Learning approach to solve a variety of community problems are:

- Providence College. Here, students studying American Public Policy learn first hand the *consequences* of public policy, both good and bad (although that is something they must often decide for themselves). Students can serve meals at a homeless shelter, tutor in an urban school, interview welfare recipients and prepare case profiles for welfare reform.
- Rhode Island School of Design. Students conduct weekly art classes at the bedsides of hospitalized children, and for senior citizens.
- Wilmington College. Business students are able to help develop business and marketing plans for local businesses and non-profit organizations.
- Shawnee State University. Science students participate in ecological projects to learn the applications for the study of science and nature.
- Calvin College. Those studying mathematics and computer science analyze demographic data from several food pantries to find patterns in the pantries' patrons. Seasonal and other variations were also considered to help predict when periods of high demand would arise.

Each institution's program is usually much different from those found at other schools. For instance, college credit is usually granted to students participating in Service Learning projects. But not all schools offer credit. There are many reasons why Service Learning programs differ from school to school and even department to department. Often, the difference occurs *because the program itself is in its infancy.* Service Learning is a relatively new philosophy in higher education. Different schools have different levels of funding available, as well as various numbers of people behind it. Most often, a college will become involved in Service Learning when an individual or small group of faculty members decides to try it out.

When there is an interest in Service Learning at a college, but one does not exist, students can be the impetus for starting one. Since many educators and administrators are becoming more interested in Service Learning, it should not be difficult to find people who would support it and help design a program. The secret is recognizing opportunity and acting upon it. For instance:

- An accounting student may see an opportunity to investigate loan and credit discrimination on behalf of the poor or help a local organization obtain financing for community improvement projects.
- An agriculture student can help establish a community gardening project or aid in dietary planning for local agencies.
- A person studying to be an architect can help coordinate a local fix-up project.
- Students majoring in marketing or business can do much to increase the bottom line of local groups, organizations and small businesses.

- Chemistry students can learn some of the effects that substance abuse has on individuals by serving in counseling and drug-treatment centers.
- Those students majoring in computer science have a chance to teach computer basics at just about any community center in any town in the country. People are desperate to learn these skills, which are crucial to job market-ability. These students can also show people the right and wrong way to use computer technology.
- Students majoring in economics have a tremendous doorway to opportunity. They can professionally serve consumer groups, small business organizations and local Goodwill agencies. Their knowledge of economics can help troubled people see new solutions to their money problems.
- The education major can open up another gold mine of opportunities. Head Start programs, for example, will welcome those with teaching skills. Tutoring for older adults or prison inmates is another area needing people with teaching backgrounds.
- Students studying engineering may find some interesting needs for their design talents in helping those who are disabled or use their scientific and environmental skills in working to improve the environment.
- Fine Arts students may wish to consider art therapy for those with mental or physical disabilities. For example, students may assist at art therapy sessions for criminal offenders.
- History majors may find use for their abilities at a local historical society, museum or library.
- Psychology students can also begin working professionally in many ways. Activities include research, counseling and organizational work.

Here are some steps that you might take to initiate a Service Learning opportunity:

1. Talk to your advisor, your professors or other people on staff at your college. Find out what kind of Service Learning opportunities are available. Ask about getting involved.
2. If you have friends who go to other colleges and universities, find out what kind of Service Learning programs are offered at your friends' schools. This could give you some good ideas about how to start and design a similar program.
3. Look around your community. Are there any obvious problems which need solving? Can you think of a way to help? If so, in addition to talking about your proposal with your advisor or professor, you might present your Service Learning ideas to community leaders like the local mayor or city council. These leaders could marshal community support for your program.

What Service Learning comes down to is students and teachers recognizing a community need and responding to it.

 Vocabulary

As you think about this essay, this definition may be helpful to you:
1. **watershed**   a turning point

 Discussion Questions

1. How does service learning differ from internships or voluntary action?
2. What does the term *praxis* mean? How does reflecting on a situation and sharing it with others contribute to learning?
3. What kind of service involvement would be possible in your field? Can you add ideas to the suggestions for different majors that the author outlines?
4. What steps would you need to take if you wanted to set up a service learning program at your school?

 Suggestions for Your Journal

Write an outline for a proposal for a service learning class. What details will you need to include in order to establish a class for this type of learning? What real-world work environments might provide the kind of practical experience you want? What tasks or activities within this experience might help you develop the skills that you need?

Distance Learning

Michael P. Governati, George Steele, and Kate M. Carey

Michael P. Governati, Ph.D., is the executive director of Miami University Middletown
Campus in Middletown, Ohio. Kate Carey, Ph.D., and George Steele, Ph.D., are
respectively the executive director and director of Degree Completion Programs for the
Ohio Learning Network. The Ohio Learning Network is an organization dedicated to
significantly expanding access to learning opportunities for the citizens of the state of
Ohio. It is also charged with enhancing the capacity and effectiveness of colleges and
universities in their use of technology in instruction and research, as well as collaborat-
ing with similar organizations.

I magine going back in time, to a place where the Internet is still more of
a dream rather than a reality, and to a place where all types of Web interactions are limited or do not exist. Imagine going back to the early 1990s!
The speed of the technological revolution that surrounds us is sometimes difficult to comprehend in all of its influences. All sections of our society, culture,
and economy are being transformed by it. Commenting about its impact on
commerce, futurist Peter F. Drucker describes the perceptual and intellectual
change from the industrial age to the technological age: "In the new mental geography created by the railroads, humanity mastered distance. In the mental
geography of e-commerce, distance has been eliminated. There is only one market. The competition is not local anymore; it knows no boundaries."

Just as new telecommunication, computer, and multimedia technologies
have changed the business sector and spurred the development of e-business,
they are also creating a new approach in education called distance learning.
Distance learning uses a variety of computing, telecommunication, and multimedia technologies to provide interactive learning experiences and to deliver
these experiences to students in both synchronous and asynchronous learning.
Synchronous learning is that which occurs in the same time and place. This traditional type of learning is illustrated when teachers and students are located in
the same place (a classroom) and time (periods within a schedule such as
quarters or semesters).

Asynchronous learning is learning that can occur anywhere and at any
time. Logging on to a computer and taking a course when it best fits your schedule is an example of this. Asynchronous learning did not begin with the Internet.
The attempt to remove distance and increase access to higher education in the
United States can be traced back at least to the development of correspondence courses by the private sector and public institutions at the beginning of
the 20th century. Before e-mail, correspondence courses relied on text-based in-
terchanges between teacher and student through the postal system. Asynchro-

nous learning, however, has blossomed with the advent of affordable computers and the new technologies. In the last decade of the past century, the share of U.S. households with personal computers rose from 22 percent to 53 percent. Households with access to the Internet went from 0 percent to 52 percent, and by the end of the decade 95 percent of public schools in the United States had Internet access. Higher education in the United States responded too. From 1995 to 1998, there was a 72 percent increase in distance education programs, from 690 to 1,190 with over 1.6 million students enrolled. The rate of acquisition and utilization of computer and Internet technologies compared to that of other innovative technology in the past, such as color TV, has been astounding. While it took TV nearly four decades from invention to mass-market acquisition, the personal computer enhanced by Internet access will be as *ubiquitous* as televisions in American households by 2010, only twenty years after the emergence of the World Wide Web.

Changes for Higher Education

These changes are creating a new context for higher education and providing new opportunities to different types of students. Yesterday's context for higher education shared many of the characteristics of the industrial age itself. The organizational emphasis was based on standardization of delivery (courses) that emphasized specialization of learning (majors) supported by an elaborate bureaucratic structure. The purpose of education fit neatly into one of the three boxes of life—education, work, and retirement. Education prepared people for work from which they planned to eventually retire. Education, work, and retirement created a pattern of life that was linear and easily understood. Throughout most of the last century, participation in the first box of life was limited, particularly at the higher education level. Access to higher education was dependent on socioeconomic status, geographic proximity to campuses, congruency of time available and schedules of course offerings, and one's age. The predominant pedagogy and delivery systems were synchronous teacher-centered lecture-and-discussion formats supplemented by low-tech support such as chalk and blackboards, motion pictures, overhead projectors, audio tapes, and slides. The focus of teaching centered on providing the "basics" or the "essentials" to students to prepare them for the next box of life—work. Although differences of opinion about the need for and nature of the "basics" or the "essentials" existed, society believed that education prepared individuals for work.

In the twenty-first century, new technologies will radically change the context for higher education. The greatest change will be the emergence of a life span model for education that will replace the "three boxes of life" *paradigm*. Educational emphasis will shift from preparing students for a lifetime of work in predominantly one career area, to a focus on acquisition of tailored knowledge and skill sets for people who change jobs and careers more frequently over an extended period of time. For students, learning how to learn will become more critical as continued education and learning throughout one's life will become the norm. The focus of teaching will become more student-centered as the barriers of time and place diminish and asynchronous learning becomes more quickly accessible. These efforts will be supported by the continuous development of information technology and electronic delivery systems that will make learning anywhere any time a reality. We will see a convergence of technologies—the merging of computing, telecommunications, and multimedia technologies. This convergence will draw upon the worldwide resources of both materials and people for teaching and learning.

How much will traditional higher education be affected by this? One school of thought says higher educational institutions' stakeholders will determine the impact of these changes. For example, traditional residential colleges and universities that focus on students in their late teens and early twenties will not be as radically affected as those institutions that serve commuter and adult students. Some form of traditional education will always exist for most young adults leaving home every autumn to live on campus. Classroom and social learning are equally important in this view of higher education. The new technologies will change the way teachers teach, but the difference will be more subtle, rather than revolutionary.

Another school of thought sees all of higher education being impacted by distance learning. Technological change will continuously and radically alter social, political, and business structures. These powerful forces will create an expectation and demand for information age responsiveness from all of higher education. As learning needs for the great majority of the population is spread out over their lifetimes, both personal and social costs will seriously question the value of the personal four-to-five year moratorium higher education currently exacts. This moratorium might well be an educational and pleasant experience, but is it worth the current debt often incurred to achieve it? With the barrier of distance broken, students can seek exceptional educational offerings to acquire a degree or upgrade their skills while continuing to engage in other social roles whether it is leisure pursuits, parenting, or career interests.

Types of Technology

Several new technologies will link teachers and students in both synchronous (same time) and asynchronous (anytime and anyplace) ways in the twenty-first century. The distinguishing characteristics of these technologies relate to how they permit learners to access learning opportunities anywhere and at any time. All these technologies will be Internet applicable. Today, most Internet access is limited to hard-wired networks. Tomorrow, wireless connections will greatly increase the meaning of anywhere access for distance learning. Some of the technologies used in learning will still be synchronously based: for example, instant messages, chat room discussions, and streaming video. Technologies that will enhance asynchronous learning will include e-mail, captured video, and CD-ROMs. The important difference between these two groups is that anytime/anyplace (asynchronous) technologies can more easily support learning designed to be same time (synchronous). Conversely, synchronous technologies do not adapt well to asynchronously designed learning.

Perhaps the most serious issue facing distance learning is the *digital divide*. This term refers to the unequal access to the use of technology based on primarily socio-economic factors, but also geographic factors. Computers and Internet access are seen as items that are unaffordable to many disadvantaged individuals and families. Additionally, some rural areas do not have reliable, fast Internet service.

Access to computing and information can be compounded by the rate of technological change. Moore's Law (so termed by Intel co-founder Gordon Moore) proposes that computer capabilities as measured by computer memory will double every 18 months while costs hold constant. This means that you can buy a faster computer with more memory at about the same price as your last computer. This technological advance is great, but most of us have tired of using "old" computers for "new" things. While this experience would certainly frustrate someone trying to take a course over the Internet, having no computer and no Internet access precludes this even as a possibility. Public libraries offer computer and Internet access but users are often limited so that others can share that resource.

Needed: A New Type of Learner

Although distance learning offers a more convenient and flexible way to take courses and complete a degree, it may not necessarily fit all students' learning styles or needs. Just as the current lecture and discussion approach that is predominantly used in traditional higher educational settings is better adapted to some students' learning styles (auditory and verbal learners who can commit large blocks of time to attend campus), Internet-based distance learning creates its own preferences. Some students will find it difficult to study as independently as distance learning requires and will feel more comfortable with the daily contact with an instructor and other students found in more traditional learning. Self-motivated adult learners with strong reading and writing skills have the best success with distance learning modes of instruction.

Hence, just as traditional approaches to learning have not met the needs of everyone, the challenge for distance learning educators is to design learning opportunities that have greater access, flexibility, and scope than that which is currently available. The challenge, though, must be met soon. The world is moving fast. More and more households have computers and Internet service. A new, more computer-literate generation of students is coming of age. And a new adult learner computer-literate market is emerging. Technology-enhanced learning in the classroom or offered via distance is here. Given the exponential changes in telecommunications and multimedia technologies, reliance on traditional modes of time- and place-bound education may be viewed in this century not only as quaint, but as a relic of a bygone industrial age.

Reprinted by permission of the authors.

● ●

 Vocabulary

As you think about this essay, these definitions may be helpful to you:
1. **synchronous learning**   learning that occurs in the same time and place
2. **asynchronous learning**   learning that occurs anywhere, anytime
3. **ubiquitous**   widespread
4. **paradigm**   an outstandingly clear or typical example; theoretical framework
5. **digital divide**   unequal access to the use of technology

 Discussion Questions

1. What is the difference between synchronous and asynchronous learning?
2. What are the advantages and disadvantages of learning in a classroom with a teacher and classmates versus learning in an independent computer course?
3. Can society afford to let some of its members not participate in distance learning? What would be the costs?

 Suggestions for Your Journal

Would you make a good distance learner? Why or why not? If you took a distance learning course, what subject would you take?

Are your computer skills at the level you want? What do you need to do to improve them? What resources are on your campus to assist you in developing these skills?

Distance Education

Michael L. Dertouzos

The late Michael L. Dertouzos is introduced fully at the beginning of his essay on human-centered issues in technology in Unit 5. Briefly, he adds a special perspective on the enduring issues in educating people effectively. It may surprise you to see where he, who was once in effect the webmaster for the World Wide Web, comes down on the issue of distance learning.

E ducation is the world's most important collaborative human activity. Education is so vital because is defines future society. It's also the only force strong enough to close the expanding jaws of the rich-poor gap. It is natural for people to want to join new information technology with education. Unlike the Agrarian and Industrial Revolutions, which helped learners indirectly by feeding them, transporting them to school, and providing them with electricity, the Information Revolution helps directly, because it deals with the currency of knowledge: information.

Distance education has many faces. It can be used to teach literacy in Africa; provide industrial training and certification to health professionals, maintenance engineers, and other specialists; and offer courses to university and adult populations, as in the case of Britain's Open University. The biggest hope of all, however, is that it be used to interconnect young students with their teachers and peers, forming a new breed of educational communities that straddle space and time. Yet, despite the richness and promise of distance education, there is a dearth of responsible experimentation with its educational approaches. Partly, that's due to the difficulty of measuring objectively how effective a particular approach is. But there is also another reason—a wild-frontier mentality of hope and expectation that these new technologies are bound to help.

In the late 1990s, I attended a meeting where Benjamin Netanyahu, then prime minister of Israel, explained to a group of politicians and computer professionals how he wanted to provide a quarter million of his country's toddlers with interconnected computers. He said, however, he was having trouble funding the project. I turned the tables and asked him why he wanted to do this in the first place. He was stunned, since it should have been obvious—especially to an MIT technologist—that computers are good for learning.

Throughout the world, droves of politicians, led by those in the United States, are repeating the fashionable *mantra* that millions of children in thousands of schools must be interconnected. You can feel their rush: "Isn't it so reasonable and modern to put an emerging technology to work toward the noblest of social goals: the education of our children?"

Not quite.

After 35 years of experimenting with computers in various aspects of learning, the jury is still out with respect to the central question, "Are computers truly effective in learning?" The evidence from numerous studies on whether computers improve the actual learning process is overwhelmingly ... inconclusive.

Certainly, the promise is impressive. Simulators can help teach the kinetic and quantitative skills needed to drive, ski, swim, sail, even operate on humans. Computers can help learners write, compose music, generate designs, and create new objects. Speech understanding machines can be used as literacy tutors teaching adults who feel too embarrassed to fumble along in front of people, to read.

Collaboration at a distance can help teachers and students discuss homework on the Web, debate issues, examine problems, pursue joint projects, and get useful information from other people. At a more ambitious level, collaboration techniques can bridge schools that lack certain teaching specialties with schools that have the right people. Students in different countries can collect information on local customs and then assemble, share, and compare the results.

But potential does not equal actual results. Just to pick one statistic from a pile of evidence, U.S. high school students consistently rank from 12th to 18th, internationally, in physics and math abilities, whereas Asian students rank 1st. Yet U.S. students have far greater access to computers than their Asian counterparts. What are Asian educators doing, without technology, that American educators would do well to emulate? Another of the many reasons the jury is out is that learning depends critically on what human teachers do best—lighting a fire in a student's heart, nurturing a student, being a role model. None of these attributes is easily conveyed over the Information Marketplace.

So what should we do with this highest form of collaboration? I suggest the same answer I gave to Prime Minister Netanyahu, scaled up here to encompass the world: Let us interconnect students, and experiment with human-centric collaborative education, creatively and widely (in the hundreds of thousands to a few million students), but refrain from deploying it massively (in the hundreds of millions)—at least until the jury reaches some better conclusions. This won't make politicians shine as bright, but our children may shine brighter.

· · · · · · · · · · · · · · · · · · · ·

 Vocabulary

As you think about this essay, this definition may be helpful to you:

1. **mantra**   a mystical chant believed to change the world if repeated often enough

 Discussion Questions

1. Compare Dertouzos on distance education with Governati, Steele, and Carey
   (the authors of the preceding reading). What is the major difference in their
   expressed attitude toward distance education?
2. Dertouzos asserts that distance education has many possible strengths but
   also some limitations. Identify those strengths and weaknesses and add your
   own ideas to each list. What do you see as the true potential benefits of distance education?

 Suggestions for Your Journal

What personal experience have you had with distance education? Was that a
good experience for you? Could it have been better? If so, how?

Are We Going to Get Smarter?

Roger C. Schank

Roger C. Schank, a leading researcher in artificial intelligence, is the Distinguished
Career Professor in the School of Computer Science at Carnegie Mellon, where he is
also chair and chief technology officer for the Department of Cognitive Arts.

Is intelligence an absolute? Does mankind get smarter as time goes by? It depends on what you mean by intelligence, of course. Certainly we are getting more knowledgeable. Or at least it seems that way. While the average child has access to a wealth of information, considerably more than was available to children fifty years ago, there are people who claim that our children are not as well educated as they were fifty years ago and that our schools have failed us.

Today, questions about what it means to be intelligent and what it means to be educated are not at the center of our scientific inquiry, nor are they at the center of our popular discourse. Still we live our lives according to implicitly understood ideas about intelligence and about education. Those ideas will be seriously challenged in the next fifty years.

Over ten years ago, I was asked to join the board of editors of *Encyclopaedia Britannica*. The other members were mostly *octogenarians* and mostly humanists. Because I was both a scientist and much younger than everyone else, most of what I said was met with odd stares. When I asked the board if they would be happy to put out an encyclopedia ten times the size of the current one if the costs involved remained the same, they replied that, no, the current encyclopedia had just the right amount of information. I responded that they would be out of business in ten years if that were their belief. They had no idea what I meant—although I tried to explain the coming of what is now called the World Wide Web. At a later meeting, after having heard me make similar assertions about the future, Clifton Fadiman, a literary hero of the 1940's, responded, "I guess we will all have to accept the fact that minds less well educated than our own will soon be in charge of institutions like the encyclopaedia."

The chairman of the board of the *Encyclopaedia Britannica* at the time was the late Mortimer Adler. He was also responsible for a series called The Great Books of the Western World, which was (and is) sold as a set. These books represent all the great written works of the world's wisdom—according to Adler and his colleagues, anyhow—and the series consisted mostly of books written prior to the twentieth century. I asked Adler whether he thought there might be some new books that could be included, and he replied that most of the important thoughts had already been written down.

This idea, that all the great thoughts have already been thought, has been prevalent in the American idea of education and intelligence for a long time.

Here are the admission requirements for Harvard College in 1745:

> When any Schollar is able to read Tully or such like clasicall Latin Author *ex temporare*, and make and speake true Latin verse and Prose *Suo (ut aiunt) Marte*, and decline perfectly the paradigms of Nounes and verbes ine the Greeke tongue, then may hee bee admitted into the Colledge, nor shall any claim admission before such qualification.

What the Great Books series and Harvard of 1745 have in common is an underlying assumption that the study of man and his institutions had been sufficiently mastered in ancient times and therefore education required you to be well read and well versed in the thoughts of those who preceded you. An educated person in this view is one who is able to discuss, with *erudition*, a variety of historical, philosophical, and literary topics. Being educated—and therefore being intelligent—has, for the last century and many centuries before that, been about the accumulation of facts, the ability to quote the ideas of others, and a familiarity with certain ideas. Education has meant accumulating information and intelligence has often meant little more in the popular imagination than the ability to show off what one has accumulated.

But what happens when the facts are in the walls?

Fifty years from now, knowledge will be so easy to acquire that one will be able simply to say aloud whatever one wants to know and hear an instantaneous response from the walls—enhanced by a great deal of technology from the walls, of course. Knowing offhand what Freud had to say about the superego won't mean much when you can turn to the nearest appliance and ask what Freud had to say and hear Freud (or someone who looks and sounds a lot like him) saying it and finding five opposing thought leaders from throughout time ready to propose alternative ideas if you want to hear them and discuss them together.

But is intelligence simply the ability to be informed of answers to your questions, or is it the ability to know what questions to ask? As answers become devalued, questions become more valued. We have lived for a very long time in an answer-based society. Signs of it are everywhere: in the television shows that people watch such as *Jeopardy* and *Who Wants to Be a Millionaire?*; in the games that people play, such as Trivial Pursuit; and most of all in school, where answers are king. Increasingly, the chief concern of our schools is testing. School has become a *regimen* for learning answers rather than learning to inquire.

New technologies will change all this. When the pocket calculator was introduced, people asked whether calculators might as well be used in math tests, since from now on such devices would always be available. As a result, math tests began to focus on more substantive issues than long division. The introduction of artificial intelligence into everyday devices will have the same effect. As machines become omnipresent and able to answer questions about whatever concerns us, the values we place on each individual's being a repository of factual knowledge will diminish. The old idea of school, based on the notion that the most knowledgeable person in town had information to impart and the rest of us were forced to sit and memorize that information, will give way to new ideas of knowledge acquisition. Knowledge will no longer be seen as a commodity to be acquired. Anything obtained easily is devalued in society, and it will be the same with knowledge.

What will be valued will be good questions. *Computers can only take you so far*, we will hear people say.

Imagine the following: You're sitting in your living room, talking with your friend, and an issue comes up between you. You turn to the wall for a response. "Who was right?" you demand. The wall points out that it has a number of virtual people available to join your conversation. You choose some characters that you have heard about or conversed with before. A lively discussion ensues. Eventually the limits of the computer's collective knowledge are reached. The walls know no more of relevance. "This, then, is an exciting question!" you exclaim. Knowing a good question makes you ready to enter into a discussion with other live humans interested in similar questions. You tell that to the walls, and suddenly the people interested in such questions—those who have gone beyond the software in the same way that you have—are all there in your living room (virtually). In a world where this is possible, what does it mean to be educated? What does it mean to be intelligent?

To think about the education part of that question, we have to ask what a child's life would be like in that world. Fifty years from now school, as we know it, will have atrophied from lack of interest. Why go to school to learn facts, when virtual experiences are readily available and the world's best teachers are virtually available at any moment? Education will mean—even from the age of two—exploring worlds of interest with intelligent guides available to answer your questions and pose new ones. World upon world will open to the child who is curious. Education in such a society will be a matter of what virtual (and later real) worlds you have entered and how much you have learned to do in those worlds.

To Fadiman's remark quoted above, I responded that minds would not be less well educated, just differently educated. In the world of Clifton Fadiman, an educated mind was one that had been trained at Harvard (or its equivalent) and was conversant with the major ideas in Western thought. His idea of education did not include, for example, being able to program in Java, or understanding the basics of neuroscience. In fifty years, there will still be Harvard, but the value of its *imprimatur* will have been altered tremendously.

Education in its deepest sense has always been about doing, rather than about knowing. Many scholars throughout the years have pointed this out, from Aristotle ("For the things we have to learn before we can do them, we learn by doing them") to Galileo ("You cannot teach a man anything; you can only help him discover it within himself") to A. S. Neill ("I hear and I forget; I see and I remember; I do and I understand") to Einstein ("The only source of knowledge is experience"). Nevertheless, schools have ignored this wisdom and chosen—in the words of John Dewey—to "teach by pouring in."

The virtual schools that will arise to take the place of current institutions will attract students less because of the credentials they bestow than because of the experiences they offer. Since these experiences will be there for the taking when a learner decides to learn, most students will start college long before the age of eighteen. Success in various virtual experiences will encourage us to encounter new ones, much as video games do today. Certifying agencies will worry more about what you can do—what virtual merit badges you have achieved—than what courses you have taken.

Fields of endeavor will create experiences in those fields. Instead of Harvard or Columbia offering courses in physics, physicists from around the world will work with virtual-educational–world designers who will build software to create physics experiences. Those experiences will be available to everyone. The old idea that the smartest people were those who received the best grades from schools that tested them to see how well they had learned the lessons will morph into a notion that the smartest students are the ones who pose questions for the software that have to be sent to humans in order to be answered. Intelligence will mean the ability to reach the limits of an educational experience.

Will we collectively be smarter as a society because of all these innovations? In terms of raw capacity for thought, people are as smart now as they ever were or ever will be. But a brilliant cave dweller who had available to him limited knowledge of the world and limited wisdom from the ages, could work only within the *parameters* of the tools he knew. He may have understood the nature of humans and their institutions as well as the Greeks who followed him. But in any absolute sense he wasn't too smart, because there was so much that he hadn't experienced.

Each generation improves on the experiences it opens up to the next. But a leap of tremendous proportions is coming in the next generation. The fact that we still have teachers and classrooms and textbooks will be almost laughable in fifty years. People will look back at us and ask why it took so long for us to change our notions of education, why we thought SAT scores mattered, or why we thought memorizing answers was a mark of intelligence in any way. The notion that education is about indoctrination by the state—an idea boldly stated in the 1700s and little acknowledged today—will seem scary. The governmental control of information—still popular in some countries and still possible in those countries without computer access—will become an archaic notion. Too much experience will be available too readily and too cheaply to prevent anyone from experiencing anything. Governments will have to give up even imagining that they are in the education business, an area they dominate today, and will be unable to control the broad distribution of virtual experiences in much the way that they are failing to control television and computer access in country after country today.

We will begin to understand in the next fifty years that experience and one's ability to extend its range is the ultimate measure of intelligence and the ultimate expression of freedom. The creation of virtual experience will become a major industry; our homes will be dominated by virtual experiences; our schools will have been replaced by them. What we see today in video games and science fiction movies will become our reality. Today, games like Everquest attract hundreds of thousands of players, who inhabit virtual worlds in an effort to gain status, form relationships, and acquire various virtual objects. These games are so real to the participants that the virtual objects they employ are for sale (for hefty prices) on e-Bay. Many players of these games have a social life entirely based upon them. In the future, these worlds will become much more sophisticated and even more intertwined with the real world.

It is what we can do, not what we know, that will matter in an educational system based on realistic performance environments. The important intellectual issues will revolve around questions arising from the nature of students' interactions in the virtual educational world.

When educational environments demand questions, ask how questions were obtained, and demand to know the experiences that brought on those questions, then the profound change that computers offer will have been realized. We will all be smarter—a great deal smarter—in the sense that we will not be afraid of new experiences. We will know how to find those experiences and will grow from them. Our minds will be differently educated and our intellectual world will be dominated neither by humanists nor by scientists but by experientialists, those who have been there and have become curious as a result.

From *The Next Fifty Years*, ed. John Brockman. Copyright © 2002 by John Brockman. Used by permission of Vintage Books, a division of Random House, Inc.

● ●

Vocabulary

As you think about this essay, these definitions may be helpful to you:
1. **octogenarians** persons whose age is in the eighties
2. **ex temporare** extemporaneous
3. **erudition** extensive knowledge acquired chiefly from books
4. **regimen** a regular course of action
5. **imprimatur** a Latin word meaning "let it be printed"; official sanction
6. **parameters** boundaries

Discussion Questions

1. What is the difference between intelligence and knowledge? According to the author, how will our ideas about intelligence and education change in the next 50 years?
2. What does Schank mean when he talks about hearing "an instantaneous response from the walls—enhanced by a great deal of technology from the walls, of course"?

3. Do you agree with Fadiman that all the great thoughts and ideas have already been thought and written down? Why or why not?
4. Schank says school has become a regimen for learning answers rather than learning to inquire. Why does he think that good questions will be valued over answers in the future? Do you agree? Why?
5. Explain Schank's claim that the smartest students in the future will be those "who pose questions for the software that have to be sent to humans in order to be answered."
6. Is Schank correct when he says that future "governments will have to give up even imagining that they are in the education business"?

 # Suggestions for Your Journal

Imagine yourself in 50 years, taking part in an educational experience "from the wall" as the author describes it. What area would you be curious about? What are some questions about this topic you would pose for the wall to answer?

How would you feel about conversing with virtual experts in this fashion? Or conversing virtually with others who have the same interest in the topic you do? Would you prefer this method of learning to society's current way of teaching and learning? If so, why? If not, why?

UNIT SUMMARY

The writers in this unit describe the learning process from many different perspectives. Because learning is the central mission of the college experience, understanding learning is essential to college success. The readings in this unit have offered an overview of different learning approaches from which every student can benefit.

Summary Questions

1. What specific approaches to learning do the readings in this unit describe? Which ones would you like to experience in more depth? Why?
2. What tasks or strategies described in the readings could you adopt to improve the learning skills needed in your academic work?
3. What implications for your own lifelong learning are suggested in these readings?

Suggested Writing Assignments

1. Write a brief essay describing the advantages and disadvantages of either service learning or distance learning.
2. Select one reading in this unit and write about how your personal experience has been the same as or different from what the writer describes.
3. Has the use of the Internet influenced how you learn? In what ways?

Suggested Readings

Brown, Neil, and Stuart Keeley. *Asking the Right Questions: A Guide to Critical Thinking.* Upper Saddle River, NJ: Prenctice Hall, 2001.

Donald, Janet. *Learning to Think: Disciplinary Perspectives.* San Francisco: Jossey-Bass, 2002.

Goleman, Daniel. *Working with Emotional Intelligence.* New York: Bantam Books, 1998.

What About Technology?

Higher education is in transition, and technology is a major force driving the change. As the first essay on distance learning in Unit 4 (pp. 118–121) suggests, some colleges are expanding beyond their traditional buildings and campuses into cyberspace in order to reach out to students who want or need to study in nontraditional ways. Technology will not replace colleges, but it is already affecting how we learn. In the next decades, many new information technologies will emerge. As a result, students will experience new and exciting methods of teaching and learning.

As you begin your college experience, you will witness many of these changes. How you adapt to and learn about technology in college will affect how well you later adapt and learn in the workplace. Information technology is changing the nature of jobs and how workers do those jobs. It is projected that by 2010, 90 percent of all workers will be affected.

This unit touches on some interesting facts, applications, and opinions about technology and the

The information revolution has changed people's perception of wealth. We originally said that land was wealth. Then we thought it was industrial production. Now we realize it is intellectual capital.

—WALTER WRISTON,
FORMER CEO OF CITICORP

133

influence it has on our lives. Starting with a comparison between imaginary classes—one at the University of Bologna in 1349 and a second taught via distance learning from a yacht off Vancouver Island in 2003—A. W. Bates and Gary Poole sketch some foreseeable challenges of new educational technology. Steven McDonald deals with practical implications—especially your legal rights and responsibilities—of using the Internet. Clifford Stoll offers a different perspective as he writes about how libraries and librarians are reinventing themselves. Ellen Goodman describes her foray into the new technological age by recounting her past experience with old systems. She points out how, much to her sorrow, new technology is changing the way we communicate, or fail to communicate, with each other. Finally, Michael Dertouzos anticipates and explains the need for future technologies to be "human-centric."

The Challenge of Technology

A. W. Bates and Gary Poole

- A. W. Bates is director of distance education and technology in the Department of
- Continuing Studies at the University of British Columbia in Vancouver. Gary Poole is
- director of the Centre for Teaching and Academic Growth at the University of British
- Columbia. This reading is from their book *Effective Teaching with Technology in Higher*
- *Education,* published in 2003. To know why they selected the University of Bologna in
- the 14th century, read the essay by Frank H. T. Rhodes in
- Unit 1, "The Rise of the American University."

I magine the medieval city of Bologna in 1349. At the university, Professor Ricardus Angelicus is giving a lecture on the differences between the four epistles in the Christian Bible's New Testament, drawing especially on the work of St. Augustine and Thomas Aquinas. The lecture is entirely in Latin. He depends very heavily on the manuscripts collected by the library of the University of Bologna.

Indeed, the session is called a *lecture*, which stems from the Latin word for a "reading," because it is mainly based on readings in Latin from ancient handwritten manuscripts. The philosophical position underpinning the teaching methodology is scholasticism, "training the students to consider a text according to certain pre-established officially approved criteria which are painstakingly and painfully drilled into them" (Manguel 117).

The professor is moving on to the University of Paris at the end of the semester, then will return to his position as a senior administrator in the Vatican in Rome. Later he becomes Bishop of Chichester in England.

There are nine students in the class, and they come from many parts of Europe. They pay a fee directly to the professor. Most are younger sons of nobility or high-ranking clergy, although one or two may also be sons of wealthy merchants. Most are destined for careers in the church or law.

Students are given oral examinations by the professor. The examination contains mainly factual questions around interpretations of the Bible. There is a heavy emphasis on memorization and *rote* learning, as many of the manuscripts are unique or very rare. Also the Roman Catholic Church is anxious that religious texts are interpreted "correctly."

Now let's switch to a small yacht just off the coast of Vancouver Island in Canada in 2003. Roger Boshier, a professor at the University of British Columbia, is online to graduate students in the Masters of Educational Technology program being offered jointly with Tec de Monterrey in Mexico. He is discussing with his students in an online forum the impact of globalization and information technology on national cultures. Roger has been directed to an online article by one of the Australian students and is commenting on it. The session is in English but includes several students from Latin America. An instructor from Tec de Monterrey is offering a similar online discussion forum at the same time in Spanish. Students who are bilingual often switch between the two forums.

The philosophical position underpinning the teaching methodology is *constructivism,* whereby students are encouraged to construct their own meaning through discussion and reflection.

Roger has to return to Vancouver the next day, as he also teaches several on-campus courses, although most of these also have an online component. He will be taking a *sabbatical* next year in New Zealand but plans to continue to teach the Masters in Educational Technology course while away.

He has twenty students in his seminar group, and they are from all over the world. Most are working professionals: teachers in secondary schools or instructors in universities and colleges. Most already have a graduate degree but are taking this program because of the rapid changes occurring in the field....

Which of these two *scenarios* matches most closely your own learning experiences at your university or college? Which of these scenarios would most suit your comfort level (assuming you know Latin)? If Rip van Winkle awoke from his sleep of eight hundred years, would he feel out of place in your typical university or college class?

Our point is not that universities today are old-fashioned. Much has changed and more is changing. We are not suggesting either that newer is better. Does the "modern" scenario challenge the basic values and tenets of higher education? We don't think so. But the two scenarios do indicate the close interrelationship between technological development and the practice of teaching in universities.

We deliberately pitched our first scenario just before the invention of the Gutenberg press. The invention of the mechanical printing press was a product of changing times but further became a major influence on change in society. Information technology, and particularly the Internet, is a similar consequence and cause of major change in our society, including how we teach and learn.

We believe that technology has an important place in university and college teaching, but it needs to be used with care and discrimination. The question then is not, Should we use technology? The questions are: In what contexts and for what purposes is technology appropriate for learning and teaching? What do we need to do to ensure that when we use technology for learning and teaching purposes we use it effectively? ...

Over the last ten years the Internet has become a major influence on a wide range of activities. It is now used for communications (e-mail, World Wide Web), banking, hotel and travel reservations, entertainment, news, and a host of other applications. The Internet is now an essential feature of work, leisure, and study for many people, and its influence is likely to grow as more and more people are able to access the technology on a global basis.

Its impact on education and training has been as great as on any other area. Web sites provide instant access to data from active volcanoes, Web cameras record events as they happen, and Web databases provide access to a multitude of academic resources. More online courses are becoming available.

Students need to learn how to use technology to seek, organize, analyze, and apply information appropriately. It will become increasingly difficult to accept someone as being fully educated if they do not know how to use the Internet to communicate with other professionals, if they do not know how to find Web sites that will provide relevant and reliable information within their field of study, or if they do not know how to develop their own multimedia reports for communicating their knowledge or research. Therefore, we cannot ignore technology in learning and teaching. The best way to help students understand the strengths— and weaknesses—of technology in their field of study is to use it in teaching.

One frequent criticism of the use of technology in teaching is that we are being driven by a technological *imperative*: we have to use technology because of a blind belief that it is good for us. If we don't agree to the use of technology, we will be considered out of date and may lose our credibility.

Those who challenge the technological imperative do so from a variety of perspectives. Some ask, *What is technology doing to our ways of thinking and understanding?* Those who ask this question usually answer that technology weakens our ability to think rationally or logically. Others go further and suggest that the pressure to use technology in education is a conspiracy by multinational companies and big business to sell technology and hook young people forever into being technology consumers.

Some supporters of the use of technology in teaching believe that there are important educational benefits in using technology but recognize the pressure, especially on senior management, to be fashionable and to have the latest "toys," and they lever that pressure to win support for their technology-based teaching initiatives.

Finally, many postsecondary teachers are aware that whereas technology ought to be able to help them in teaching students, their knowledge of technology is often less than that of their students, and in particular they are unsure of how best to use it to achieve their teaching goals.

Those who believe that technology can play a valuable role in teaching and learning, understand the "technological imperative" arguments. They accept that some of these arguments are valid, but believe that they are insufficient for a blanket denial of the use of technology. We recognize that there is a great deal of hyperbole and exaggeration about the benefits of technology in education. There are pressures from the commercial sector to use technologies for teaching that are based on profit, not educational benefits. And without major changes in the way we work, technology will be time-consuming and require an unreasonable amount of dedication to learn new skills.

Nevertheless, such arguments should not blind us to the genuine benefits technology can bring when used wisely. Pressures for change on the university and college from both within and outside require us to look afresh at how students learn and how teaching is organized and delivered if quality is to be maintained or even improved.

Work Cited

Manguel, Alberto. *A History of Reading*. New York: HarperCollins, 1996.

 Vocabulary

As you think about this essay, these definitions may be helpful to you:

1. **rote**   to learn "by rote" is to learn with the use of memory but little intelligence or understanding.
2. **constructivism**   a philosophy (or system of thinking) in which meaning is not inherent in a word or object but is attached to that word or object ("constructed") by the author or creator
3. **sabbatical**   short for "sabbatical year"; a leave of absence from regular teaching duties, often with pay, granted to professors usually every seventh year, for rest, travel, or research
4. **scenario**   a possible course of action, usually imagined or projected
5. **imperative**   necessary, not to be avoided

 Discussion Questions

1. Compare the two scenarios that these authors use to open their essay. What are the major points of difference? Of similarity?
2. How do Bates and Poole feel about the use of up-to-date technology in college teaching? Do you agree?
3. What benefits do Bates and Poole identify for the use of technology in the classroom?

 Suggestions for Your Journal

It may not be possible for you to imagine yourself back in the University of Bologna in 1349, but try to imagine what it was like to attend school before the advent of the personal computer. If you are 18 or so, talk first with someone old enough to have attended school before, say, 1970. Would you have preferred their classroom environment to the one you have now, or do you prefer school in the 21st century?

Have you decided on a future career? For the purpose of your journal, select one and discuss some of the ways that, in your view, college should prepare you for the technological demands of that profession.

Virtual Legality: An Overview of Your Rights and Responsibilities in Cyberspace

Steven J. McDonald

Steven J. McDonald is an associate legal counsel in the Office of Legal Affairs at The Ohio State University. In this essay he discusses legal implications important to those who use the Internet. His focus is especially on college students.

The Internet is a powerful and revolutionary tool for communication—powerful in its ability to reach a global audience and revolutionary in its accessibility to those who formerly were only at the receiving end of mass communications. With access to the Internet, *anyone,* even a preschool child, can now effectively be an international publisher and broadcaster. By posting to Usenet or establishing a web page, for example, an Internet user can speak to a larger and wider audience than does the *New York Times,* NBC or National Public Radio. Many Internet users, however, do not realize that that is what they are doing.

Not surprisingly, given these facts, the Internet also has a powerful and revolutionary potential for misuse. Such misuse is particularly prevalent on college and university campuses, where free *access* to computing resources is often mistakenly thought to be the equivalent of free *speech,* and where free speech rights are in turn often mistakenly thought to include the right to do whatever is technically possible.

The rights of academic freedom and freedom of expression do apply to the use of college and university computing resources. So, too, however, do the responsibilities and limitations associated with those rights. Thus, legitimate use of institutional computing resources does *not* extend to whatever is technically possible. In addition, while some restrictions are built into the institution's computer operating systems and networks, those restrictions are not the only restrictions on what is permissible. Users of college and university computing resources must abide by all applicable restrictions, whether or not they are built into the operating system or network and whether or not they can be *circumvented* by technical means. Moreover, it is not the responsibility of a college or university to prevent computer users from exceeding those restrictions; rather, it is the computer user's responsibility to know and comply with them. When you're pulled over to the side of the Information Superhighway, "I'm sorry, officer—I didn't realize I was over the speed limit" is not a valid defense.

So just what are the applicable restrictions? The same laws and policies that apply in every other context. "Cyberspace" is not a separate legal jurisdiction, and it is not exempt from the normal requirements of legal and ethical behavior within the college or university community. *A good rule of thumb to keep in mind is that conduct that would be illegal or a violation of institutional policy in the "offline" world will still be illegal or a violation of institutional policy when it occurs online.* Remember, too, that the online world is not limited to your college or university, to the state in which it is located, or even to the United States. *Computer users who engage in electronic communications with persons in other states or countries or on other systems or networks may also be subject to the laws of those other states and countries and the rules and policies of those other systems and networks.*

It is impossible to list and describe every law and policy that applies to the use of college and university computing resources and the Internet—since, by and large, they all do—but the following are some of the ones that most frequently cause problems.

Copyright

Copyright law generally gives authors, artists, composers, and other such creators the exclusive right to copy, distribute, modify, and display their works or to authorize other people to do so. Moreover, their works are protected by copyright law from the very moment that they are created—regardless of whether they are registered with the Copyright Office and regardless of whether they are marked with a copyright notice or symbol (©). That means that virtually every e-mail message, Usenet posting, web page, or other computer work you have ever created—or seen—is copyrighted. That also means that, if you are not the copyright owner of a particular e-mail message, Usenet posting, web page, or other computer work, you may not copy, distribute, modify, or display it unless:

- its copyright owner has given you permission to do so, or
- it is in the *"public domain,"* or
- doing so would constitute "fair use," or
- you have an "implied license" to do so.

If none of these exceptions applies, your use of the work constitutes copyright infringement, and you could be liable for as much as $100,000 in damages for each use. In addition, if you reproduce or distribute copies of a copyrighted work having a total retail value of at least $1,000 (which could include, for example, posting a $50 software program on a web page or newsgroup from which it is downloaded 20 times), your action may also be criminal, even if you do it for free.

It's usually easy to tell whether you have permission to make a particular use of a work: The copyright owner will have told you so expressly, either in writing or orally. However, it is not always so easy to tell whether the work is in the public domain or whether what you want to do constitutes fair use or is covered by an implied license.

Placing a work on the Internet is not the same thing as granting that work to the public domain. Generally speaking, a work found on the Internet, like a work found anywhere else, is in the public domain only if (a) its creator has expressly disclaimed any copyright interest in the work, or (b) it was created by the federal government, or (c) it is very old. Unfortunately, how old a particular work must be to be "in the public domain" depends in part upon when the work was created, in part upon whether and when it was formally published, in part upon whether and when its creator died, and in part on still other factors. Consequently, there is no one specific cutoff date that you can use for all works to determine whether or not they are in the public domain. As a rule of thumb, however, works that were created *and published* before 1923 are now in the public domain....Works that have never been published *might* be in the public domain, but if you don't know for sure, it is best to assume that they are not.

In very general terms, a particular use of a work is considered "fair use" if it involves only a relatively small portion of the work, is for educational or other noncommercial purposes, and is unlikely to interfere with the copyright owner's ability to market the original work. A classic example is quoting a few sentences or paragraphs of a book in a class paper. Other uses may also be fair, but it is almost never fair to use an entire work, and it is not enough that you aren't charging anyone for your particular use. It also is not enough simply to cite your source (though it may be *plagiarism* if you don't).

An implied license may exist if the copyright owner has acted in such a way that it is reasonable for you to assume that you may make a particular use. For example, if you are the moderator of a mailing list and someone sends you a message for that list, it's reasonable to assume that you may post the message to the list, even if its author didn't expressly say that you may do so. The copyright owner can always "revoke" an implied license, however, simply by saying that further use is prohibited.

In addition, facts and ideas cannot be copyrighted. Copyright law protects only the expression of the creator's idea—the specific words or notes or brushstrokes or computer code that the creator used—and not the underlying idea itself. Thus, for example, it is not copyright infringement to state in a history paper that the Declaration of Independence was actually signed on August 2, 1776, or to argue in an English paper that Francis Bacon is the real author of Shakespeare's plays, even though someone else has already done so, as long as you use your own words. (Again, however, if you don't cite your sources, it may still be plagiarism even if you paraphrase.)

Exactly how copyright law applies to the Internet is still not entirely clear, but there are some rules of thumb:

- You *may* look at another person's web page, even though your computer makes a temporary copy when you do so, but you may not redistribute it or incorporate it into your own web page without permission, except as fair use may allow.

- You *probably may* quote all or part of another person's Usenet or listserv message in your response to that message, unless the original message says that copying is prohibited.
- You *probably may not* copy and redistribute a private e-mail message you have received without the author's permission, except as fair use may allow.
- You *probably may* print out a single copy of a web page or of a Usenet, listserv, or private e-mail message for your own, personal, noncommercial use.
- You *may not* post another person's book, article, graphic, image, music, or other such material on your web page or use them in your Usenet, listserv, or private e-mail messages without permission, except as fair use may allow.
- You *may not* download materials from Lexis-Nexis, the Clarinet news service, or other such services and copy or redistribute them without permission, unless the applicable license agreement expressly permits you to do so or unless your particular use would constitute fair use.
- You *may not* copy or redistribute software without permission, unless the applicable license agreement expressly permits you to do so.

Libel

Libel is the "publication" of a false statement of fact that harms another person's reputation. For example, it is libel to say that "John beat up his roommate" or "Mary is a thief" if these statements are not true. If a statement doesn't harm the other person's reputation—for example, "Joe got an 'A' on the test"—it is not libel even if it's false. In addition, a statement of pure opinion—for example, "I don't like John"—cannot be libelous. But you cannot turn a statement of fact into an opinion simply by adding "I think" or "in my opinion" to it. "IMHO [In my honest opinion], John beat up his roommate" is still libelous if John didn't beat up his roommate. If you honestly believed that what you said was true, however, you *might* not be liable if it later turns out that you were wrong.

A libel is "published" whenever it is communicated to a third person. In other words, if you say "Mary is a thief" to anyone other than Mary, you have "published" that libel. That means that almost anything you post or send on the Internet, except an e-mail that you send *only to the person about whom you are talking*, is "published" for purposes of libel law.

A person who has been libeled can sue for whatever damages are caused by the publication of the libel. Since a libel on the Internet could potentially reach millions of people, the damages could be quite large.

A good rule of thumb to follow: If you would be upset if someone else made the same statement about you, think carefully before you send or post that statement to the Internet, because it might be libelous.

Invasion of Privacy

There are a number of different laws that protect the "right to privacy" in a number of different ways. For example, under the Electronic Communications Privacy Act, which is a federal statute, it generally is a crime to intercept someone else's private e-mail message or to look into someone else's private computer account without appropriate authorization. The fact that you may have the technical ability to do so, or that the other person may not have properly safeguarded his or her account, does not mean that you have authorization. If you don't know for sure whether you have authorization, you probably don't.

Invasion of privacy, like libel, is also a "*tort,*" which means that you can also be sued for monetary damages. In addition to the sorts of things prohibited by the Electronic Communications Privacy Act, it can be an invasion of privacy to disclose intensely personal information about another person that that person has chosen not to make public and that the public has no legitimate need or reason to know: for example, the fact that someone has AIDS, if he or she has not revealed that information publicly. Unlike with libel, a statement can be an invasion of privacy even if it is true.

Obscenity, Child Pornography, and "Indecency"

Under both state and federal law, it is a crime to publish, sell, distribute, display, or, in some cases, merely possess obscene materials or child pornography. These laws also apply equally to the Internet, and a number of people have been prosecuted and convicted for violating them in that context.

The line between what is obscene and what is not is hard to draw with any precision—as one Supreme Court Justice said, "I could never succeed in intelligibly" defining obscenity, "[b]ut I know it when I see it"—but the term basically means hardcore pornography that has no literary, artistic, political, or other socially redeeming value. One reason that it is so hard to define obscenity is that it depends in part on local community standards; what is considered obscene in one community may not be considered obscene in another. That makes it particularly difficult to determine whether materials on the Internet are obscene, since such materials are, in a sense, everywhere, and it is therefore not enough that the materials are legal wherever you are. In one case, the operators of a bulletin board service in California posted materials that were not considered obscene there, but [they] were convicted of violating the obscenity statutes in Tennessee when the materials were downloaded there.

Child pornography is the visual depiction of minors engaged in sexually explicit activity. Unlike obscenity, child pornography is illegal regardless of whether it has any literary, artistic, political, or other socially redeeming value.

Sexually oriented materials that do not constitute either obscenity or child pornography generally are legal. Still, it is illegal in most cases to provide such materials to minors, and displaying or sending such materials to people who do not wish to see them may be a violation of your college or university's sexual harassment policy.

"Hacking," "Cracking," and Similar Activities

Under the federal Computer Fraud and Abuse Act, and under a variety of similar other state and federal statutes, it can also be a crime to access or use a computer without authorization, to alter data in a computer without authorization, to transmit computer viruses and "worms" over computer networks, to conduct "e-mail bombing," and to engage in other such activities. Engaging in such activities can also make you liable for monetary damages to any person who is harmed by your activities. Again, the fact that you may have the technical ability to do any of these things, or that another computer owner may not have properly safeguarded his or her computer, does not mean that you have authorization. If you don't know for sure whether you have authorization, you probably don't.

Institutional Policies

Use of college and university computing resources is also normally subject to the institution's rules and regulations—for example, its code of student conduct, policy on academic misconduct, sexual harassment policy, and all other generally applicable institutional policies. In addition, institutional computer use policies often contain the following types of additional, specific prohibitions:

- Institutional computer accounts and passwords may not, under any circumstances, be shared with, or used by, persons other than those to whom they have been assigned by the institution—even family and friends. Users are responsible for all use of their accounts.
- Users must limit their use of institutional computing resources so as not to consume an unreasonable amount of those resources or to interfere with the activity of other users.
- Institutional computing resources are intended for institution-related use and therefore may not be used for personal commercial or business purposes or for other personal gain. Personal use of institutional computing resources for *other* purposes may be permitted when it does not consume a significant amount of those resources, does not interfere with the performance of the user's job or other institutional responsibilities, and is otherwise in compliance with institutional policies.
- Users of institutional computing resources may not state or imply that they are speaking on behalf of the institution and may not use institutional trademarks and logos in connection with their use of those resources without specific authorization to do so.

For Further Information

If you have questions about the legality of your specific use of institutional computing resources, it is best to ask before proceeding. *The resolution of specific legal issues requires an analysis of all the facts and circumstances; the general guidelines in this document do not constitute, and should not be relied upon as, specific legal advice.* You may be able to get general advice (but, again, not specific legal advice) from your academic advisor, from computer lab site managers, or from your institution's computer help desk.

In addition, you can find more information on these and related topics at the following web sites:

- "Cyberspace Law for Non-Lawyers," which is located at:
  http://www.ssrn.com/update/lsn/cyberspace/csl-lessons.html

- "Law and the Web," which is located at:
  http://www.Cnet.com/Content/Features/Dlife/Law/index.html
- "10 Big Myths About Copyright Explained," which is located at:
  http://www.clari.net/brad/copymyths.html
- "Soundbyting: Music on the Internet," which is located at:
  http://www.soundbyting.com

Reprinted by permission of The Ohio State University Office of Legal Affairs.

 Vocabulary

As you think about this essay, these definitions may be helpful to you:
1. **circumvent**   to get around, evade
2. **public domain**   the legal realm embracing property that belongs to the community at large
3. **plagiarism**   to steal or pass off words or ideas of another as one's own
4. **libel**   defamation of a person by written or presentational means
5. **tort**   a wrongful act that may lead to legal action

 Discussion Questions

1. Why, according to the author, does the Internet have such potential for misuse?
2. How does the author suggest you can judge what is legal or illegal in cyberspace?
3. How do copyright laws affect the Internet?
4. Why is your online "right to privacy" so important?
5. Why are "hacking," "cracking," and similar activities illegal?

Suggestions for Your Journal

As you think about the legal questions involved in using the Internet, two major issues should be your privacy and your safety as an individual. What steps can you take to protect yourself against identity theft? What practices should you follow consistently in order to be safe from persons who want to take advantage of you in cyberspace?

The Connected Library

Clifford Stoll

Clifford Stoll, commentator, lecturer, and Berkeley astronomer, is the author of many best-selling books. In this essay, he describes his reactions to the changes taking place in libraries today because of automation and other technological advances.

• • • • • • • • • • • • • • • • • • •

Sandi Webb, a councilperson in Simi Valley, California, wants to close the community library system: "We need to rip out those useless bookcases, filled with outdated books that are seldom opened, and replace them with low-cost computers and CD-ROMs and high-speed Internet access lines."

Yee-haw! Computers will eliminate those pesky libraries. Get rid of them books. After the book-burning festival, let's eliminate local politicians, now that computers and telephones let us instantly vote on issues.

Alongside churches and day-care centers, libraries are about the most underfunded and underappreciated of our society's institutions. The field receives so little respect that library schools are changing their names to "schools of information management." Apparently embarrassed by their lack of status, many librarians now call themselves information specialists.

Of course, practically every person is an information specialist. A baker specializes in information about breads and cakes. A historian is certainly an information specialist. So is a doctor. Taxicab drivers, too. "Information specialist" is a meaningless, generic title.

I may not know what an information specialist does, but I sure know what a librarian oughta do. For two millennia, they've been stewards of books, charged with organizing, cataloging, preserving, and making books available. Our *cornucopia* of historical appreciation, technological progress, and cultural awareness isn't the result of a team of information specialists; rather it's due to centuries of rarely thanked librarians.

Yet as librarians turn away from their heritage and toward computers, our book collections become less well preserved, less organized, and less available. Their name change symbolizes a transformation of librarians from stewards of our cultural endowment to professional information handlers. They're now at home answering e-mail, reading Internet mailing lists, and surfing the Web. Can't blame them: I'd rather check out some Usenet scuttlebutt than deal with a confused patron at the reference desk.

Libraries, of course, are riding the information age bandwagon. With great fanfare, the University of California opened their version of the library of the future, a brand-new library facility. The official reason for moving the library was seismic strengthening—Berkeley's in earthquake territory and someone worried about books falling off shelves. But pretty quickly, the library reconstruction got hijacked by library automation folks. These are information management types—typically with degrees in computer science—who feel they know more about how libraries should be run than librarians.

The old friendly library of stacks and study tables morphed into an information-age *monolith,* sprouting hundreds of computers. A cumbersome spiral staircase showcases the importance of appearance over function. It's admired by administrators, architects, and technologists. Of course—they don't have to use it.

To make room for the computers and spiral staircase, half the books were shipped ten miles off campus, into a book warehouse. The books available at the actual library are just an echo of the entire collection. Sandi Webb's wishes have come true: Any book that hasn't been checked out in a year gets warehoused. Thus, there's a complete set of Tom Clancy novels on the shelf, but if you're searching for anything over twenty years old, your book has to be hauled in on tomorrow's bus.

And don't think that you can go to the warehouse to read. You'll discover that you can't browse the shelves—books aren't filed by subject, title, or author. They're warehoused by size. Perfect for a computer call system. Impossible for the researcher.

Ever hear of a bookshelf that has stopped working? I've witnessed it. To save space, my library put its shelves on rollers, called compact shelving. To get a book, you turn a wheel and roll several bookshelves, in order to open up an aisle to reach your volume. Nice idea, so long as the mechanism works. When a wheel gets jammed, you can't move the shelves, so your book's out of reach. If several people want books, they wait in line for an aisle to open up. Wait in an aisle next to a bookshelf and nobody can get to any other shelf. It's a storage system designed to provide only the book you're hunting for. Nothing else.

Library administrators love compact shelving; open shelves take up more space than rolling bookcases. Combined with offsite warehousing of books, research libraries are becoming systems which will deliver only the book which you request . . . a fiendish way to prevent both browsing and serendipitous research.

Of course, the big library improvement is universal Internet availability. Not just dozens of workstations. My university's library of the future features four Ethernet ports at every table. Sprouting from some study carrels are eight computer ports and sixteen power outlets. Every work space has a high-speed link to the Internet.

These connections let you hook up your laptop computer to the Internet. Of course, you have to supply the computer, cable, software, and account. That's never a problem for the information specialists who'll happily give you a tour.

Who's using all those library ports? At the University of California library, almost nobody. Walking past carrels and tables, I've seen about five students linking their laptops to the network. Practically everyone at the library is reading books. Curiously, all of the library's public terminals are in use—often by students playing Internet games—but the hundreds of computer connections remain unused.

Well, not quite unused. About half of the library Ethernet ports have been broken. Some outlets have pencils stuffed into them. Others show broken faceplates or have been pried apart. Many connectors are missing, leaving a rectangular hole and a colorful bouquet of Class-V communications wires.

Maybe I'm seeing the effect of bored students, curious to see how connectors work. Maybe campus lowlifes infest the library, seeking to vandalize pricey computer networks. Perhaps it's the result of a conspiracy of *Luddite* librarians who object to technology pushing aside their jobs.

Whatever the explanation, so far the electronically wired library has been a dud for students, researchers, and librarians. The only ones who really celebrate this boondoggle are the library automation promoters. They, of course, call it a model for future libraries.

Once, the University of California's library ranked second only to Harvard. But since the library renovation and computerization, the Association of Research Libraries dropped its ranking from second to fifth place. Local librarians feel it will drop another few notches next year, since it is no longer adding as many books as it once did. Sad news for library automation hucksters: College ratings bureaus take into account such outmoded ideas as how many books a library has, how available they are, and the staffing of the library. They don't count unused Ethernet ports.

What about public libraries? Worried that I was just considering the needs of researchers, I conducted a spur-of-the-moment, utterly unsystematic survey in Berkeley. I stood on a street corner and asked a dozen passersby, "What do you want in a public library?"

Fully half of those questioned replied, "I don't have any money to give you," and kept walking.

Of the half dozen who took me seriously, the most common answer was "I want books in the library. Lots of books." A few asked for magazines, newspapers, and journals. Several insisted on a good librarian. Evening hours. A harried mom wanted Saturday morning storytelling. Nobody mentioned . . . CD-ROMs, multimedia software, and network connections. Which is odd, given that these are expensive and quickly become obsolete. And, at least in my limited survey, hardly in demand.

According to a survey in *School Library Journal,* 1994 school expenditures on audiovisual and computer equipment roughly equaled book costs . . . each about five thousand dollars. By 1998, computers were way ahead of books.

For some reason, librarians—oops, I mean information specialists—feel that their library isn't doing a good job unless it has plenty of electronic *gizmos* and a flashy Web site. American Library Association conferences hold dozens of sessions on how to make library Web pages. Does this serve library patrons? Local communities? Or does it mainly advertise to distant Internet surfers, who never visit the library and only rarely read books?

Moreover, as librarians get replaced by techno-literate infospecs, you'll find fewer helpful faces behind the library counter. Rhonda Neagle is a library media specialist and technology facilitator at Logan High School in New Haven, California. "It's only the rare moment in any day when I'm on the floor helping kids," she reports. The rest of the time, she's troubleshooting laser printers and VCRs, serving on committees, and overseeing networks, according to the June 1997 *Electronic Learning* magazine.

Rapid *obsolescence* hits libraries hard. Twenty-five years ago, Fort Worth installed the newest and most expensive computers in their library. The modern replacements cost three million dollars, so they dipped into their endowment. A decade from now, there will be no nest egg to replace the obsolete 1997 computers.

Compare a well-cataloged collection of books, magazines, and newspapers with two dozen high-tech Internet workstations, complete with multimedia software. Which will last longer? Which better serves a neighborhood of children, young adults, adults, and elderly? Which promotes reading, study, and reflection? Which is more likely to be seen as a toy? Which will better preserve our heritage and foster a sense of scholarship and friendship?

Library bureaucrats adopt a gee-whiz attitude toward the Internet: "Libraries must develop a new paradigm," writes Brown University library administrator Brian Hawkins. He wants more computers, more networks, and fewer books.

Meanwhile, librarians politely yawn at traditional library tasks, such as cataloging works, storing books, and staffing reference desks. Berkeley's library committee seeks a "fundamental shift in emphasis from being a warehouse to becoming a gateway for information." Translation: Give 'em computers and get rid of books.

The result of this technolust is that libraries—public and private—are hiring lots of computer specialists. Meanwhile, they're laying off librarians. They're spending money on new databases, but not new books. There's no librarian to help you figure out the thousands of available databases. Gateway to information, indeed.

It's odd to read articles in *Forbes* and *Fortune* on how information is the career of the future. Yet librarians, who have taken care of information for millennia, can't find jobs.

During the 1960s, libraries spent zillions on what was then new media: 16mm films, phonograph records, and filmstrips. Then, as now, the stuff was expensive, quickly went out of date, and [was] tough to archive. What happened to all those phonograph records purchased by your library in 1965?

Today, the closest thing we have to a digital archive medium is the CD-ROM. Yet it has a life span of thirty to fifty years. Within a few decades, newer devices will make CD-ROM readers obsolete. And when manufacturers no longer build reading devices, libraries won't be able to access their collection of CD-ROMs. They'll wind up in a landfill. But a book? It's universally accessible, easily stored, immediately readable, completely portable. Thousands of years have demonstrated the book's importance and permanence.

And that's what the high-tech library reformers are out to gut. As librarians get laid off, branches run understaffed. They're open perhaps one or two nights a week. They don't subscribe to out-of-town papers. They quietly cancel story hours. Instead of a librarian helping you look up a book, you're pointed to a computer.

Our technologists are working to change our libraries into sterile information warehouses, filled with workstations yet devoid of books. What'll happen when the Internet is universally available and nobody needs to visit the library to search for information? Will libraries close up because trendy "information gateway" grants aren't available and they no longer have any books?

I can't think of a more effective way to eliminate libraries. Burning books won't work—centuries of fanatics, censors, and dictators have tried and failed. And you can't close down libraries by political fiat: They're far too popular in neighborhoods.

No, the best way to gut our libraries is to ship the books off to distant warehouses, supplant librarians with generic information specialists, and replace bookshelves with gleaming computer workstations. Donate computers and software which will quickly become obsolete. Provide patrons with CD-ROMs and high-speed Internet ports. Encourage kids to surf the Web rather than read books. Count hits on your Web page instead of visitors to the stacks. Pretty soon, traffic to the stacks will evaporate and the library will fossilize.

In the struggle for liberty and literacy, books and libraries are the best weapons we've got. Use them. Appreciate them. Support them.

From *High Tech Heretic* by Clifford Stoll, © 1999 by Clifford Stoll. Used by permission of Doubleday, a division of Random House, Inc.

● ●

 Vocabulary

As you think about this essay, these definitions may be helpful to you:
1. **cornucopia**   a symbol of abundance
2. **monolith**   an organized whole that acts as a unified powerful force
3. **Luddite**   someone who fights technological change
4. **gizmos**   gadgets
5. **obsolescence**   the process of going out of use or losing usefulness

 Discussion Questions

1. What do you think of the writing style the author uses to share his view of the current direction of libraries?
2. What does the author claim is happening to our library systems in general?

3. The author is assessing his library system based on his need for research functions. Are there other functions for which the automated library might be more useful and effective?

4. Upon what does the author base his opinion about the obsolescence of tomorrow's libraries? Do you agree?

 # Suggestions for Your Journal

When you are doing research on a project for class or for your personal activities, when do you turn to the Internet and when do you prefer to use print media—a newspaper or a library book, for example? Write about the habits that you have developed in these activities and try to explain them to yourself and a friendly reader.

What do you expect a library at your college or university to provide for you that you don't expect to find on the Internet?

Technology Eliminating Conversation

Ellen Goodman

Ellen Goodman, a columnist whose essays regularly appear in more than 200
newspapers across the country, began her journalistic career as a reporter for
Newsweek and the *Detroit Free Press,* then joined the *Boston Globe.* She has won a
Pulitzer Prize for distinguished commentary and is the author of several books. In this
essay she describes her initiation into new telephone technology and how it has
affected face-to-face conversation.

• • • • • • • • • • • • • • • • • •

We are at lunch when my friend leans over the table to share his latest
encounter with telephone technology.

It all began with a voice mail message, which wasn't in itself so startling.
But my friend was at his desk when the phone didn't ring. A colleague, it seems,
had learned how to dial directly into voice mail—avoiding the middleman, or
middle ear, entirely.

Was my friend, a man who *parses* moral dilemmas for a living, insulted
that this caller didn't want to speak to the real, live and available him? Were either of us aghast at some new techno-wrinkle of rudeness? Appalled by the
state of the art of message-dropping?

No, we were delighted, curious, envious. How on Earth did he do that?

I am old enough to remember black rotary phones, the Model T of this
technology. I remember when the telephone was a beloved instrument of conversation. Furthermore, I was raised to believe in courtesy as one of the cardinal
virtues.

But we are in the middle of a communications revolution that feels increasingly like guerrilla warfare. Everywhere you turn in this revolution, machines are pointed at you. Today, anyone near a phone can end up feeling like
the target of snipers.

Half a dozen years ago when I read that Martha Stewart had something
like six or seven voice mail numbers, I was bug-eyed in astonishment. Now I
have three voice mails, three e-mails, three fax machines all collecting messages
in assorted buildings that are nowhere nearly as well decorated as Martha's, but
you get the point.

To understand how the world has changed, think back to the warm and
fuzzy telephone ads that once encouraged us to reach out and touch someone.
Compare that to my favorite telephone ad of this season. It features Paul Revere
in his full midnight ride *regalia* trying to reach John Adams, who is of course
screening his calls: "John, John, this is Paul. Pick up. It's important."

In this revolutionary atmosphere, it isn't a new communications weapon that is lusted over by patriots seeking their personal freedom. It's an anti-communications weapon.

We want technology that enhances our ability to not talk to people. We want a personal Star Wars defense system to screen and shoot down, avert and disarm the incoming missives. We long for the ability to be out of touch.

This has created a whole new etiquette called "etiquette be damned." The dirty little secret of corporate America is the number of people for whom phone tag is actually dodge ball. All over the various midtowns of our country, people wait to return calls until they are pretty sure the other person is at lunch. Who hasn't picked up a phone to have a startled caller exhale: "Oh, I just wanted to leave a message"?

Of course, the invasion of the dinner snatchers has created an additional wrinkle. People who know the words to "Solidarity Forever" and are generally sympathetic to the plight of the new working class now greet marketing callers by snarling, "Why don't you give me your home number since you have mine?"

This is now leading to a high-tech arms race, a kind of mutually assured destruction. First you pay to put a phone in your house-office-car. Now you can also pay to keep the calls out.

Just last month, Ameritech announced a service to let customers reject the sort of unwanted telephone calls that come from telemarketers. "Customers are screaming for this," said the company's chief executive officer.

We are also "screaming" for what I would call, in *oxymoronic* fashion, one-way conversations. The linguistic types call this *asynchronous* talk. In that sense the phone is becoming more and more like e-mail. One person leaves a message for the other who leaves a message—look ma, no hands. It's like playing virtual tennis.

But such is the reality of modern life. All the advances have *ratcheted* up the number of "exchanges" we're expected to make until our own circuits are overloaded. Efficiency trumps courtesy. We don't just talk, we use the phone as a drop-off center.

Remember Alexander Graham Bell's first words over the newfangled phone? "Mr. Watson, come here, I want you." What would he say today? "Watson old boy, when you get a minute, have your voice mail call my voice mail."

 Vocabulary

As you think about this essay, these definitions may be helpful to you:
1. **parses**   resolves component parts of speech and describes them grammatically; analyzes closely

2. **regalia**   special dress, generally very formal, like an admiral's best uniform or a priest's robes for conducting a high mass
3. **oxymoron**   a figure of speech that combines apparently contradictory or incongruous ideas
4. **asynchronous**   happening at different times
5. **ratcheted**   changed by stages

 Discussion Questions

1. How does Ellen Goodman compare her current involvement with technology with her past experiences?
2. What is the "new etiquette" associated with increased telephone technology, according to the author?
3. What does the author mean by "efficiency trumps courtesy"?

 Suggestions for Your Journal

Do you make or receive telephone calls when you are driving? Do you notice when other drivers are on the phone? How have such calls changed the quality of your conversations? The use of cellular phones while driving is highly controversial. In many places it is illegal. Take a stand for or against making such telephone activity illegal in the town where you now reside.

Human-Centric Issues in the Information Marketplace

Michael L. Dertouzos

The late Michael Dertouzos was the author of eight books, including *The Unfinished Revolution: Human-Centered Computers and What They Can Do for Us*, from which this essay is taken. Dertouzos joined the MIT faculty in 1964 and became director of the MIT Laboratory for Computer Science in 1974. Under his leadership, it became one of the largest research labs at MIT, with 400 faculty members, graduate students, and research staff. Dertouzos introduced the concept of human-centered computing and, as this essay shows, had a special talent for putting complicated technology into human terms and making it accessible to nontechnical audiences. "We made a big mistake 300 years ago when we separated technology and humanism," Dertouzos said in an interview in *Scientific American*. "It's time to put the two back together."

By 2010, over a billion people and their computers, along with some 100 billion appliances, will be interconnected. What will they all do? They will buy, sell, and freely exchange information and information services.

Make no mistake: The sharing of information and e-commerce over today's Internet is only the tip of the Information Marketplace iceberg. Take, for example, the "content" that the press and Wall Street were hyperventilating about throughout the late 1990s, in the wake of proposed megamergers like that between America Online and Time Warner. All the content you can imagine—TV, movies, theater, radio, newspapers, magazines, books—accounts for less than 5 percent of the world's industrial economy. On the other hand, a whopping 50 percent of that economy—some $10 trillion—is office work, or, as it used to be called, white-collar work. This includes buy and sell transactions, reviewing mortgage applications, processing insurance forms, dealing with medical information, filling and reviewing millions of government forms, teaching and learning, selling customer services, and a myriad of business-to-business services. That's information work—the processing of information by skilled humans, and secondarily by machines, and the delivery of that work where and when it is needed. This is barely happening over the Internet today, so no one talks about it. But it will be everywhere on tomorrow's Information Marketplace. Human-centric computing must make it easy for people to offer their work across space and time if the Information Marketplace is to reach its full potential.

By 2020, and by my reckoning, some $4 trillion of this information work will flow over the Information Marketplace, shaking up the distribution of labor. Just imagine what 50 million Indians could do to the English-speaking industrial world using their ability to read and write English and offer their office skills, at a distance, for about one-third of what the West pays today. Such a move would have colossal economic consequences, in the redistribution of work, internationally. It would also mark a *poetic comeback* for India, which may then be in a position to exert economic power on a nation like England that taught the Indians English to dominate them. As much as information work will flow from poor to rich, even more will flow from rich to rich—services that will be increasingly delivered via the Net because of speed and convenience. By the time this activity and the electronic commerce in goods level out, the "buy-and-sell" part of the Information Marketplace will grow from some $200 billion in 2000 to some $5 trillion annually, roughly one-fourth of the world industrial economy.

The "free exchange" part of the Information Marketplace will be just as important, because people have as much free time as work time, and they value what they do with it just as much. Already the lives of many people are affected through family e-mail; collaboration, playing, and dating; entertainment through listening to music and viewing images and videos; accessing information of personal interest; engaging in discussions about literature, hobbies, and social issues; publishing their views; and much more. These uses will grow. When I speak publicly, I always ask those people in the audience who use e-mail to communicate with family members to raise their hands. The ratio, largely invisible in 1995, was consistently over 90 percent in 2000. Many new activities will arise as well that we can't predict today.

Taken together, the monetary and nonmonetary activities of the Information Marketplace, driven by the onrush of faster computers and communications, computerized appliances, mobile gadgets, and portable software, will propel us toward a world overflowing with information and information-related activities. The question is, "How can we build this world so we are ensured of doing more by doing less?" rather than drowning in information overload and computer complexity. Only by throwing out last century's model for computing and adopting—indeed, demanding—a new computing philosophy, a new master plan, that lets people interact naturally, easily, and purposefully with each other and the surrounding physical world.

Human-centric computing will transform today's individual computers, the Internet, and the Web into a true Information Marketplace, where we'll buy, sell, and freely exchange information and information services using systems that will talk with us, do things for us, get the information we want, help us work with other people, and adapt to our individual needs. Indeed, it is these five basic capabilities of computer and communications systems that are the pivotal forces of human-centric computing.

As builders of computer systems start turning these forces into useful technologies, the rest of us who are collectively frustrated by today's computers can accelerate the process by tirelessly repeating the rallying cry of human-centric computing: "Information technology should help people do more by doing less!" If we shout loud enough, *entrepreneurial* companies will make this request their goal. They will recognize the huge, pent-up demand for human-centric systems, and will build them, upstaging the massive computer-communications establishment and shifting the market in their direction.

Much as we like to tout it, the Information Revolution is not yet here. It started innocently enough in the 1950s with a handful of laboratory curiosities dedicated to mathematical calculations. The 1960s brought time-shared computers, each used in round-robin fashion by tens of people to spread the high computer cost. Universities and other organizations soon discovered that the real benefit was not the money saved but the information shared through e-mail and document transfers within each group sharing a machine. The 1970s brought the Arpanet, which interconnected tens of time-shared machines, mostly at universities; again, this was built to spread computing costs, and again, the real benefit turned out to be expansion of the community that could share information, this time to a few thousand people. The personal computer's arrival in the 1980s made computer power affordable to millions of people who used their machines for office work and for play at home. The Ethernet, which arrived at the same time, made possible the interconnection of hundreds of PCs in local networks, mostly within organizations. The growing demand to bridge together the thousands of these local nets was addressed by the Internet, which had been already developed as a method for interconnecting networks of computers. These changes increased the community of people who could share information through e-mail and file transfers to a few million people. Then, in the 1990s, when networking advances seemed to be leveling out, and it looked like nothing big could possibly happen, the biggest change of all took place—the World Wide Web arrived as a software application for Internetted computers. It hit the steadily growing community of interconnected users with a quantitative and qualitative jolt. Creating and browsing Web sites captivated the world so much that the number of interconnected users shot up to 300 million by the end of the 20th century, as they and the rest of the world began experiencing the awesome socioeconomic potential of the Information Marketplace.

Unlike the Industrial Revolution, which has run its course, the Information Revolution is still growing. All we have today is several practical activities, an abundance of exciting promises, and a gigantic tangle of complexities, confusions, and fads—to be sure, a revolution in the making, but one that is unfinished. The missing ingredient is human-centric computing. To put it into action requires three big steps: changing the mind-set of users and designers; ensuring that our machines are easier to use and make us more productive; and insisting that new technology reach many more people.

Integrate Computers into Our Lives

The need to change the mind-set of computer users and designers sounds obvious, but we are marching in the opposite direction. Everywhere we turn we hear about almighty "cyberspace"! The hype promises that we will leave our boring lives, don goggles and body suits, and enter some metallic, three-dimensional, multimedia, terabyte-infested, gigahertz-adorned otherworld.

To which I respond with the technical term: Baloney!

When the Industrial Revolution arrived with its great innovation, the motor, we didn't leave our world to go to some remote motor-space! On the contrary, we brought the motors into our lives, as automobiles, refrigerators, drill presses, and pencil sharpeners. This absorption has been so complete that we refer to all these tools with names that declare their usage, not their "motorness." These innovations led to a major socioeconomic movement precisely because they entered and affected profoundly our everyday lives. People have not changed fundamentally in thousands of years. Technology changes constantly. It's the one that must adapt to us.

That's exactly what will happen with information technology and its gadgets under human-centric computing. The longer we continue to believe that computers will take us to a magical new world, the longer we will delay their natural fusion with our lives, the hallmark of every major movement that aspires to be called a socioeconomic revolution.

Once we change our mind-set in earnest, we will no longer put up with the maddening computer faults we now suffer. And we will be careful about what we accept from the *proselytizers* of technology. No longer will we be seduced by fancy buzzwords like "multimedia," "intelligent agents," "push-versus-pull technologies," "convergence," "broadband," "gigahertz" and "gigabytes," and a few hundred others already with us and yet to come. Instead, we will behave more like we do when we shop for a car: "Rather than tell me how fast the engine turns or whether it has an overhead cam, tell me about how many people it seats comfortably, the gas mileage it gets, and its annual maintenance cost." We must begin asking the same kinds of questions about computers and software: "Rather than tell me about all its gigas of processor speed and memory, tell me how quickly it can find and show me any movie I want to see, or help me find a replacement part for my lawn tractor."

As users, we want to know how much more we can achieve with a given machine or software, and at what effort, compared with what we are doing now. We'll accept quantitative or qualitative answers, as long as they address these kinds of questions. First, we'll be told that computers are different and don't admit to such measures. Nonsense. If we insist, designers and manufacturers will be compelled to respond. As they do, they will gradually adopt the new mind-set too. Eventually, they will be anxious to innovate, develop measures of usefulness, and brag about the real utility their products and services bring, versus that of their competitors.

And when the computers "vanish," as motors did earlier, we'll know the Information Revolution has finished!

Give Us a Gas Pedal and Steering Wheel

The second step toward doing more by doing less is to raise the level of controls we use to interact with our systems, from their current, low, machine level to the higher human level where we operate.

Since computing began, designers and users have been catering to what machines want. Engineers design to suit what the computer, communications system, or peripheral needs. They then throw all the components at the users and expect them to make everything function together. Miraculously, we accept without protest!

As you sit in front of your computer trying to bend it to your wishes, I imagine you trying to control a very early vintage car. Instead of having a steering wheel, brake, and gas pedal, you must wear a ring on each finger. Each ring is connected with pulling cables to levers that control spark advance, fuel mixture, the valve clearance of each cylinder, the angle of each wheel, the tension on each brake drum. What you want to do, at the human level, is go from Boston to New York. But to get there you must operate at the machine level, wiggling all the wires and levers. The prospect is so *harrowing* you would not be willing to undertake the trip. Yet we do it every day when we fire up the computer. We need to replace the low-level controls with the equivalents of the steering wheel, gas pedal, and brake.

Finally, computers will be easier to use and make us more productive if we can stick to a few common and consistent commands to do what we want with information, regardless of where the information resides. It's inconceivable to me that we are still using different commands between operating systems and browsers, just because operating systems work on information that is local to our personal computers while browsers work on distant information that sits on the Web. In both cases we want to do exactly the same things: enter information, see it or hear it, move it around, transform it, use it as a program to accomplish a task, and so on. Human-centric computing requires that we have the same set of commands for both of these cases, as well as for other gadgets and auxiliary systems that, inevitably, do the same things with information. This situation is as ridiculous as using your steering wheel to turn your car on city streets, but having to use the brake pedal to turn the car out in the country. Today's systems not only force us to learn different commands, but also entirely different ways of working each time a system changes or is "upgraded."

Many people confuse wishes with claims. Computer vendors have abused the phrases "ease of use" and "user-friendly." What they usually mean is that you can change a few colors or icons on the screen, which is supposed to give the impression that the system is bending to your commands. Such feeble cosmetics are *tantamount* to painting a smelly trash can in pretty colors to chase away the bad smell. You would be better off if all the multicolor, multimedia bells and whistles were replaced by a thin, noisy pipe, through which you could speak with a wise old man at the other end. Unfortunately, we do not know how to make machines behave intelligently, except in extremely limited contexts. Nor can we create "intelligent agents"—another darling of the spin doctors—that can act in our stead, behaving the way people expect an intelligent surrogate to act. When I say we must improve ease of use and increase productivity, I mean improve the fundamental communication between people and machines, not *wax* commercial about unrealistic desires.

We have complicated things enough. It's time we change our machine-oriented mind-set and invent controls that are much closer to what people want to do. We need the steering wheel, gas pedal, and brake of the Information Age. New technology can help us in this quest.

Reach All People

The third step needed to make computers human-centered and help us finish the Information Revolution is to reach more people. Many more.

At the beginning of the 21st century there were some 300 million people interconnected over the Internet. That big number makes us feel pretty smug. Yet it represents only 5 percent of the world's population. It's scandalous to characterize the Web as "worldwide" when it spans such a tiny portion of humankind. The voices of billions of people in the developing world and the poor regions of the industrial world cannot be heard through anything other than television news tidbits and government information feeds.

If we do nothing, matters will get worse. The rich, who can afford to buy the new technologies, will use them to become increasingly more productive and therefore even richer. The poor will be left standing still. The outcome is inescapable: Left to its own devices, the Information Revolution will increase the gap between rich and poor nations, and between rich and poor people within nations.

This gap is already huge. In the U.S. economy, an average of $3,000 in hardware, software, and related services is spent each year per citizen. In Bangladesh it's $1, according to that country's embassy. I suspect that if I could find an "embassy" representing poor Americans, or the poor of any industrial nation, I would get an equally screeching dissonance between information technology expenditures in the ghetto and the suburbs.

Some people believe the gap will close by itself, because of the growing reach and potential benefits of the Internet. It can't. The poor could have a crack at these benefits if, somehow, they were provided with the communications systems, hardware, software, training, and other help they need to join the club. Absent such help, they can't even get started.

We cannot let this gap widen. It's high time we begin closing it. Not just to be compassionate, but also to avoid the bloodshed that, historically, follows every widening rich-poor gap.

This may sound like a worthwhile social goal, but not something that will necessarily help the rest of us. Not so. First of all, if engineers begin to design computers so simple that they can be used easily by people with limited skills, the machines will be easier to use for everyone! The World Wide Web Consortium is already using this important principle in its Web Accessibility Initiative, which is creating technology to help people with visual, auditory, and other impairments to use the Web. These improvements also make the Web easier to use for people without these limitations. The history of technology shows many more examples like this; whenever designers build utility for the least-skilled user, they enhance utility for all users.

Second, if we can increase the number of people who will benefit from the technologies of information, the productivity of the entire planet will rise. New technologies will not only help the poor become literate, learn how to plant, and take care of their health, but will also help them sell their goods and services over an expanding Information Marketplace. The potential is immense. Companies in developed economies could buy information work from people in less-developed countries at greatly reduced prices, as is now done with manufacturing. Entrepreneurs in developing countries could even help those in developed countries. Imagine a new breed of useful counseling exchanges between the rich people of the West, who are often troubled by depression, divorce, and family problems, and the poor people of the East, who seem to counterbalance lack of money with strong family ties and inner peace: Older, experienced Indian women could spend a lot of time over the Net chatting with Western divorcées, who could benefit from their advice at costs substantially below the psychologist's counseling fee. The lack of time that characterizes Westerners would be counterbalanced by the plentiful time of people in India.

There is little we can do to help people become interconnected except call attention to the disparity. Yet we must not let this important objective be forgotten, for it is essential to our broader quest. We must also persist because the Information Marketplace is huge and largely unexplored. If even a small number of Nepalese or a few inner city people found a way to become productively interconnected, they would serve as role models to their peers. A timid experiment could turn into a beneficial economic spiral.

From Michael L. Dertouzos, *The Unfinished Revolution: Human-Centered Computers and What They Can Do for Us*, pp. 120–122. Copyright © 2002 by Michael Dertouzos. Reprinted by permission of HarperCollins Publishers, Inc.

• •

 ## Vocabulary

As you think about this essay, these definitions may be helpful to you:
1. **poetic comeback**   referring to the idea of "poetic justice," which describes a situation in which vice is punished and virtue rewarded, usually in a manner peculiarly or ironically appropriate
2. **entrepreneurial**   acting in the manner of someone who sees an opportunity and takes advantage of it, usually by starting a business
3. **proselytizers**   people who attempt to convert others to their point of view or cause; often used about people who attempt to convert others to their own religion
4. **harrowing**   from a harrow, which is a farm implement that uses spikes or disks to pulverize the soil; thus, a harrowing experience is harsh and dangerous to its victim
5. **tantamount**   equivalent to
6. **wax**   to become a specified way

 ## Discussion Questions

1. What does Dertouzos mean by the "Information Marketplace"? How does this concept differ from the Internet and the World Wide Web?

2. Give some examples from this essay to define the idea of human-centric computing. Then suggest some examples out of your own experience with computers.

3. Is it surprising that Michael Dertouzos, who was fluent in understanding the technologies involved in computers and the Web, expresses so much frustration at the lack of human-centric concerns in the delivery of technological services? If so, examine some of your assumptions about technology and technicians in the light of this surprise.

4. What does Dertouzos mean when he says, "Give us a gas pedal and a steering wheel"?

5. The final section of this essay expresses a need to extend the benefits of technology in what amounts to a worldwide social revolution. Dertouzos writes: "The third step needed to make computers human-centered and help us finish the Information Revolution is to reach more people. Many more." What actions would such a step require? Why does Dertouzos believe such actions are necessary?

 # Suggestions for Your Journal

What is the difference between human intelligence and computer intelligence? Can computers be trained to "think"? If so, on what level?

Two persistent strongly human-centric concerns about computer technologies are that they will lead (1) to loss of individual privacy and (2) to the redistribution of jobs, causing many in developed countries like the United States to face unemployment. Do you share these concerns? What can you do to protect yourself from their negative effects?

Discuss your own experiences with technology. Write about the uses of technology that you expect to take part in.

UNIT SUMMARY

The readings in this unit have covered a wide variety of topics and ideas about technology and how it is changing our school, work, and personal lives.

Summary Questions

1. When you enter your campus library, do you encounter the situations that Stoll writes about in his essay? How are they the same? Different?
2. How has technology influenced your role as a student? How is it different from past generations' experiences?
3. What skills described in this unit's readings can you learn while in college?

Suggested Writing Assignments

1. A major blackout in the Northeastern United States showed how dependent Americans are on electricity for their technology. Write an essay in which you assess this dependency: Is it tolerable in a risky world?
2. Visualize the world 25 years from now and write an essay about how you think technology will have changed the college campus and its students' ways of learning.

Suggested Readings

Canter, Lawrence, and Martha Siegel. *How to Make a Fortune on the Information Superhighway: Everyone's Guerrilla Guide to Marketing on the Internet and Other On-Line Services.* New York: Harper Reference, 1994.

Celente, Gerald. *Trends 2000.* New York: Time Warner, 1997.

Dertouzos, Michael. *The Unfinished Revolution.* New York: HarperCollins, 2001.

Levine, John, Carol Baroudi, and Margaret Levine Young. *The Internet for Dummies.* Foster City, CA: IDG Books, 1997.

What Are My Rights and Responsibilities as a Student?

In many ways, the modern university forms its own community. Like a small town, a university or a college often has its own residential areas, business centers, spaces designed for sports and other recreation, food services including "fast food" options and some that are fancier, centers of government, a hospital or health service center, a security office, and so on. The resemblance is not limited to physical settings, because comparable lines of authority and responsibility can be found in both civil governments (as in villages or towns) and university structures. Like cities, colleges and universities have the authority to establish their own laws—codes of acceptable behavior—and penalties for violating those codes. As well, the state and federal laws apply both to cities and to colleges located within a given state or nation. Each of us is familiar with such laws—those against violence, theft of property, indecent or threatening behavior, excessive noise or other activities that constitute a public nuisance, and the like.

The freedom from work, from restraint, from accountability, wondrous in its inception, becomes banal and counterfeit. Without rules there is no way to say no, and worse, no way to say yes.

—THOMAS FARBER

165

Because many new college students are near or at the age when civil laws apply to them in a new way, they need to keep in mind that the older we are, the higher the level of responsibility for our actions the law is likely to expect of us. Some behavior that may be cute from a 2-year-old and merely annoying from a 10-year-old might well be illegal from someone 18 or older. Moreover, the cities and states we live in give us greater freedom when we reach 18 or 21, and with that freedom comes a higher degree of accountability. If you drove your parents' car illegally when you were 13, your parents were usually held responsible (though they may have, in turn, imposed their own regulations on you!), but if at 18 you drive illegally (under the influence of alcohol, for example, or faster than the speed limit allows), it is your own license that will be affected, and your own record that starts accumulating.

Other laws relate specifically to the people who make up the university community. These are generally developed, implemented, and enforced within the university itself. Such laws authorized by a university community usually include the expectation that students, faculty, and staff members will obey and respect the civil laws of their city, state, and nation, but they go further as well. Because a university has special characteristics, its code of prohibited behavior will take its special characteristics into account. We begin Unit 6 with an essay about the special characteristics that make a university unique, "On Academic Freedom" by Halverson and Carter. With that essay to establish the context, the remaining essays in this unit take up the question of your rights and responsibilities as a student member of your college community. Krutch and Minnick each consider the ethical dimensions of your role as a student. Like many ethical questions, these essays raise issues that are perennially debatable, for which you may find only provisional answers. George Will suggests a change in the emphasis of discussions about these and other ethical issues. All of this is to be expected in a university setting, where the search for truth is constant and the searchers are continually hopeful of better, clearer, wiser answers to such age-old questions as "What is the best way to proceed?" and "How can we make a stronger community?"

On Academic Freedom

William H. Halverson and James R. Carter

William H. Halverson is associate dean emeritus of University College at The Ohio State University. After completing academic studies focused on philosophy, Halverson authored well-known textbooks for college philosophy classes. More recently, he has translated several books from Norwegian into English. James R. Carter, also a philosopher by education, is assistant dean of the College of Arts and Sciences at the University of Louisville, where he directs the Advising Center. In the following essay, Halverson and Carter define the notion of academic freedom, which is at the heart of a university as established and perpetuated in Western cultures.

People create institutions to serve a variety of purposes that they regard as important. They establish hospitals in order to care for the sick, retail stores to sell goods to consumers, banks to manage transactions involving the exchange of money, radio and TV stations to provide various sorts of program materials to the public, and so on. An institution is a means to an end, a way of doing something that society has decided needs to be done.

The Purpose of a University

What, then, is the purpose for which society has created universities? Why do people spend millions of dollars to build buildings—libraries, laboratories, classrooms, and the like—and additional millions to enable people like us (students, teachers) to occupy those buildings? What is a university for? What is its mission?

Try this: *the unique mission of a university is the discovery, preservation, and dissemination of truth.*

The discovery of truth: that is the heart and soul of the university. You must not think of professors and students as, respectively, those who already know the truth and those who do not. Professors have an edge on students by virtue of having been at the business of learning a bit longer than most students—but they would be the first to tell you, if they are candid, that even after many years of diligent study, their knowledge of the truth is limited, fragmentary, and mixed with error.

Our Common Ignorance

The professor's problem is the problem of human beings generally: we can rarely be certain that what we have learned, what we believe, is the *truth*. For many thousands of years, scholars believed that the earth was flat, and that it was stationary in the center of the universe, and that the sun, the planets, and the stars revolved around it. These beliefs, we now know with a high degree of certainty, were in error. We may be inclined to laugh at those silly people of yesterday who held such childish views. But let us not laugh too loudly, for it is highly likely that among the beliefs you and I hold today are some that will appear as foolish to future generations as the flat-earth theory does to us. Truth and error do not wear labels that enable us easily to distinguish between them.

Our situation, then, may be described as follows. We (that is, all people) hold many opinions, some of which are probably true and some of which are probably false. In addition, there are many matters about which we are totally ignorant, and about which we therefore have no opinions at all. Our task, if we wish to know the truth, is to rid ourselves so far as possible of both ignorance (no opinions) and error (false opinions), to exchange ignorance and error for the truth.

Seeking the Truth

How does one go about this? How does one attempt to determine the truth or falsity of any assertion? Clearly, one must look to the evidence that appears to be relevant to the truth or falsity of that assertion. *Paradoxically, the surest way to establish the truth of an assertion is to try to disprove it.* If there is some evidence in support of an assertion, and if nobody can find any evidence against it after making a reasonable effort to do so, then there is at least some reason to believe that the assertion may be true. Until, of course, some contrary evidence turns up, in which case one has to start all over again.

Thus we arrive at the following *axiom:* one who desires to know the truth concerning any matter must be persuaded by the evidence, and by the evidence alone. Anything or anybody who attempts to compel a conclusion based on anything other than the evidence is to that extent an enemy of truth.

Academic Freedom

Academic freedom is the opportunity to hold opinions based on the best evidence one has and to speak those opinions without fear of reprisal. Academic freedom means free and open discussion, a liberty to read what you want, to debate any issue, to defend new views and reinterpret or criticize old ones in an open forum.

Academic freedom can exist only when two conditions are met. First, it can exist only in a community of open and intelligent individuals who recognize that in principle every legitimate question deserves an answer, and that the legitimacy of question and answer cannot merely be assumed but must be shown capable of withstanding criticism. Second, academic freedom requires that this community make truth its common purpose, and free and open discussion the means to it. Unless both conditions are met, any freedom that there is will be purely accidental, and not very secure.

It is therefore an essential part of this idea to promote and provide for the intellectual development of every member of the academic community. In this community, it is not only those who have already cultivated a high degree of intellectual understanding who have a place. There must also be room for those who are just beginning their intellectual development. Students in each new generation must be allowed their skepticism; they must have time to examine and criticize even the most fundamental, most widely held views. But they in turn must be open to criticism and direction from their teachers and peers.

How does this notion of academic freedom affect your life? The university's need to maintain academic freedom means that *your* freedom to inquire is essential. You cannot be free if there is prejudice in the academic community. The idea of academic freedom requires that the individuals in the university actively help one another through the basic intellectual tactic of challenge and response. In his essay *On Liberty,* John Stuart Mill reminds us of this, and of the unique mission of an academic community, when he writes, "Complete liberty of contradicting and disproving our opinion, is the very condition which justifies us in assuming its truth…."

Enemies of Academic Freedom

Anyone or anything that tends to inhibit free inquiry and discussion concerning any matter, or that attempts to compel a conclusion based on anything other than the relevant evidence, is by definition an enemy of academic freedom. And there are, unfortunately, many such enemies.

Some of these enemies are purely internal, within the individual. They can be rooted out only by great effort on the part of that individual.

One of these is *fear.* The most comfortable opinions to hold are those that we have held the longest, and so we fear the discomfort of abandoning long-held opinions. The most comfortable opinions to hold are those that are widely held by those whose esteem we crave, and so we fear to adopt opinions that we know will be unpopular. A sage once said, "I never learned anything of importance without feeling a sense of loss because of the old and familiar but mistaken view that had to be abandoned." But we are human, and we fear such loss—even though it be for the sake of truth.

Sheer laziness is an enemy of academic freedom. It is easier, it takes less effort, simply to adopt a view that one has heard expressed by someone else than to study the evidence and draw one's own conclusion. But the easy way, unfortunately, is not the best way, for it gives us no basis for distinguishing between opinions that are true and those that are false.

Undue respect for tradition is yet another internal enemy of academic freedom. Indeed, the opinions of one's forebears deserve considerable respect, for they represent the accumulated wisdom of many generations. Still we must not be bound by them, and we must be willing to abandon them if the weight of the available evidence suggests that they are mistaken. For we, too, will pass on a fund of accumulated wisdom to the next generation, and those who receive it have a right to expect of us that it will contain relatively more truth and less error than that with which we began.

Perhaps the more obvious enemies of academic freedom are the external enemies. Every one of us is capable of being such an enemy and probably has in fact acted as one at one time or another. If in the course of a discussion one shouts down a would-be participant instead of allowing him or her to speak, one is playing the enemy. The same is true if one heckles, and so prevents from being heard, a speaker who holds views with which one disagrees. An instructor who uses the threat of a bad grade to compel agreement (or the *appearance* of agreement) with his or her own views is violating the academic freedom of students.

The administrator who denies promotion or *tenure* or a salary increase to an instructor because the instructor advocates views with which the administrator disagrees is violating the academic freedom of that instructor. A citizen who demands the ouster of a faculty member on the grounds that he or she holds views that are "dangerous" or "unorthodox" is asking (usually without realizing it) that academic freedom be abolished.

We repeat: anyone or anything that tends to inhibit free inquiry and discussion concerning any matter, or attempts to compel a conclusion based on anything other than the relevant evidence, is by definition an enemy of academic freedom. That academic freedom has so many enemies, both internal and external, underscores the important fact that the pathway to truth is not an easy one to find or to follow.

Academic freedom, then, is by no means a cloak for nonsense. It does not confer approval upon ideas that are *demonstrably* false, unsupported by evidence, or just downright silly. To the contrary: academic freedom makes it more likely that in due course such ideas will be shown up for what they are, and that views that are supported by the evidence—that is, truth—will prevail. In an institution whose business is the discovery, preservation, and *dissemination* of truth, academic freedom is the *sine qua non*—the "without which nothing," the essential condition in the absence of which it would cease to be a university.

Reprinted by permission of the authors.

●　●

Vocabulary

As you think about this essay, these definitions may be helpful to you:
1. **paradoxically**   in a manner seemingly contradictory to common sense and yet perhaps true.
2. **axiom**   a fundamental notion or idea that is assumed to be true
3. **tenure**   used within universities, this term denotes an earned privilege of assured continued employment following a long period—usually seven years—of probation during which a faculty member is evaluated on teaching ability, research productivity, and community service
4. **demonstrably**   capable of being proved, either logically or by reference to the real world
5. **dissemination**   dispersal; thus, universities are said here to exist for spreading the truth (by teaching and publishing, for example), not hiding it

 Discussion Questions

1. Identify and explain the paradox in the statement, "the surest way to establish the truth of an assertion is to try to disprove it."
2. What, according to Halverson and Carter, are the two necessary conditions without which academic freedom cannot exist?
3. Halverson and Carter argue that "one who desires to know the truth concerning any matter must be persuaded by the evidence, and by the evidence alone." What else are people persuaded by?
4. What, according to Halverson and Carter, are the enemies of academic freedom?
5. How, according to Halverson and Carter, should we regard the opinions we have received from people we respect?

 Suggestions for Your Journal

Fear, laziness, and undue respect for tradition—have you ever struggled with these internal enemies of academic freedom? Write a journal entry in which you select one of these and advise a younger friend how to deal with them successfully.

Academic freedom seems to be in conflict with the idea of majority rule. Is it?

How does the university differ from other institutions that seem to be, or ought to be, concerned about the truth—churches, for example, or the federal government?

The New Immorality

Joseph Wood Krutch

Joseph Wood Krutch was a distinguished professor of literature at Columbia University.
The author of many books, Krutch was highly respected for his understanding of the
ethical dimensions of literature. In the following essay, he comments on observations
he made as a teacher and observer of students.

• • • • • • • • • • • • • • • • • • • •

The provost of one of our largest and most honored institutions told me not
long ago that a questionnaire was distributed to his undergraduates and
that 40 percent refused to acknowledge that they believed cheating on examinations to be *reprehensible.*

Recently a reporter for a New York newspaper stopped six people on the
street and asked them if they would consent to take part in a rigged television
quiz for money. He reported that five of the six said yes. Yet most of these five,
like most college cheaters, would probably profess a strong social consciousness. They may cheat, but they vote for foreign aid and for enlightened social
measures.

These two examples exhibit a paradox of our age. It is often said, and my
observation leads me to believe it true, that our seemingly great growth in social
morality has oddly enough taken place in a world where private morality—a
sense of the supreme importance of purely personal honor, honesty, and integrity—seems to be declining. *Beneficent* and benevolent social institutions are
administered by people who all too frequently turn out to be accepting "gifts."
The world of popular entertainment is rocked by scandals. College students, put
on their honor, cheat on examinations. Candidates for the Ph.D. hire ghost writers to prepare their *theses.*

But, one may object, haven't all these things always been true? Is there really any evidence that personal dishonesty is more prevalent than it always was?

I have no way of making a historical measurement. Perhaps these things
are not actually more prevalent. What I do know is that there is an increasing
tendency to accept and take for granted such personal dishonesty. The bureau-
crat and disk jockey say, "Well, yes, I took presents, but I assure you that I made
just decisions anyway." The college student caught cheating does not even
blush but shrugs his shoulders and comments: "Everybody does it, and besides,
I can't see that it really hurts anybody."

Jonathan Swift once said: "I have never been surprised to find men
wicked, but I have often been surprised to find them not ashamed." It is my
conviction that though people may be no more wicked than they always have
been, they seem less likely to be ashamed. If everybody does it, it must be right.
Honest, moral, decent mean only what is usual. This is not really a wicked

world, because morality means *mores* or manners and usual conduct is the only standard.

The second part of the defense, "It really doesn't hurt anybody," is equally revealing. "It doesn't hurt anybody" means it doesn't do that abstraction called society any harm. The harm it did the bribe-taker and the cheater isn't important; it is purely personal. And personal as opposed to social decency doesn't count for much. Sometimes I am inclined to blame sociology for part of this *paradox*. Sociology has tended too often to define good and evil as merely the "socially useful" or its reverse.

What social morality and social conscience leave out is the narrower but very significant concept of honor—as opposed to what is sometimes called merely "socially desirable conduct." The persons of honor are not content to ask merely whether this or that will hurt society, or whether it is what most people would permit themselves to do. They ask, and ask first of all, would it hurt them and their self-respect? Would it dishonor them personally?

It was a favorite and no doubt sound argument among early twentieth-century reformers that "playing the game" as the gentleman was supposed to play it was not enough to make a decent society. They were right; it is not enough. But the time has come to add that it is nevertheless indispensable. I hold that it is indeed inevitable that the so-called social conscience unsupported by the concept of personal honor will create a corrupt society. But suppose that it doesn't? Suppose that no one except the individual suffers from the fact that he sees nothing wrong in doing what everybody else does? Even so, I still insist that for the individual himself nothing is more important than this personal, interior sense of right and wrong and his determination to follow that—rather than to be guided by what everybody does or merely the criterion of "social usefulness." It is impossible for me to imagine a good society composed of persons without honor.

We hear it said frequently that what present-day people most desire is security. If that is so, then they have a wrong notion of what the real, the ultimate, security is. No one who is dependent on anything outside himself, upon money, power, fame, or whatnot, is or ever can be secure. Only he who possesses himself and is content with himself is actually secure. Too much is being said about the importance of adjustment and "participation in the group." Even cooperation, to give this thing its most favorable designation, is no more important than the ability to stand alone when the choice must be made between the sacrifice of one's own integrity and adjustment to or participation in group activity.

No matter how bad the world may become, no matter how much the mass man of the future may lose such of the virtues as he still has, one fact remains. If one person alone refuses to go along with him, if one person alone asserts his individual and inner right to believe in and be loyal to what his fellow men seem to have given up, then at least he will still retain what is perhaps the most important part of humanity.

 Vocabulary

As you think about this essay, these definitions may be helpful to you:
1. **reprehensible**   deserving censure
2. **beneficent**   performing acts of kindness and charity
3. **theses**   long essays that incorporate the results of original thinking or research
4. **mores**   moral or ethical attitudes
5. **paradox**   a statement that is perhaps true, even though it seems to be contradictory

 Discussion Questions

1. Define "honor" as you think Krutch means it.
2. How might you attempt to answer the question "Is there really any evidence that personal dishonesty is more prevalent than it always was?" How does Krutch attempt to answer it?
3. Underlying Krutch's beliefs as expressed in this essay is the insistence that "for the individual himself nothing is more important than this personal, interior sense of right and wrong." Others might respond that such an internal sense is learned from those around us and therefore that different cultures are likely to result in different "personal, interior" senses of right and wrong. Which of these positions do you agree with? Why?
4. What does Krutch mean by the assertion that "Only he who possesses himself and is content with himself is actually secure"?
5. This essay was written more than 35 years ago. Have society's views on ethical and moral behavior changed for better or worse from that time to now? Discuss.

 Suggestions for Your Journal

Describe your personal code of ethics. Have you seen students cheat in class? Should you care if they do? Why or why not?

Discuss why you, as that "one person alone who refuses to go along," might or might not make a difference.

Ideas as Property

Thomas L. Minnick

Thomas L. Minnick, an English teacher who admits to having graded more than 25,000
English composition papers, has served as an expert witness and researcher on issues
relating to intellectual property and plagiarism in cases tried in New York, Ohio, and
California. In this essay he emphasizes the positive value of ideas and other intellectual
creations as property and draws attention to the fact that as property, under the law,
ideas can be stolen or mistreated with serious consequences for the thief.

• • • • • • • • • • • • • • • • •

The idea of "property"—that is, something owned by one person or group
and therefore *not* owned by anyone else—is among the oldest, most widespread notions that humans share. Even cultures that believe that all things are
owned jointly and equally by all members of the society (usually a tribe or
clan) also believe that no single individual can claim ownership of those things.
For example, because they believe that the land belongs to all, they also regard
any individual who claims to own a part of it as violating the property rights of
the group. The notions of "thieves" and "theft" depend on the idea of property,
since stealing is defined as the act of taking something that does not belong to
the thief. The ownership of property is also one of our most important ideas:
many of our laws are based on the principle that three rights guaranteed to individuals living in a society are the right to life, the right to liberty, and the right
to own property. Thomas Jefferson, writing the Declaration of Independence,
paraphrased this already well-established principle when he identified "life, liberty, and the pursuit of happiness" as three *inalienable* rights of Americans.

We take for granted certain categories of property and, along with them,
certain kinds of theft or other violations of property rights. For example, if you
(or you and your local lending agency together) own a car, then a person who
steals your car, drives it carelessly until the fuel is almost gone, then wrecks it,
is unquestionably a thief, because he or she has taken your property without
your permission and deprived you of it. Even if the car is returned to you no
worse for wear, your rights have been violated, and no reasonable person
would disagree that a theft has occurred. The same is true if someone takes
your watch, your bookbag, your pet, or your starter jacket identifying your favorite sports team. Furthermore, if someone takes your credit card and buys a
substantial amount of merchandise in your name, even if the physical merchandise was never yours (and wouldn't fit you anyway), those items have
been stolen from you since your property—in this example, your credit line
and the dollars from it that will go to pay the bills—has been taken without
your knowledge or approval.

Sometimes it may be less clear that *your ideas are your property,* but that is exactly what they are, and the courts recognize them as such. A specialization in legal studies is the field of intellectual property law, which is based on the premise that an idea belongs to the person who created it, and therefore that any profit, financial or otherwise, derived from that idea also belongs to the originator. The theft of ideas takes many forms. Suppose you design and *patent* an important new drug for the treatment of arthritis and, learning of your research, others market that drug under a different name. Unless you and they have entered into a prior agreement about distributing your drug and sharing the profits, their action violates your rights to your intellectual property. Or again, suppose you write a song, both words and music, and someone else, hearing it, decides the words are effective but that the music is not—then adapts your words to new music of their own. Given adequate evidence to establish your claim of prior ownership, you should be able to show that your intellectual property rights have been violated, and you should further be able to claim a monetary award for damages due to the violation of those rights.

Universities, whose defining reason to exist includes the development and teaching of ideas,* have a special stake in the principle that an idea belongs to the person who first conceived it. The integrity of a university depends on a strong belief in this principle, and so universities defend this principle in all they do. For what would a degree from your college or university be worth if students could be caught cheating and nevertheless receive credit for the courses where that offense took place? Undergraduates writing English compositions or research papers for courses in psychology or history, graduate students preparing their master's or doctoral theses, faculty members engaged in leading-edge research—all these participants in the university have a stake in preserving the principle of a creator's right to his or her ideas as property. If they misrepresent themselves as originating ideas that do not belong to them, they are violating the intellectual property rights of others. If they themselves are victims of plagiarists (people who copy their ideas, word-for-word or in paraphrases), then they are deprived of meaningful ownership of what they have created. Even if a particular idea is not worth much money on the open market, the theft of that idea means that the true originator may not receive the *intangible* credit or respect that that idea has earned. So it is essential to the credibility and integrity of a university, and therefore of the degrees that it confers, that it provide the best defense it can for the intellectual property of the members of its community. People who create new ideas should be respected for doing so, and people who claim as theirs those ideas that truly belong to others should be condemned.

Unfortunately, it is part of the nature of ideas that we find it harder to prove ownership of a new idea than, say, of a microwave oven. When someone has stolen your microwave oven, two statements are true: first, you no longer have your microwave, and second, someone else probably does. Ideas are not

---

*See the essay "On Academic Freedom" by William H. Halverson and James R. Carter earlier in this unit—Ed.

like that: it is in the nature of ideas that I can tell you my idea, and then you and I both will have it. If I tell you my answer to the third question on our final examination in American history, I will know that answer and so will you. For that matter, I could tell my answer to everyone in our class and we all could produce the same answer on request. And so on: I could tell everyone at my college, or everyone in my state, or everyone in our country, or in the world—and yet I would still have the idea in the same way that I did before, while everyone else also now has it. Moreover, if someone steals your microwave oven, you will probably be able to identify it by brand, size, model number, and condition. If you have had the foresight to mark it as yours—by engraving it with your social security number, for example—then identifying it as your stolen property will be substantially easier. But it is very difficult to mark an idea as yours. Usually the proof of ownership for intellectual property takes the form of a patent or copyright, although it is possible to document prior ownership of an idea in other ways as well.

How can a university protect ideas from thieves? The first step is to make clear to every member of the university that ideas are a kind of property, and that the protection of those ideas really does matter to the well-being of the university. A second step is to teach students at all levels the conventions for acknowledging when they adopt or develop the ideas of someone else. The third is to deal seriously with instances of the theft of ideas, which in an academic setting commonly takes one of two forms—cheating (that is, copying someone else's answers during an examination) and *plagiarism,* the unacknowledged dependence on someone else's ideas in writing, usually in out-of-class assignments. That you are reading this essay is part of your university's effort to make clear that it values and protects ideas as property.

The second step, training in common academic procedures for acknowledging sources, involves learning the accepted forms for footnotes, bibliographies, and citations to other authors in the text of your work. If you have had to write a research paper as a composition exercise in high school or previous college work, then you have probably learned one of the many conventional systems available for acknowledging sources you have used and identifying the specific ideas and language from others that you cite in your own work.[1] What matters is that your reader should be able to tell what ideas are your own original work and what ideas you have adopted or adapted from others. If you quote a section of someone else's writing verbatim, you must enclose the quoted material within quotation marks *and* tell your reader where the original statement appeared. If you rely on someone else's ideas, even if you do not quote them

---

[1]Perhaps the most widely used guide for authors using footnotes and bibliographies is "Turabian"—which is the shorthand way that writers refer to Kate L. Turabian, *A Manual for Writers of Term Papers, Theses, and Dissertations,* 6th ed. (Chicago: The University of Chicago Press, 1996). Other well-regarded guides of this sort include *MLA Handbook for Writers of Research Papers,* 6th ed. (New York: Modern Language Association, 2003); *The Chicago Manual of Style,* 15th ed. (Chicago: The University of Chicago Press, 2003); and *Publication Manual,* 5th ed. (Washington, D.C.: American Psychological Association, 2001). Your instructor can help you decide among them.

word for word, then a footnote identifying your source and indicating the extent of your indebtedness is appropriate.

The third step a college or university must take to ensure that ideas are credited to their true creators—namely, dealing seriously with instances of the theft of ideas—will be evident in the ways that instructors and the systems of the university react when a case of cheating or plagiarism is suspected. If an instructor suspects that a student has cheated on a test or copied someone else's essay, the easiest action to take will always be no action at all. But would such a lack of action be the right way to proceed? If cheating or plagiarism mean so little that they can be ignored, then the instructor is contributing to the institution's loss of integrity and the weakening of the degree—of *your* degree. Indeed, by such inaction an instructor would become an accessory to the theft. The right way to proceed is to put the investigation of the facts of the alleged case into the authority of a separate group of people—often called the Honor Board or the Committee on Academic Misconduct. By hearing many cases of this kind, such a group becomes familiar with the kinds of questions that should be pursued, the kinds of evidence that can be gathered, and the appropriate resolution of the incident. Since effective teachers make a commitment to put forth their own best efforts for their students, those teachers may feel a degree of betrayal when a student knowingly tries to misrepresent someone else's work as his or her own. Therefore, it is usually wiser for a neutral party or group to investigate and *adjudicate* a case of suspected misconduct.

Some schools automatically suspend a student who has been found in violation of the rules on cheating or plagiarizing. Such a suspension may be in effect for a term or several terms, and the student will not be permitted to re-enroll until that assigned time period has passed. Other schools dismiss a student permanently for violating the rules of proper academic conduct. The consequences of academic misconduct can be devastating: law schools, medical schools, and the other professional programs available to you may be permanently closed if your record contains a notation about academic misconduct. You need to know what your college considers to be academic misconduct, and you need to know what the penalties for committing such misconduct can be. At many colleges and universities, students are bound by an "honor code" that requires them to notify instructors of any cheating they may be aware of. In such places, the failure to notify an official about suspected misconduct also qualifies as a violation and is grounds for disciplinary action.

Know the relevant policies at your institution, but do not let the seriousness of those policies paralyze you when you start to write an essay or a research paper for one of your classes. Some students ask, with justification, "How can I be sure that my ideas are original? Surely someone else has had almost every idea before me at some time or another. How can I be safe from misconduct accusations?" When you are told to be original, your teacher does not expect that every idea in your essay will be unique in the history of human thought. But a teacher does have the right to expect that *when you knowingly depend* on the thinking of someone else, you will acknowledge that in the conventional way (using quotation marks, footnotes, and a bibliography). You can express your own original turn of thought by seeing an idea in a new light, or combining ideas that you have not read before in the same combination, or by modifying the acknowledged ideas of someone else with critical commentary or new emphasis, and so on. And just to be sure, if you really have any doubts about the originality of your work, talk to your instructor about them before you turn the work in for a grade.[2]

Reprinted by permission of the author.

 Vocabulary

As you think about this essay, these definitions may be helpful to you:
1. **inalienable**   incapable of being surrendered or transferred
2. **patent**   a license securing for an inventor the exclusive right to make, use, or sell an invention for a term of years
3. **intangible**   not capable of being precisely identified; abstract
4. **plagiarism**   stealing or passing off the ideas or words of another as one's own
5. **adjudicate**   to act as judge

 Discussion Questions

1. What is the historical basis for ownership of property?
2. How does the author define ideas as property? How do ideas and material property differ?
3. Why is the concept of ideas as property so important in a university setting?
4. What steps can be taken by a university to ensure ideas as property are protected, according to the author?
5. What can happen to a student who is found to have cheated or plagiarized?

 Suggestions for Your Journal

Find out and write down in your own words your college's policies and procedures for deciding cases of alleged academic misconduct. This exercise is important so that you know what those policies and procedures are: They identify your responsibilities and your rights. Then comment on whether, in your judgment, those policies are justified and those procedures are fair.

[2]I am pleased to record my gratitude to my colleagues Professor Sara Garnes and Dean Virginia Gordon for their conversations with me about the topic of this essay.

Please Stop This Talk About Values

George F. Will

- George F. Will is a well-known and highly respected conservative columnist and
- political analyst. In recent years he has been an articulate critic of higher education,
- arguing on behalf of the "traditional" curriculum that has been under fire for at least
- the last decade. In this essay, Will takes on a more general ethical issue, urging that
- writers and teachers focus less on "values" and more on virtues.

• • • • • • • • • • • • • • • • •

Here at Lafayette College in Easton, Pa., as elsewhere in our republic, the birth of which was nobly assisted by the Frenchman for whom the university is named, today's peace and prosperity allow a preoccupation with the problem of teaching what are nowadays called "values." Talk of values is a new, and regrettable, vocabulary for discussing a recurring American concern.

When the Marquis de Lafayette returned to America in 1824, his tour catalyzed the young republic's unease about what it sensed was a decline from the pinnacle of virtue achieved by the Revolutionary generation that was then passing. Then, as now, the nation was feeling its oats economically, was feeling queasy about whether its character was as strong as its economy and, thus, was wondering about whether prosperity constituted progress.

Today it would be progress if everyone would stop talking about values. Instead, let us talk, as the Founding Fathers did, about virtues.

Historian Gertrude Himmelfarb rightly says the ubiquity of talk about values causes us to forget how new such talk is. It began in Britain's 1983 election campaign, when Prime Minister Margaret Thatcher embraced the accusation, which is what it was, that she favored "Victorian values."

Time was, "value" was used mostly as a verb, meaning to esteem. It also was a singular noun, as in "the value of the currency." In today's politics, it is primarily a plural noun, denoting beliefs or attitudes. And Friedrich Nietzsche's *nihilistic* intention—the demoralization of society—is advanced when the word "values" supplants "virtues" in political and ethical discourse. When we move beyond talk about good and evil, we are left with the thin gruel of values-talk.

How very democratic values-talk is: Unlike virtues, everyone has lots of values, as many as they choose. Adolf Hitler had scads of values. George Washington had virtues. Who among those who knew him would have spoken of Washington's "values"?

Values-talk comes naturally to a nonjudgmental age—an age judgmental primarily about the cardinal sin of being judgmental. It is considered broadminded to say, "One person's values are as good as another's."

Values are an equal-opportunity business: They are mere choices. Virtues are habits, difficult to develop and therefore not equally accessible to all. Speaking of virtues rather than values is elitist, offensive to democracy's *egalitarian*, leveling ethos.

Which is why talk of virtues should be revived. Alexis de Tocqueville, who toured America not long after Lafayette did, noted that although much is gained by replacing aristocratic with democratic institutions and suppositions, something valuable is often lost: the ability to recognize, and the hunger to honor, *hierarchies* of achievement and character. So democracy requires the cultivation of certain tendencies of democracy.

So says Professor Harvey C. Mansfield, Harvard's conservative (who because of his opposition to grade inflation is known there as Harvey "C-minus" Mansfield). He notes that a theme of American literature, *writ large* in the works of Mark Twain, is the effect of democracy on the higher qualities of people. To counter democracy's leveling ethos, universities, Mansfield says, should teach students how to praise.

Students should learn to look up to the heroic—in thought and action, in politics and literature, in science and faith. After all, the few men and women who become heroes do so by looking up and being pulled up by a vision of nobility. Which makes a hero quite unlike a *role model*. A very democratic notion, role model: It is something anyone can successfully emulate.

Here, then, is higher education's special purpose in a democracy: It is to turn young people toward what is high.

A wit has said that in the 19th century, England's ruling class developed the system of elite secondary schools for the purpose of making sure that Byron and Shelley could never happen again. The proper purpose of American higher education is not to serve as a values cafeteria, where young people are encouraged to pick whatever strikes their fancies. Rather, the purpose of higher education for citizens of a democracy should be to help them identify that rarity, excellence in various realms.

These thoughts for commencement season are pertinent to the political season. Whenever you hear politicians speaking of "values," you are in the presence of America's problem, not its solution.

 Vocabulary

As you think about this essay, these definitions may be helpful to you:
1. **nihilism**   the belief that nothing has meaning or importance
2. **egalitarian**   the belief that all people should have equal social and political rights
3. **hierarchy**   a group of people arranged by rank or class, often related to political power
4. **writ large**   signified or expressed in a more prominent magnitude, or taken to a higher degree

Discussion Questions

1. What is the fundamental difference that Will draws between values and virtues? What are his best examples of this difference, in your view? Can you suggest other examples?
2. Why does Will refer to Lafayette and Washington in this brief essay?
3. Did Hitler have "values," as Will claims? If so, what might they have been?

Suggestions for Your Journal

Identify two or three virtues that you believe are important. Do you possess those virtues? Give examples that show you have used them in action.

UNIT SUMMARY

The essays in this unit focus on ethical values, especially those that relate to institutions of higher education. Halverson and Carter, Krutch, and Minnick discuss aspects of intellectual honesty as they relate to academic study, and Will encourages readers to substitute "virtues" for "values" in talk about ethics.

Summary Questions

1. Do you agree with the essentially intellectual picture of the university that the authors in this unit share? What are some alternative views of the purpose of a university or college education? Can your alternatives fit compatibly with the views these authors offer?
2. An important qualification in most ethical theories is the belief that "ought implies can"—that is, that we cannot be expected to measure up to impossible standards. In the essays in this unit, do any of the authors ask you to do what you cannot reasonably be expected to do?
3. What university courses might you take to further explore the kinds of moral and ethical issues discussed in these essays?

Suggested Writing Assignments

1. Write a short essay connecting your ethical beliefs to those given in one of the essays in this unit. Show how your beliefs significantly differ or coincide with those expressed here.
2. The authors in this unit agree that acts of intellectual dishonesty, like cheating on tests and plagiarizing, are not acceptable at a university. Write a short essay identifying some other forms of behavior that are inappropriate at a university. Suggest a plan for limiting such inappropriate activities.
3. Might you expect your sense of values or virtues to change as you complete an undergraduate degree? Why? How?

Suggested Readings

Emmons, M. L., and R. E. Alberti. *Your Perfect Right.* San Luis Obispo, CA: Impact, 1974.
Lewis, H. *A Question of Values.* New York: Harper & Row, 1990.
Pojman, L. P. *Ethics: Discovering Right and Wrong.* Belmont, CA: Wadsworth, 1990.

What Is Diversity and Why Is It Important to Me?

Just about anyone interested in American higher education can start an argument these days by bringing up the topic of "political correctness." The phrase is highly specific to our times and became important largely because of changes in the way that educators think about how to design a college curriculum.

Before 1980, the question of what to include in a well-designed college program of studies would have had different answers from different scholars, but most of them would have differed only in matters of degree. The questions people asked were "How much science should be required? How many courses of European, English, or American literature should be expected? Should Faulkner receive as much emphasis as Melville?" More recently, debates on the appropriate content of a required curriculum in general studies have grown louder, more political, and nastier. The questions people now tend to raise include "Why have you omitted literature by women and people of color? How can you prefer courses

We reason deeply when we forcibly feel.

—MARY WOLLSTONECRAFT

about the European cultural tradition when students will increasingly need to deal with Asian, African, and Hispanic cultures in their daily lives in the 21st century? Do the courses you propose to require prepare students to improve the world, or just to describe it?" The "gentleman's agreement" (to use a phrase that some would argue expresses the problem) about what to include in a college degree program and how to talk about it is no longer in effect.

Detachment from political considerations used to be thought of, among scholars, as an ideal to be cultivated by educated people. Now many regard such detachment as an illusion and say that every author, teacher, and speaker should begin by identifying his or her political assumptions. So let us say up front that without abandoning the rich history of Western thought, we value diversity and believe that the free expression of diverse points of view is essential to the well-being of a university.

We do not regard that as a predominantly political point of view, though it certainly is a notion with political consequences. On this principle, for example, we oppose all intellectual straitjackets—such as those the Nazis imposed on German universities in the period from their rise to power until the end of World War II, a time when faculty members and students alike suffered imprisonment and death for expressing ideas that were politically incorrect according to the ruling powers of the time. Further, we believe that argument and dissent need to proceed within a civilized framework—that there are reasonable constraints on behavior that all members of a community need to observe and respect. But the essential nature of a university cannot long survive in the presence of restraints on thinking and expressing ideas.

We value diversity of opinions and cultures because the free exchange of ideas is the surest way to expose bad thinking and to find the good. The essay on academic freedom by Halverson and Carter in Unit 6 provides the rationale for this belief.

We also value diversity on the fundamental ground of our shared nature as human beings: We all want to be treated fairly, and we all object to unearned punishments and rewards. So Unit 7 continues with essays in which many individuals speak about why the fact that they are different from the majority—in race, religion, gender, looks, sexual preference—should not disqualify them from the respect accorded to us all in a civilized environment, especially in a free democratic nation. In these essays, students talk about the ways that thoughtless or premeditated comments or other forms of behavior have affected them and made them feel like outsiders. This feeling of alienation is often the motivation that opens the dialogue among diverse groups, a dialogue that is most evident on our campuses perhaps because no other class of institutions is better suited for carrying on just such a dialogue.

Defining dialogue is not an easy task. The sort of dialogue we mean is not merely a conversation. Rather, we intend this term in the way that thinkers such as the 19th-century Catholic philosopher John Henry, Cardinal Newman, and the early 20th-century Jewish teacher Martin Buber have meant it: one person speaking to another, heart to heart, and listening. Universities and colleges offer unequaled opportunities for students to meet others who are different from themselves and to enter into dialogue with them. The goal of dialogue is understanding and connecting with another person, and the result of dialogue is often to understand oneself better through understanding someone else. International students, students from different religions and cultures, students who share your goals in education but may differ from you in almost every other way—these are people worth seeking out for what they can teach you about themselves and about yourself. Dialogue is the means by which we discover and evaluate truth, and diversity is the starting point for dialogue.

Among the most powerful statements of the reasons that America—and especially American universities—needs to keep this dialogue alive will be found in the speech, "I Have a Dream," which Reverend Martin Luther King Jr. delivered a few years before his assassination. His vision of a society free at last from judgments based narrowly on the accidents of birth joins in perpetuity such other classic statements of the need for freedom of expression as "Areopagitica," the poet John Milton's defense of a free press, and "On Liberty," philosopher John Stuart Mill's reasoned explanation of the essential character of a free society. To close the unit, Ingram and Parks comment on racial developments since 1963, when King delivered that speech.

Learning from Differences

Richard J. Light

Richard J. Light is professor in the Graduate School of Education and the John F. Kennedy School of Government at Harvard University. He and colleagues interviewed seniors over a ten-year period to develop the information and anecdotes on which he based his 2001 study, *Making the Most of College: Students Speak Their Minds*. This reading suggests that much can be learned from listening to students talk about their college experiences.

• • • • • • • • • • • • • • • • •

The topic of ethnic and racial diversity is a highly charged political issue on many campuses. Students may want to think about how they will approach this issue in their years at college. If their parents attended an American college or university, the modern version will probably be noticeably different. Not just in terms of course coverage, but perhaps most of all in terms of campus atmosphere. What can any student from any background learn from the experience of studying and living and working on campus in this new atmosphere? ...

One key theme is that diversity on campus exerts an impact on learning both in and out of classes. A second theme is that interactions among students often have powerful effects on people from many different backgrounds—not just any one subgroup. A third theme is that while many interactions are positive, some are clearly the opposite. About two-thirds of the examples students give are strikingly positive. Some tell about discussions with fellow students from different racial and ethnic groups that enhance academic learning. Others describe a process of interpersonal growth. Yet several tell of troubling encounters.

Several of the findings are unexpected, at least to me. I did not expect so many students to respond to questions about the educational impact of diversity by describing complex incidents that led simultaneously to academic and personal growth. I did not expect students to identify so many incidents that occur outside of classes, often in residence halls, as the ones they remember most vividly. And I had no idea of the importance of religious life and religious diversity for many undergraduates. Student after student characterizes religious diversity as an especially powerful source of learning. Let us begin with that finding.

Religious Diversity as a Positive Force

When I ask students about the impact of diversity, many bring some aspect of religious diversity into their response. At the outset I focused primarily on racial and ethnic diversity. But I quickly learned that these are intertwined with religion. Understanding the power of students' religious convictions offers some insight into the impact of ethnic diversity.

Religious diversity plays a role in classroom discussions and debates that can serve a powerful educational function. This is most likely to happen when students are able to integrate their religious perspectives into their classes and express them directly. Faculty members who are comfortable inviting and dealing with such comments can capitalize on them to enhance classroom discussion. And students who feel comfortable integrating a spiritual aspect of their life with what may sometimes seem like abstract academic concepts may find that this combination leads to powerful learning.

Why are students so convinced of the educational value of religious diversity? Some report being surprised, taken aback, or even shocked by what other students say in class. Yet when a remark is put into a broader context, such as the context of a religious tradition, it may take on a whole new meaning. Students note that they don't feel they must agree with all religious remarks or observations. Rather, they value the way discussions can be enriched by religious perspectives.

What features do students bring with them when they first arrive on campus? First, if they are religious, regardless of the denomination, they bring a core set of beliefs and traditions. Many bring certain religious rituals that other students may not have encountered before. In classes, such students may interpret literary, historical, or cross-cultural readings in light of their religious upbringing.

And what of students who are not religious? There are many, and, perhaps surprisingly, they show every bit as much enthusiasm for religious diversity as do their more devout friends. Most students who are not religious did not become that way thoughtlessly. They arrived at their views with some reflection. And they are delighted to be informed by fellow students who know more about certain religious traditions. Not proselytized—just informed.

Religious diversity is a bit different from ethnic or other types of diversity among undergraduates. Sara Goldhaber, a student interviewer, concludes from her in-depth interviews with forty religious undergraduates that "given the personal nature of religion, most students learn much more about the religious diversity of their peers through social interactions than they do in class discussions." The students I interviewed echoed this point strongly. And most felt it would be difficult, if not impossible, for the sharing of beliefs and experiences that leads to this personal sort of learning to be built into class discussions. They noted that the nature of classroom discussion at a rigorous college pushes people, understandably, to more academic and abstract conversations and analyses.

Nearly all of the anecdotes students related about learning from religious diversity took place outside of classes. The deeply positive interactions among people of different religions are a striking confirmation of a particular value of a residential college community. Bringing together people from different backgrounds and religions, so that they live together, work together, and play together, leads to an enormous amount of strong positive learning. The evidence is compelling. Goldhaber and I found several kinds of learning from religious diversity.

Reaffirming a Religious Commitment

For some students, living in close proximity to others of different religions, or of no religion at all, leads to reflection and insights that reaffirm their own religious faith. One Catholic student told Goldhaber:

> I have reevaluated my beliefs. The independence of college life and growing intellectually have been the largest influences for me. These things have made me think more critically about my religious beliefs. They are no longer simply the tradition I was brought up in, and all I know to do. Now, at college, there are people of different religions all around me. And some people have chosen the path of no faith. Living and interacting with these people marks an important difference. Simply seeing myself in contrast to other students, and noticing our differences, has made me reconsider and ultimately reaffirm my faith.
>
> Discussions with other students have challenged my beliefs and forced me to explain them. In order to do this well, I have searched for the intellectual bases for my beliefs. I feel I have found them through talking with priests, reading literature, praying, and thinking about issues myself. Part of college is deciding who you are and what you want to be. I think it's the responsibility of every Catholic to seriously consider the priesthood as a vocation. Thinking about this has forced me to think about what is important to me and what drives my life. Friends often come to me to ask about "the Catholic position" on an issue.
>
> For example, in terms of premarital sex, I have learned why the Catholic Church feels it is wrong, rather than just accepting it as dogma. The reasons are both religious and intellectual in basis. Catholics believe that marriage is a sacrament in which man and woman are blessed by God in a special way and only then can engage in sexual intercourse. Also, marriage is a lasting institution, and so sex—as the most intimate expression of physical love—is only appropriate in that context. On other topics, I struggle with the Catholic Church's position, and have questions about the official view. I don't think it is all right to flippantly throw Catholic views out the window, though I do sometimes disagree with the official viewpoint after long consideration of, and struggle over, an issue.

Understanding and Respecting Other Religions

It is natural on a college campus to discuss and examine ideas. And who better to do it with than people who are different from you in some way? When that difference happens to be in religion, students report that they learn a great deal about religions other than their own. Few students have grown up with in-depth knowledge of the customs, traditions, and beliefs of other religions. Living together at college thus provides an ideal environment in which to discuss differing religious perspectives and, even better, to see fellow students practicing their religions. Nearly every student we interviewed expressed respect for fellow students who remain true to their religious traditions even when doing so requires making certain social sacrifices. Seeing friends and colleagues actually implementing customs and beliefs leads to a particularly strong kind of learning.

This theme is brought up repeatedly by students from all religions. It depends heavily on living arrangements, where on a day-to-day basis students from different religious backgrounds and traditions mix and mingle routinely. On a campus where almost any generalization has many exceptions, this learning

about different religious traditions seems to be a nearly unanimous feature of
residential life.

> I grew up in a Christian community, and had never met anyone Jewish before
> Harvard. When I moved in with a roommate freshman year who observed the
> major holidays, I learned a lot about the Jewish tradition. It was eye-opening to
> see the perspective of a different calendar, rules about food, and observance of
> holiday traditions.
>
> During Passover, I went with my Jewish roommate and another Christian
> roommate to an interfaith *Seder* organized by a semi-observant Jew and an
> Orthodox Jew who were our friends. They invited a Muslim, a Buddhist, a bunch of
> Christians, and several Jewish friends, so it was a really neat group at the table. We
> all had the books [Haggadahs], and every time a prayer was read they would go
> around the table and ask if there was anything similar in our religious traditions.
>
> That was also Holy Week, so I had just come the day before from Good Friday.
> We had had a similar meal that day to commemorate the Last Supper. I had never
> really made the connection between the Last Supper and Passover. In Sunday
> School we had learned that Christ was at a Passover Seder, but if you've never
> been to one, that means nothing, and is just a trivia fact to pull out. So making
> connections between these two celebrations, and being with a diverse group of
> people who were interested in sharing their traditions, was fascinating. It took us
> hours. We did the entire Passover Seder and in addition all of our interfaith
> discussions, so we went way longer than the *Hillel* ones did.
>
> That evening gave me an insight into the figure of Christ that I had never
> really had. I knew he was Jewish, but realizing that he was at the same type of
> dinner that I had just experienced for the first time helped me to make sense of
> why all of his apostles were together and drinking wine and eating bread—
> actually, *matzo.* In the prayer book there's a line the priest says every week during
> *Eucharist* that quotes Christ saying, "Take, eat, and every time you do this, do this in
> remembrance of me," or something to that effect. I had never understood that
> choice of wording. First of all, I thought "this" meant eating in general, and then I
> realized that it came from the Passover meal, which of course happens only once
> a year and so had a more special origin.
>
> In addition, I had thought his words were a bit egotistical and should have
> been ringing alarm bells in the disciples' heads about Christ's coming death. But I
> realized in the context of the Passover Seder that saying something so important
> would not be unusual because the rest of the Seder is also of tremendous import.
> Seeing this special and spiritual meal put Christ's words in a context that made
> more sense and had new meaning to me. I feel that now I have a whole basis for
> understanding another religion.

Exploring One's Own Beliefs

The college years are a time of change, introspection, questioning, and exploration of what a student believes in—and religious diversity can help this exploration. One woman spoke to Goldhaber from the midst of this process:

> Everything that I have learned by observing and interacting with my more
> religious roommates has helped me to decide what is important and not
> important to me in a belief system, or more generally in a spiritual outlook. I have
> a specific example.

My observant Protestant roommate got married to a very religious person who wants to be a minister and to participate in religion within a framework that I feel is blatantly sexist. When my roommate was deciding to marry him, I felt very uncomfortable with the idea. Her wedding made me realize that what is important to me in my religious quest is not to find fault with the religions of other people, but rather to interact with people in a loving, caring way. I learned to look past, and to forgive, the aspects of other people's religions and beliefs that I may disagree with.

This process forced me to think hard about what I believe. If I really believe that people carry God within them and are sentient beings, oppression didn't matter. To think that a sexist attitude would oppress people would be to deny the spiritual power of individuals. Yet I am still uncomfortable with this view that I came to, because it commits me to a view of the world that is counterintuitive for me. I am a liberal, and I work to decrease poverty and suffering and oppression in many situations. So it is hard to justify my work while believing in the spiritual framework I just described. I think this all requires a transformation of my perception of suffering, one which I am far from mastering.

...

Living and Learning Together

When preparing to ask about learning related to students' different ethnic and racial backgrounds, I expected to find that most "academic" learning took place in classes and most "personal" learning happened in interactions outside of classes. Student interviewers predicted that the interviews would confound my expectations. They were right. Learning does not take place in such a partitioned way.

Perhaps because of this crossover between in-class and out-of-class learning, when students interact with fellow students from different racial and ethnic backgrounds in day-to-day living, it makes a strong impression. This finding drives home the importance of creating residential living arrangements that bring students from different backgrounds together, rather than creating separation by racial or ethnic background. If students from different backgrounds live apart from one another, a precious kind of learning may be lost.

Students give myriad examples of such crossovers between in-class learning and residential living, and they characterize them as highlights of their life at college. One striking story comes from a junior:

> I'm an African-American guy who grew up in a pretty middle-class home. I went to an integrated high school. I thought I knew exactly what to expect here at college when I got my freshman roommate mailing. There were going to be four of us—two white and two black, in a suite with three small bedrooms. So two guys get singles, and two share a bedroom. I wondered how that would work, and expected it might cause some tension. I especially hoped the tension wouldn't be anything racial.
>
> As it turns out, I was completely wrong about what would happen. We quickly resolved the room arrangements by agreeing to split the year with two of us sharing for the first half and the other two sharing for the second half. So that potential dilemma vanished quickly. For the first few weeks the four of all got along quite well.

But it was the connection with our classes that created some tensions. One of my white roommates and I both enrolled in a literature class where we read work by a diverse group of writers. And this was where the academic work and our living together intersected. It made for some difficult moments.

I remember two examples in particular. We read two black authors, and, to say the least, their styles were very different. One was a piece by Imamu Amiri Baraka called "The Toilet." The other was an essay by James Baldwin, written when he lived in Paris. I thought Baraka was a challenging and complex writer, while I was disappointed with Baldwin. My white roommate had exactly the opposite reaction.

Now you could say that this is entirely normal. Why would anyone be surprised that two students would have different takes on two authors? But somehow when we talked about it, we both got very offended. I had assumed he would agree with me, and he had assumed I would agree with him. Then he called the Baraka piece "absolute trash," and I took it as a racial remark. So I clammed up and stopped talking to him. Our relationship became very strained.

Thank goodness for our two other roommates. It was pretty obvious to both of them what was happening. One evening a few days later they just couldn't stand the tension. So when we had our regular weekly "group grousing time" they pressed each of us.

I first realized that evening that if I become angry with a white guy who really is a good guy, it's pretty foolish for me to think he is a racist just because he doesn't like a particular piece of writing by a black man. How would I feel if I told my white roommate I didn't enjoy reading James Joyce, and he accused me of making a racist remark? I would get upset with him, and I think I would be right to get upset with him.

The good news is that the four of us are still living together now, as juniors. And thanks to those awkward moments we had together as freshmen, now I feel completely free to criticize James Michener or James Joyce or Henry James, and my white roommate feels completely free to say what he really thinks about any black author. We even laugh about it now because it's kind of a bond. It's hard for me to advise other people to live together the way our group has done. But I can certainly say that for me, as one guy, the intersection of living arrangement and academic work has been a big learning experience, a big winner.

Another student in his junior year gave the following example to inter-viewer Anna Fincke:

Freshman year I had one roommate who was black. We became very close friends. We find each other easier to associate with than many other people. Being white, I think having a black roommate freshman year has had an impact on the mix of people I know. I met people he knew. I don't think that's unusual—any roommate who runs in a different crowd will bring that. He was from Georgia and had a very strong tradition of African-American culture. He was quite religious and conservative. He really represents to me some especially interesting, valuable, and worthy aspects of African-American traditions. In discussions I became aware of some of his struggles and the circumstances he encounters. Like in my high school there was a considerable rift between blacks and whites in terms of academics. It's interesting to see how he dealt with those difficulties.

I don't think anyone comes to college without preconceived notions. They arise from your life experience. And they always change with your new experi-ences. The high school I went to was racially mixed—it was just over half black.

The chance to get to know students of other races here, and have challenging, searching discussions with them, has raised my confidence in asserting who I am and what I believe, without respect to race. In a small town in Texas, where I'm from, it's easy to fall into certain unfortunate patterns of talking to people of different races. There are certain formalisms used to smooth over tensions. Now I'm more willing to be direct and inclined to say what I think is the truth about one issue or another.

For each student, the tone of college life is set early. Much of that tone depends upon roommates, neighbors, and dorm supervisors. Again, living arrangements go a long way toward shaping both attitudes and relationships. A young woman told Sara Goldhaber about an unexpected friendship:

Moving into our dorms freshman year, we all got together the first night in our proctor's room. She had asked us to bring something along that was important to us, and to introduce it along with ourselves. I had just come back from spending a summer traveling through Eastern Europe and Israel. My object was a pillow. When I was young, my best friend was an Israeli girl whose family had moved to America for a few years. That summer I had visited them in Israel. When I left, the younger kids presented me with a red, heart-shaped pillow they had made. It said in Hebrew, "Have a safe trip. We love you," and it had all their names on it. It really meant something to me. I thought the pillow was very emblematic of both my relationships with people and my religious experiences.

Just before my turn, the guy next to me introduced himself as a *Shiite* Muslim from Pakistan. His object was a necklace with several pendants of *Koranic* verses and a curved sword. I was stunned. I hadn't ever had direct contact with a Muslim before, and I had such a historical prejudice and fear of negative interactions between Jews and Muslims. Shocked and frightened a bit, I went on anyway with what I was going to say, and explained that I was a religious Jew. He turned to me with a big grin and said, "Great! It's always hard to find somebody else who doesn't want pepperoni on their pizza." We became fast friends and it was always a big joke that we could go out to dinner together, because we had similar dietary restrictions.

Meeting the Muslim guy in my dorm turned Islam into a real religion for me. After being a fanatical ideal, it became something which real people practiced and believed in. This experience made me realize the prejudices that I held about religion in general, and Islam in particular. Before meeting him, I was frankly unwilling to believe that he could keep his Muslim views out of any discussion. I see people make this misguided assumption all the time, because when someone says they are religious, it is easy to jump to the conclusion that that is the only thing which defines them.

Living with students from different backgrounds can actually change behavior. In the spirit of pressing students to go beyond platitudes when talking about the impact of residential living, I asked interviewees to give examples of interactions from their residential living experience that changed their behavior. Two seniors who lived in the same residence hall both told me of a particular incident. It illustrates the power of roommates, the value of choosing wisely, and how residential living experiences can change behavior. One of the seniors described the incident this way:

Eight of us blocked together. Eight guys. Four of us are white, one is black, three are Asian. We were all just chatting on a weekend afternoon. We had known each other since freshman year. Saw each other practically every day. Didn't expect any big surprises. We feel entirely comfortable with each other.

It was last October. I remember one of the Asian guys asked, "How are you going to handle voting in the November election? Are you going home, or are you going to use an absentee ballot?" All five of us non-Asian guys responded that we hadn't thought about it yet. The truth is that a couple of us might just have let the election slide. We are pretty busy. And since none of us come from cities or towns right near campus, I guess we would have just let this one election pass.

The Asian-American guys became visibly upset. They asked how much we knew about [Daw Aung San Suu Kyi]. Two of us knew she was the Burmese woman under house arrest who had won a Nobel Peace Prize while fighting for democracy in Burma. They asked us if we had heard about Wang Dan, who was arrested in China's Tiananmen Square student uprising for democracy. They asked about Wei Jing [Sheng], sitting in jail because of his speaking out and writing for democracy in China. They pressed us how, knowing about these people and what they were risking for the chance to vote, while we were taking so much for granted—how could we just take a pass on voting that year?

Well, it didn't take them long to embarrass us. Big time. They didn't try to rub our noses in it, or anything like that. But they felt strongly about it. They certainly changed our behavior. So the five of us all made a big point of sending away for absentee ballots that very afternoon. And all five of us voted. Now that I think back on that afternoon, it seemed like a small thing at the time. But it really affected me. I bet you I will never pass on another election in my lifetime.

For learning—and behavior change—to take place, students must mix and mingle and interact. Ideally students from different backgrounds should work together to accomplish a common task. Sometimes formally in a classroom. Often less formally outside of classes. The key point is that extensive contact, preferably both inside and outside of class, is what allows students to benefit and learn from ethnic differences on campus—and that residential arrangements can foster this contact in a way that encourages such learning....

In the context of residential living, some students inevitably encounter situations in which they are uncomfortable. This characterizes life at any college. And it was true long before colleges began to strive for diversity in their student bodies. Yet when students from different racial or ethnic backgrounds live together, new kinds of delicate moments and personal interactions inevitably arise. While some of these circumstances can be difficult for students to cope with, students from all backgrounds report that they learn something. Often that something is about themselves.

Several graduating seniors commented on the importance of the simple principle of bringing good will to all personal encounters. For example, a young white woman suggested that one way to enhance good will among people of different backgrounds is to encourage each student to be reflective about himself. Especially when racial or ethnic differences raise a delicate issue or lead to an awkward moment. Inevitably these awkward moments will occur. It is up to each student to transform them into an educational opportunity—a learning experience. When a student is willing to be reflective and assume good will, the results can be powerful.

 Vocabulary

As you think about this essay, these definitions may be helpful to you:
1. **Seder**   a Jewish home or community service including a ceremonial dinner. This ritual meal is held on the first or first and second evenings of the Passover in commemoration of the exodus from Egypt. The Last Supper of Christian tradition was a Seder on the first night of Passover.
2. **Hillel**   a greatly revered Jewish teacher who lived about the time of Christ. Most campuses with Jewish students also have a gathering place with programs for them, often named in Hillel's memory.
3. **matzo**   the unleavened bread eaten at a Seder and remembered in the Christian communion service
4. **Eucharist**   a Christian sacrament at which bread and wine are taken in remembrance of the Last Supper
5. **Shiite**   One of the major branches of Islam, the religion in which Allah is the one god and Muhammad is His prophet
6. **Koranic**   The Koran is the book of sacred writings accepted by Muslims as revelations made to Muhammad by Allah through the angel Gabriel. Koranic verse are verses from the Koran.

 Discussion Questions

1. Most of the examples that Light gives in this reading are positive, even if they do not seem to start out that way. But Light says that "some are clearly the opposite. About two-thirds of the examples students give are strikingly positive. Some tell about discussions with fellow students from different racial and ethnic groups that enhance academic learning. Others describe a process of interpersonal growth. Yet several tell of troubling encounters." Discuss some instances in which dealing with fellow students who are different was either positive or negative.
2. Much of the literature about diversity acknowledges that people need to feel safe in their environment before they can talk about those differences with candor. What needs to be true for an environment to be "safe" for such discussions?

3. Light reports, "Student after student characterizes religious diversity as an especially powerful source of learning." Do you agree? Suggest some reasons why this appears to be true.

 ## Suggestions for Your Journal

Most students who live on campus find that they have to make several adjustments to their new college environment. Write about some of the adjustments that you had to confront. Were they routine or difficult?

What kind of difference in others is the hardest for you to come to terms with—religious? ethnic? geographical? racial? sexual orientation? or some other kind? Compare differences that you manage easily with those you find hard to handle.

How Discrimination Works and Why It Matters: Five Personal Statements

Chana Schoenberger, from Bethesda, Maryland, was a high school student when she wrote her comments and published them in *Newsweek*. Joy Weeber was a graduate student in a doctoral program in Psychology at North Carolina State in Raleigh. Edward Delgado-Romero is a psychologist at the University of Florida Counseling Center in Gainesville. Donna Talbot coordinates the student affairs graduate programs in the Department of Counselor Education and Counseling Psychology at Western Michigan University, Kalamazoo. And Lisa J. Brandyberry is a senior psychologist and director of adult outpatient and emergency services at Piedmont Behavioral Health Care in Albemarle, North Carolina.

   Discussion Questions and Suggestions for Your Journal for these five essays appear on pages 219–220.

Getting to Know About You and Me
Chana Schoenberger

A religious holiday approaches; students at my high school who will be celebrating the holiday prepare a presentation on it for an assembly. The Diversity Committee, which sponsors the assemblies to increase religious awareness, asked me last spring if I would help with the presentation on Passover, the Jewish holiday that *commemorates* the Exodus from Egypt. I was too busy with other things, and I never got around to helping. I didn't realize then how important those presentations really are, or I definitely would have done something.

This summer I was one of 20 teens who spent five weeks at the University of Wisconsin at Superior studying acid rain with a National Science Foundation Young Scholars program. With such a small group in such a small town, we soon became close friends and had a good deal of fun together. We learned about the science of acid rain, went on field trips, found the best and cheapest restaurants in Superior and ate in them frequently to escape the lousy cafeteria food. We were a happy, bonded group.

Represented among us were eight religions: Jewish, Roman Catholic, Muslim, Hindu, Methodist, Mormon, Jehovah's Witness, and Lutheran. It was amazing, given the variety of backgrounds, to see the ignorance of some of the smartest young scholars on the subject of other religions.

On the first day, one girl mentioned that she had nine brothers and sisters. "Oh, are you Mormon?" asked another girl, who I knew was a Mormon herself. The first girl, shocked, replied, "No, I dress normal!" She thought Mormon was the same as Mennonite, and the only thing she knew about either religion was that Mennonites don't, in her opinion, "dress normal."

My friends, ever curious about Judaism, asked me about everything from our basic theology to food preferences. "How come, if Jesus was a Jew, Jews aren't Christian?" my Catholic roommate asked me in all seriousness. Brought up in a small Wisconsin town, she had never met a Jew before, nor had she met people from most of the other "strange" religions (anything but Catholic or mainstream Protestant). Many of the other kids were the same way.

"Do you all still practice animal sacrifices?" a girl from a small town in Minnesota asked me once. I said no, laughed, and pointed out that this was the 20th century, but she had been absolutely serious. The only Jews she knew were the ones from the Bible.

Nobody was deliberately rude or *anti-Semitic,* but I got the feeling that I was representing the entire Jewish people through my actions. I realized that many of my friends would go back to their small towns thinking that all Jews liked Dairy Queen Blizzards and grilled cheese sandwiches. After all, that was true of all the Jews they knew (in most cases, me and the only other Jewish young scholar, period).

The most awful thing for me, however, was not the *benign* ignorance of my friends. Our biology professor had taken us on a field trip to the EPA field site where he worked, and he was telling us about the project he was working on. He said that they had to make sure the EPA got its money's worth from the study—he "wouldn't want them to get Jewed."

I was astounded. The professor had a doctorate, various other degrees and seemed to be a very intelligent man. He apparently had no idea that he had just made an anti-Semitic remark. The other Jewish girl in the group and I debated whether or not to say something to him about it, and although we agreed we would, neither of us ever did. Personally, it made me feel uncomfortable. For a high-school student to tell a professor who taught her class that he was a *bigot* seemed out of place to me, even if he was one.

What scares me about that experience, in fact about my whole visit to Wisconsin, was that I never met a really vicious anti-Semite or a *malignantly* prejudiced person. Many of the people I met had been brought up to think that Jews (or Mormons or any other religion that's not mainstream Christian) were different and that difference was not good.

Difference, in America, is supposed to be good. We are expected—at least, I always thought we were expected—to respect each other's traditions. Respect requires some knowledge about people's backgrounds. Singing Christmas carols as a kid in school did not make me Christian, but it taught me to appreciate beautiful music and someone else's holiday. It's not necessary or desirable for all ethnic groups in America to assimilate into one traditionless mass. Rather, we all need to learn about other cultures so that we can understand one another and not feel threatened by others.

In the little multicultural universe that I live in, it's safe not to worry about explaining the story of Passover because if people don't hear it from me, they'll hear it some other way. Now I realize that's not true everywhere.

Ignorance was the problem I faced this summer. By itself, ignorance is not always a problem, but it leads to misunderstandings, prejudice and hatred. Many of today's problems involve hatred. If there weren't so much ignorance about other people's backgrounds, would people still hate each other as badly as they do now? Maybe so, but at least that hatred would be based on facts and not flawed beliefs.

I'm now back at school, and I plan to apply for the Diversity Committee. I'm going to get up and tell the whole school about my religion and the tradition I'm proud of. I see now how important it is to celebrate your heritage and to educate others about it. I can no longer take for granted that everyone knows about my religion, or that I know about theirs. People who are suspicious when they find out I'm Jewish usually don't know much about Judaism. I would much prefer them to hate or distrust me because of something I've done, instead of them hating me on the basis of prejudice.

 Vocabulary   • • • • • • • • • • • • • • • • • • •

As you think about this essay, these definitions may be helpful to you:
1. **commemorate**   to mark by some ceremony or observation
2. **anti-Semitic**   discriminating against Jews as a religious or racial group
3. **benign**   mild or harmless disposition
4. **bigot**   one who is intolerantly devoted to one's own opinions or prejudices
5. **malignantly**   injuriously, intentionally harmful

: **What Could I Know of Racism?**
: *Joy E. Weeber*

• • • • • • • • • • • • • • • • •

W hat could I know of racism, being a middle-class, college-educated White woman? What could I know of the pain of being rendered invisible because of a single characteristic? What could I know of having the complexity of myself, a Dutch American from a large extended family living around the world, reduced to that feature which marks me as "different" from the dominant culture? What could I know of being denied entrance to public facilities or required to sit in segregated places because of that characteristic? What could I know of being forced to use a back service entrance, like a second-class citizen? What could I know about being told that if I "work hard enough" I could make it, although getting in the front door for an interview seems an impossibility? What could I know about having to endure painful procedures to make my appearance more acceptable? What could I know of being charged a higher price for services because of the way I look? What could I know about not being able to ride a bus with dignity? What could I know of having a hard time finding a place to live because of housing discrimination or being unable to visit in the homes of my classmates? What could I know of growing up in a society that never portrays my people with positive images in the media, except for those exceptional, inspirational heroes who have more than made it? What could I know of being viewed as less intelligent simply because of the way I look? What could I know of being educated in a segregated school setting, not expected to amount to much and denied opportunities because of it? What could I know of being thought of as less than acceptable because of the way that I speak? What could I know of having to work twice as hard as others just to prove I am as good as they are? What could I know of being viewed as a charity case, rather than one who possesses civil rights?

I can know the pain of all of these things because I am disabled. My disabled brothers and sisters and I experience such acts of discrimination on a daily basis, and the pain these encounters cause is the same pain that racism causes people of color. It is the pain caused by the unconscious beliefs of a society that assumes everyone is, or should be, "normal" (i.e., White and very able-bodied). It is the pain caused by the assumption that everyone should be capable of total independence and "pulling themselves up by their own bootstraps." It is a belief in the superiority of being nondisabled that assumes everyone who is disabled wishes they could be nondisabled—at any cost. In the disability community, we call this "ableism," a form of prejudice and bigotry that marks us as less than those who are nondisabled. In this narrative, I use language the disability community claims in naming its own lived experience. And although it may not be "politically correct," it is meant as a true reflection of how many of us view ourselves and our lives as members of the disability community.

Ableism causes pain because it convinces us that there is something fundamentally wrong with us, that we are not acceptable just as we are. After all, we are the ones who are "defective," with bodies, speech, hearing, vision and emotional or cognitive functioning to be fixed by doctors and therapists. Ableism also causes pain to nondisabled people who are unprepared to deal with their own vulnerability and mortality when accidents and aging require that they do so. I did not understand the pain these attitudes had caused me until I was 35, despite having lived with the effects of polio since I was an infant. Until then, I did not know that I had spent my entire life trying to prove how I had "overcome" my polio, which is no more possible than overcoming being female or African American! I did not understand that these ableist attitudes and acts devalued my body and denied an essential element of who I am.

I only began to understand all of this when I read an essay, "The Myth of the Perfect Body," by Roberta Galler (1984),[1] who also had polio as a child. I felt as if I were reading my own diary! I was not an alien; I had a disability! I was the "supercrip" she wrote about, the defiant opposite of the pathetic cripple I had been made so deathly afraid of being. I had spent enormous amounts of my energy proving how "able" I was, to counter society's belief that I am "unable." I thought I had "passed" as normal in my nondisabled world (despite my crutches and braces), because I was often "complimented" by strangers and friends who "did not think of me as handicapped." Only when I read this woman's words did I begin to understand how my life had been shaped by living with a disability, even though my family and I had not been able to acknowledge that it existed! Only then did I begin to understand how my sense of self had been constructed by how my body had been touched, treated, and talked about by those who had been my "caregivers." Only then did I begin to understand how my life had been lived as an outsider, struggling unconsciously for acceptance.

Throughout my childhood, I had successfully resisted sincerely religious strangers' urgings for me to get "healed," people who thought of me as sick and infirm. Although these encounters left me feeling violated and nauseated, I knew I was fine and intact the way I was! Why did they think I was sick? I lived in a tight-knit community that accepted me as a whole person; they did not see me as sick. Not once had I been stopped from living life fully by anyone's low expectations, fear, or lack of imagination in how to change the world to meet my needs. I had been allowed to participate on my terms and discover my own physical limitations. My parents understood the stigma that society places on people with disabilities and were determined to nurture a sense of self that could deflect such negativity.

And yet, at the age of 10, I was marked as "other" by a diagnosis of scoliosis, found to be "defective" with a curving spine and weak leg muscles, and in need

---

[1] R. Galler, "The Myth of the Perfect Body," in C. Vance (ed.), *Pleasure and Danger: Exploring Female Sexuality* (Boston: Routledge and Kegan Paul, 1984), pp. 165–172.

of "corrective" surgery. Thus began my searing journey into a medical world that would teach me well what it really means to be disabled in this society! It was a world that taught me I was invisible, a defective body part to be talked about as if not connected to a lonely, hurting child. It was a world that taught me I had to be tough to survive, cut off from the emotional support of my family for all but 2-hour visits a week. It was a world that taught me that it was okay for others to inflict pain on me—if their goal was to make me more "normal." This world taught me that what I felt or wanted had nothing to do with what happened to my body, that it was okay to publicly strip children and parade their defects in front of strangers. The result of seven surgeries and innumerable scars was a girl who was numb, disconnected from both body and soul. I was fragmented and lost to a family who had no clue of my inner devastation. The emotional isolation of the hospital followed me home, as I heard in my family's lack of understanding that something was "wrong" with how I responded to life—emotionally, psychologically, spiritually, and politically!

My response to the horror of those years was to make myself outdo everyone, need help from no one, and take care of everyone else's needs. I was constantly proving I was the "exception," not one of those dependent cripples society cannot tolerate. Never mind that I spent my entire adult life struggling with devastating bouts of exhaustion-induced depression—although others only ever saw my bright, cheerful self. Never mind that I was alone, unable to sustain any vital romantic relationships, ever untouchable and independent. I became the angry one who spoke out against social injustice and felt the sexism in our community and family. I was the one who felt the arrogance and violence of racism. I was the one who felt the fragmentation of only seeking spiritual and physical sustenance, while psychological and emotional needs went unacknowledged. Being alone in the hospital, and the thought of seeking the company of those who might share them never crossed my mind.

At no time did I connect my different ways of perceiving and responding to the world with my experience of living with a disability. I couldn't. There was no disabled person in my world to help me understand that my empathy for those who suffered from injustice or were devalued because of race was rooted in my own experience of being devalued because of my disability. In the 7 years since my first encounter with a disabled person who understood, I have never felt alone. I have come to know the healing of belonging, of being understood without a word in a community of people who validate my feelings. I did not know how fragmented I was, and I needed other disabled people to teach me to love myself wholly! I had needed them to teach me how to embrace that part of myself that society so devalues. I needed them to show me the commonalities between our experiences of ableism and others' experiences of racism. I needed them to give words to the feelings I had never had reflected back to my self in my nondisabled world.

Most of us with disabilities learn to survive alone and silently in our nondisabled families and worlds, never knowing a disability community exists. I was the only disabled person in my family, my community, schools, and my adult social world. As a child, I had learned an aversion to the company of other disabled people because they were associated with being "defective" and stigmatized, and I was neither of those! My only experiences with other disabled people had been in situations in which nondisabled professionals "medicalized" our lives, defining us negatively. I even had my own turn at working in such settings, "helping" others in sheltered workshops and group homes, although always quitting for emotional reasons I only now understand. I had never been in an environment in which disabled people defined themselves in their own terms and celebrated their uniqueness. And now, in the written words and in the company of disabled people, I have found brothers and sisters who are teaching me that there are powerful ways of dealing with the pain of being "other." They are helping me find the words to express what I have always "known" in my body, but had no language to express.

James Baldwin (1972) wrote that "to be liberated from the stigma of blackness by embracing it, is to cease, forever, one's interior argument and collaboration with the authors of one's degradation (p. 190)."[2] It has been my experience that learning to embrace my whole self, disability and all, was not a task I could do alone. I needed the support and guidance of others who not only had lived my experience but also had ceased their internal collaboration with the negative voices of society. It is the same process that bell hooks (1989) speaks of in *Talking Back: Thinking Feminist, Thinking Black*,[3] as the need to "decolonialize" one's mind by rooting out all that does not honor one's own experience. I have found that in addition to decolonializing my mind, I have also needed to decolonialize my body. I have had to cease my interior argument with society's negative messages that I am not as good as everybody else by no longer pushing my body beyond its limits. As I have learned to listen to my body's limits, honoring them as a source of wisdom and strength, I have experienced the healing and liberation of the embrace, and I have begun to thrive.

A most profound way that I have begun to thrive is that I no longer require that I spend most of my energy walking to get around—I have begun to use a scooter for mobility. What an act of liberation—and resistance—this has been! I felt like a bird let out of a cage, the first time I used one! I could go and go and not be exhausted! I was able to fully participate in the conference I was attending, rather that just be dully present. To choose to use a scooter, when I can still walk, flies in the face of all the "wisdom" of those without disabilities. We are taught that to walk, no matter how distorted or exhausting it is, is far more virtuous than using a chair—because it is closer to "normal." Never mind that my galumphing polio-gait twists my muscles into iron-like sinew that only the hardiest of masseuses can "unknot." Never mind that my shoulders and hands, never meant for walking, have their future usefulness limited by 40 years of misuse on crutches. To choose to use a scooter also places me squarely in that stigmatized group of "pitiful unfortunates" who are "confined" to their chairs. It removes me

[2] J. Baldwin, *No Name in the Street* (New York: Doubleday, 1972).
[3] b. hooks, *Talking Back: Thinking Feminist, Thinking Black* (Boston, MA: South End Press, 1989).

from the ranks of "overcomers," such as Franklin Delano Roosevelt, Wilma Rudolph, or Helen Keller, whom society mistakenly believes actually "got over" their disabilities. My using a scooter is an act that scares my family. They are afraid that somehow giving up walking will make me give up—period! It makes them think that I am losing ground, becoming dependent on the scooter, when they and society need me to act as if I am strong and virile. Only now that I am embracing my limitations do I know how I spent much life-energy protecting my family from them. I rarely slowed them down or burdened them with feelings they could not understand. Only now can I celebrate my unavoidable need for interdependence in a society that oppresses everyone with its unattainable standard of independence!

Traditionally, families are taught by professionals that their child's disability is an individual functional problem that can only be remedied by individualized medical interventions. And so it remains the focus of many families to adapt their child to a society that needs them to be "normal." The larger social and cultural oppression that some of those interventions represent is only now being raised by those of us former disabled children who question the extreme and painful measures taken to "fix" us, measures that went beyond what may have been truly needed to ensure our full, unique development. In my scooter, I am choosing now to live by other values—the values of the disability community that require society to adapt to our needs rather than vice versa.

In using my scooter, I experience the full range of the disability experience, including those aspects I avoided when I thought I was "passing" as normal. In my scooter, I experience being denied access to places walking people enter without a thought, because they are inaccessible. In my scooter, I am eligible to use service entrances near stinking dumpsters and seating at public events that is segregated from my walking companions. Seated in my scooter, I am even more invisible to those who could never look the walking-me in the eye—an averted gaze not even required to obliterate my presence. In my scooter, I cannot visit some friends' homes because of stairs or use their bathrooms because of narrow doors. The very cost of my scooter includes a sizable "crip tax"—as the sum of its component parts is far less costly than its hefty price tag in the inflated (and captive) medical equipment market. In my scooter, I don't have full assurance that I will even be able to get on public transportation, much less treated with dignity when I do. In my scooter I feel the insult of those telethon hosts who want to paint my life as pathetic, not livable, unless I am cured. In my scooter, I know that I am viewed as far less able, needing public assistance rather than ramps and power doors to get into job interviews. Although my speech was not affected by polio, my scooter provides further reason to dismiss me, as society dismisses my brothers and sisters who use voice synthesizers to communicate their artistic vision of the world. In my scooter, I am inextricably and unavoidably a member of the disability community, with all the pain and privileges associated with that membership.

I am proud to have found my way home to the disability community. I am now able to "hang out on the porch" and hear stories from the elders of how their visions of equal justice for all took shape, how legislation acknowledging our civil rights was passed. And although it is true that we continue to struggle to define our own lives and live it on our own terms, we have also begun to create a culture that brings us together and celebrates our unique ways of being in the world. I am moved when I hear poetry that speaks my truth and read books that truly reflect my life experiences. I am healed when I see unflinchingly honest performances dealing with the reality and pain caused by ableism. I now know that I have indeed experienced the pain of ableism and I know why I felt the pain of racism when I had words for neither. I now also know the liberating power of embracing my disability and of celebrating who I am because of it.

The Face of Racism

Edward A. Delgado-Romero

When thinking of racism, people might imagine the vision of a hooded Ku Klux Klan member lighting a cross, a "skinhead" wearing swastikas, or an angry lynch mob. However, when I think of racism, one image is clear. I learned about racism in the face of my father. I learned hatred, prejudice, and contempt, and, most important, I learned how to turn that racism inward. After many years of self-reflection and healing, I have just begun to understand how deeply racism has affected my attitudes toward others and toward myself. I have begun to understand that racism works on two fronts. One is the overt and obvious racism of the Klan member. The other is the covert and subtle racism that the victim of overt racism begins to internalize, the racism my father taught me.

My father came to this country seeking to escape the personal demons that had haunted him throughout his life. He saw the United States and New York City as a new opportunity, a new beginning. Part of that beginning was rejecting all the things that he had been. My father sought to reinvent himself as an American. In those days, being an American meant being White (some people might argue that this is still true). My father felt he *was* White, because part of his family was descended from Spaniards. Somehow my father thought being Spanish (and therefore European) was better and of higher status than being a South American or a Colombian, and it was certainly better than being *Indio* or native. Our ancestral records show that the Delgado family was a virtuous family with a long tradition in Spain. However, the only records that remain of my ancestors who were native (South) Americans are a few photographs and some of their physical features that were passed along through "blood."

The United States of America taught my father to hate anyone who was not White. Richard Pryor once observed that the first English word that an immigrant is taught is "nigger." Always a quick learner, my father learned to hate "niggers," "gooks," "spics," "wetbacks," and any other "damn immigrant." However, my father soon found out that he was not excluded from the hatred. After days filled with jokes about "green cards" and "drug dealing," my father would return home to his wife and children, full of pent-up rage. We lived in fear of his anger and his explosiveness. My father tried to transform himself yet felt ambivalent about losing his security. Therefore, we were not allowed to speak Spanish to my father, and my mother was not allowed to learn English. By attempting to separate his children from their culture while denying his wife the chance to acculturate, my father replicated his divided psyche. My mother was forced to be the keeper of the culture and language, which she did with incredible bravery and pride. It was through the courage of my mother that I was eventually able to reconnect with my Latino heritage.

My father's drive to be accepted and to be acceptable knew no bounds. I remember one time as a child, we were driving a long distance to go to a restaurant (which was unusual for us). We sat and ate fried chicken and blueberry pie as my father anxiously waited for the owner of the restaurant to come over and acknowledge him. The owner finally did come over, and I remember how proud my father was to meet "a great American." It was only when I was older that I realized that this man was Georgia politician Lester Maddox. Maddox was one of the fiercest opponents of integration during the civil rights era. He was made infamous by keeping a bucket of ax handles by the door of his restaurant as a reminder of the violence that he had threatened to use against any Black person who would try to integrate his home or business. It shocks me to realize how racism had blinded my father to the fact that his fate as an immigrant and a minority group member in the United States was tied to the fate of other minorities.

As hard as he tried to fit in, my father never really succeeded. Often his physical features, his accent, or his clothes would give him away as being different. My father would react violently when confronted with his failure to become one hundred percent American. For example, during an interview for a promotion, the interviewer asked my father about the "good pot" grown in Colombia. At the time my father laughed it off. However, when he returned home he exploded in rage. These explosions became a daily event. My brother, sister, and I were a captive audience. We had no choice but to listen as he would berate us for being worthless. The angrier he became, the more pressure my father would put on us to "be American." We were wildly successful at being American, which only made my father angrier. As I became a teenager, my father became increasingly competitive with and abusive toward me. The fact that I physically resembled him only made things worse. He saw in me things he could never achieve: I spoke English without an accent, was headed toward college, and I dated Caucasian women exclusively.

I learned racism from my father, and just as he had done, I turned it inward. I came to hate the fact that I was Latino, that my parents spoke with an accent, that my skin, although light for a Latino, was darker than it should be. I wanted to be a White Anglo-American, and for many years, I actually thought I was. During my high school and college years I was in deep denial that I was Latino. I believed that America was a "color blind" society that rewarded people solely on the basis of hard work. I remember my Caucasian high school guidance counselor steering me away from minority scholarships for college and telling me "Ed, you want to get in on your own merit." At the time I believed her, and my "own merit" led to my status as a "token" at a predominantly Caucasian college, thousands of dollars in student loans, and 4 more years of denial.

I remember being deeply embarrassed by Latino music, food, customs, and history. My mother would often talk about her home country with pride and fondness. I used to get angry with her because she was being so "un-American." One time, in an attempt to share her culture with me, my mother gave me an expensive recording of Colombian music. I actually had the nerve to give it back to her because I was ashamed of everything Latino. I was particularly ashamed of my Spanish surname because of the way that my peers could mispronounce it in demeaning ways. I became so used to being called names that often I would participate in using ethnic slurs against myself and other minorities. I remember vividly a Latino varsity football player who was proud that his nickname was "Spic." Having a racial slur as a nickname was a badge of honor; it meant he was accepted. As an enthusiastic participant in the ethnic name-calling, I could continue to deny that I was different. The height of my own denial was when I told a Mexican joke to a priest, who was Mexican. The priest laughed, more out of shock than humor. The joke was, quite literally, on both of us. He confronted me, and pointed out that he was Mexican. As I stood in awkward silence, having offended someone I cared about, something began to awaken within me.

I began to realize that I was an impostor and that there was another side of me that I was denying. Although I felt intimidated and uncomfortable around people of color, there was a depth of connection that was missing in most of my relationships. I struggled to make sense of what I was feeling. My longing for connection with other minorities was first manifested in college through my participation in a fraternity. When I joined the fraternity, the membership was almost exclusively White. However, as I was able to influence member selection, the membership became increasingly diverse. I began to surround myself with other people who could understand what it felt like to be of two worlds and never fully at peace in either one. These were my first steps toward healing the racism that I felt inside.

My cultural explorations coincided with the divorce of my parents. My father eventually left our home and emotionally and financially disowned his family. This split helped me to continue the self-exploration and reclamation of my heritage that had begun in college. I learned about my ancestors, their names, and their lives. I learned my full name and the proper way to pronounce it. I was able to become friends with Latino men and Latina women. I asked my mother to give me back the recording of Colombian music I had refused to take from her and asked her to teach me about her culture. My mother saved up her money and took me on a trip to Colombia. I wish that I could say that I found my "home" in Colombia. I wish that I could say that I reconnected with my ancestors on some deep level. However, in Colombia I felt every bit the foreigner that I was. What I gained from my trip to Colombia was an understanding and appreciation for the enormous sacrifice that my mother had made for her children. In Colombia I realized that I was neither fully Colombian nor fully American. I had to find a way to make sense of my divided identity.

Many of my colleagues in psychology say that therapists enter the profession motivated in part by a need to deal with their own issues. As much as I used to argue that I was the exception to the rule, obviously I was not. In an effort to somehow identify, understand, and deal with my issues, I was drawn to graduate study in counseling psychology. I was offered a lucrative fellowship at a major university. However, only one professor (who later became my adviser and mentor) was honest enough to tell me that it was a minority fellowship. Many of the faculty and students saw the minority fellowship as a way for me to cheat the system because they did not think I was "really" a minority. One student explained his belief that I was not a real minority because I did not speak "broken English." The pressure to fit in and deny that I was different was enormous. I was faced with a choice that reminded me of dealing with my father: stay quiet and accept the status quo of the University and the program (basically "pass" as Caucasian) or assert myself and challenge a culturally oppressive system. I wish I could say that I chose to try to change the system simply because it was the moral or just thing to do. However, I think I chose to fight the system because I was tired of being quiet. Multicultural psychology became my passion and the focus of my career. I have my doubts as to how much I was able to change a deeply entrenched racist, sexist, and homophobic system, but I have no doubt that I underwent tremendous personal and professional growth.

As I progressed through my graduate training and into internship, I found that I surrounded myself with other people who could understand what it was like to face overt and covert racism. I formed a supportive network of friends and colleagues of all colors. At first I felt some animosity toward Caucasian people, but a Caucasian friend once pointed out that all people would benefit from being liberated from racism. I found that the term *liberation* captured the essence of what I was searching for: liberation from hatred and racism and, personally, a liberation from the past. I realized that liberation meant letting go of the intense anger and resentment I felt toward my father. My anger toward my father was like wearing a shrinking suit of armor: Although the anger could make me feel powerful and protected, the anger was not letting me grow and, in fact, was starting to choke me. However, I was concerned that, stripped of my armor, I would lose my motivation to fight racism. I was surprised to find that by liberating myself from my father's legacy, I was able to find peace and that from this peace I could generate more energy and motivation to face racism than I had imagined possible.

As I grow older and consider having my own children, I find myself looking in the mirror to see if I can see my father's face. There have been times when I have been both shocked and disappointed to hear his voice angrily coming out of my mouth or have seen my face contorted with his rage. I was surprised to find out that liberation did not mean I could change the facts of my past or get rid of any influence from my father. However, I gained something even more valuable: I learned that because of my experiences, I can understand why someone would be racist. I can understand what it is like to be both a perpetrator and a victim of racism. I have also come to understand that the answer to fighting racism begins with a moral inventory, a fearless look at oneself. I have come to the conclusion that I can never afford myself the luxury of asking the question "Am I racist?" Rather, I need to continually ask myself, "How racist am I?" As I struggle to deal with the reality of racism in my personal and professional life, I will continue to check my mirror and look for the face of racism.

● ●

Personal Narrative of an Asian American's Experience with Racism

Donna M. Talbot

● ● ● ● ● ● ● ● ● ● ● ● ● ● ● ● ●

Growing up in New England during the '60s and '70s had its benefits and difficulties. Although the northeast region of the country had larger pockets of people of color and immigrants than most other parts of the United States, the stiffness and arrogance of old money and elitist educational institutions created some inevitable friction among people with greatly diverse cultural backgrounds. It is in this environment (less than 5 miles from a large Air Force base) that I began my identity development, although unknowingly, as a person of color—as an Asian American.

My parents are both naturalized citizens; they were thankful to be in the United States, the land of opportunity and upward mobility. My father is French Canadian and Huron Indian and my mother is 100 percent Japanese. Although my two brothers and I were clearly raised with Japanese values and culture, my mother, our primary caretaker, insisted that we should grow up to be "good American citizens." This was driven by her pride in being a U.S. citizen and her fear of racist acts against us. What she didn't realize was that, despite her wishes, she couldn't help but raise good Japanese American citizens....

Many of my most vivid memories of what I believe to be acts of racism, sexism, and oppression took pace in "American institutions," such as schools, social organizations (Moose and Elks Clubs), and church. This fact has largely influenced my decision to become an educator, student affairs practitioner, and counselor; unfortunately, I think these experiences have also influenced my decision to move away from Christianity and to explore other forms of spirituality. In my professional roles, I address my agenda openly—to advocate for oppressed and marginalized populations so that they may not have to be subjected to the same negative experiences that I was.

My first overt experience of racism and recognition that I was "different" took place in school around the third grade. I remember waiting with my classmates in the hallway to go into social studies class. As I was standing there, several boys started to circle me while chanting that their fathers, uncles, and other male relatives had bombed my people. Then, they proceeded to pull up the corners of their eyes with their fingers, so they appeared slanted, and made funny noises like "ching," "chang," and so forth. For me this was extremely confusing because we had all grown up in the same neighborhood; but as I cried in the bathroom and looked in the mirror, it was the first time I cognitively realized that my eyes were different from theirs. Probably the most embarrassing part of this experience for me was that the teacher just stood in the doorway and laughed at the boys taunting me; he never tried to stop them or indicate that they were wrong. From that time on, through most of grade school, I hated myself and my mother for looking and being different.

A few years later, I learned how to be angry toward bias and ignorance. My older brother wanted to play baseball with his friends during the summer. To do that, my parents had to join the local Moose Club so that he could play in their leagues. Because my family would have been classified as "working class poor," this was a major commitment of which my parents were very proud. My father went to the club, completed the paperwork, and paid the application and membership fee. Everything seemed fine for about 2 weeks until we received a call from the membership person at the Moose Club; he explained to my father that the Moose, and other similar clubs, had a policy that prohibited interracial members from joining. The only apology he made was for not catching it sooner!

It wasn't until high school that I started to realize that there were benefits to being different—although I still resented being Asian. Teachers remembered me because I looked so different from my classmates, and the boys liked my long, black, straight hair and clear, olive complexion. Even colleges were interested and pursued this "high achieving" minority student. Although I was encouraged (actually, I was tracked) to take honors math and science courses, I had a strong interest in the social sciences and education. Most people were surprised, even shocked, when I turned down large scholarships from institutions with well-known engineering and computer science programs to go to a small liberal arts college. This marked the second most significant racist, or "classist," event in my educational experience. Early in my senior year, I was the first person in my local public high school ever to be accepted (early decision) to a very prestigious, liberal arts college—Amherst College. Soon, after the word was out that this had happened, I was summoned to the vice principal's office. Being the arrogant young "scholar" I thought I was, I assumed that the vice principal was calling me to give me "strokes" for my accomplishment. Several minutes into the discussion, a dark haze started to crowd my mind as I realized that this was an entirely different conversation than I had anticipated. Very confused and angry, I finally asked the vice principal what, exactly, she was trying to say to me. Her words rang loudly, almost deafeningly, in my ears, "Frankly, Donna, we're not sure you come from the *right kind of family* to be the first to represent our high school at Amherst College." At that point, I remember standing up and announcing that this meeting was over; however, as I was walking out, I suggested that this was a conversation she needed to have with my father. Although there were several other minor attempts to block my efforts to attend Amherst College, they were unsuccessful. I don't think I ever mentioned these incidents to my parents because I didn't want them ever to feel the humiliation that I had. Needless to say, the vice principal never called to have that conversation with my father.

College was an amazing experience for me—every day was a challenge to grow (personally and academically). Toward the end of my sophomore year, I was suspended, with many other Amherst students, for participating in demonstrations and a lock-out of the administration building. During that time, we had an African American dean who believed that the damage from slavery was over and that it was time to eliminate the programs and services that were created in the '60s to assist African American students. Naturally, we just labeled him an "Uncle Tom" and protested these decisions as well as demanded that the college divest its stocks in South Africa. My parents, especially my mother, were very angry with me; they were embarrassed that I would show such blatant disrespect for "authorities" and that I could jeopardize my education. During one of the many scoldings I received for this inappropriate behavior, my mother asked why I always had to be the one to stand up and challenge things, even the issues that didn't apply to me. My response to her was that I had to object twice as loud and twice as often because she wouldn't; either she was going to ride in the boat of change or she would be left behind on the shores of oppression and discontent. This response startled her and, though I didn't know until years later, pushed her into thinking about the role of "activism" and her own multicultural journey.

My faculty adviser at Amherst was a Returned Peace Corps Volunteer (RPCV-Micronesia). As well as turning me on to liberation theology through Freire's (1970) *Pedagogy of the Oppressed*,[1] he also taught me about the "toughest job I ever loved." Three weeks after graduation, despite my parents' hope that I would go to law school, I was on a plane to Ghana, West Africa. Before [I left] for the Peace Corps, friends and family would ask me what I thought about moving to an "uncivilized" country. I thought I knew what they meant, though I had no answers. After several months in my small village in Ghana, my host country friends and colleagues finally felt comfortable enough to ask me what it was like to live in an "uncivilized" country—they were referring to the United States. It suddenly became clear to me that often times we speak the same language, use the same words, and we assume that we all mean the same thing. When my family and friends in the United States used the term "uncivilized" to describe Ghana, they were making comments about the less industrialized nature of the country; when my Ghanaian friends and colleagues called the United States uncivilized, they were referring to the need to lock our doors and to never walk alone at night for fear of our personal safety. This taught me to resist assuming that I understand another person's experience well enough to casually ascribe meaning to his or her words.

When I entered the Peace Corps, I had lofty goals; these idealistic plans soon took a backseat to survival, literally and figuratively. It struck me as humorous, at some point in my service, that I felt less like an outsider here (in Ghana) than I did in my own home country. On one of my many travels across the country, I was stranded on the road without food or shelter as nighttime approached. A young Ghanaian man saw me standing by the road and realized my situation. He invited me home to his village where his family gave me a place to sleep, shared what little food they had, and fetched me drinking and bathing water

---

[1] P. Freire, *Pedagogy of the Oppressed* (New York: Continuum, 1970).

from a well nearly a mile away. When I was leaving in the morning, I asked if I could give them something for their troubles. They refused my offer, indicating that they did what anyone would do. With this comment, I became extremely embarrassed and uncomfortable as I imagined how this young "Black man" would be treated in the United States if he were stranded by the road. Stimulated by this incident and many other experiences, my time in Ghana was a time of deep introspection and what I now refer to as my "rebirth." Though returning to the States was more traumatic and painful than moving to Ghana, I knew that I had to return because there was work to do here in the United States....

● ● ● ● ● ● ● ● ● ● ● ● ● ● ● ● ● ● ● ●

Pain and Perseverance:
Perspectives from an Ally

Lisa J. Brandyberry

I grew up as "poor, White, trash" in the middle of the Midwest. The city I lived in was an industrial one—mostly union workers—and always smelled like french fries or rubber. It was mostly White, but there were a fair number of African Americans and Latinos living in various monoracial communities throughout the city. From beginning to end, the schools I went to were integrated, so there is no time I can remember that I didn't know any Black (the term I grew up with) people.

During grade school one of my best friends was Garth, a Black child in my class. We hung around a lot together during lunch hours. I don't remember being upset about the fact that when he and I played together none of my White friends would join us. Some other Black children would come over and join us from time to time. I couldn't have both his friendship and the other White kids' friendships simultaneously.

I felt good around Garth and many of the other Black children. I felt all right around most of the other White children. I was one of few working-class Whites in that particular school. I never had the right clothes because my family shopped at Kmart and hoped for blue-light specials while we were there. My mother gave me haircuts; unfortunately, it wasn't her talent. I was often too loud in my laughter, too crude in my language.

I was also fat, an automatic object of ridicule and harassment for other children. Between being too poor and too fat, there was a lot about me to pick on and many reasons to ostracize me. But, I was never totally rejected. Somehow, something in me was enough to compensate for my "failings," so I always had friends. But with most, if not all, of my White friends, I always knew I was inferior. After the sixth grade, Garth and I were shuffled to different schools, and I didn't think I'd ever see him again.

By my senior year in high school, I had become painfully aware of what made me "inferior" to my classmates. As do many people struggling with internalized oppression, I worked hard to compensate for my failings because I had grown to believe that there was something wrong with me. I worked hard at my classes and did very well; I was always smiling, always willing to do more for others, to laugh at myself when the ridicule would come my way.

My senior year the city closed down one of the other high schools, and the students were bused to different schools. Garth ended up at mine. I saw him one day walking down the hall near my locker, and I started laughing and walking toward him, remembering how good it had felt to have him for a friend. Initially, I thought he didn't recognize me, but he did. He was uncomfortable; he didn't want to be found talking to me. I tried for a few more minutes to talk with him, to find out about what had happened to him. Then I gave up, maybe too soon. After so many years of rejection from others, I was pretty aware of what it felt like to be with someone who didn't want to be with me. We ended with a "see you around" after about 2 minutes of awkwardness. That's the last time I ever spoke to him.

Being a White female, I had learned that my weight was a primary reason for rejection from others, especially males. When Garth seemed not to want to be seen with me, I assumed it was for that reason. I was too fat, too ugly. Who knows? Maybe that was part of it. But now, looking back, I believe it was probably more about race than weight. He had spent the previous 5 years in a predominantly Black school. Who knows how White people had treated him, a Black male adolescent, during those years?

My college life intensified my feelings of being an outsider. I received a scholarship to a small, private liberal arts college where the majority of the students were wealthy and White. There were a few of us paying for school through scholarships, jobs, and loans. There were even fewer Black students on campus, but they were there. All the pain I felt growing up being poor and fat was multiplied at this college, but it was there that I got angry about it. Angry about the privileges of wealthy people who seemed to believe that it was normal to have more than enough money to go to Europe on vacations, to shop for new clothes every weekend, to have cars at their disposal, to have plenty of leisure time because they weren't trying to fit in a job on top of classes and studying.

I tried reaching out to some of the few Black students on campus and became close with one woman, Doris. I cannot begin to imagine what it was like for a young Black woman from Chicago to have to survive in that small Iowa town. After we had struck up a friendship, she started pushing me to go to Black dance clubs in a nearby city. I initially refused—I didn't even go to White dance clubs. But, eventually, I agreed to go. She took charge of what I was going to wear because I couldn't dress like those "White folks," who dressed down to go out. This was time to go all out with jewelry, makeup, and hairstyles. I remember being very nervous on the long drive to the city, scared about being the only White person in the club. I was too embarrassed by this to tell my friend.

Through this experience I got my first taste of being a racial minority. Although this was unpleasant, it was vital in my development. I felt what it was like to have people be angry that I had merely walked into their place, to feel cautious about what I said and how I said it, to feel like a complete outsider, to imagine that everyone in the room must hate me because of my skin color. I am thankful that Doris didn't allow me to disappear into a corner. She pushed me out on the dance floor and pulled me around introducing me to people she knew. By the end of the night I had had a great time, and we went back together several times during the next year.

Graduate school pushed me more than any other experience to really examine myself. I was fortunate to end up in a program that emphasized diversity issues. There were many times it was painful and frightening, because I was challenged to look beyond my "liberal" attitudes to honestly examine myself. I had to go deeper than focusing on all the positive experiences I had had with people of color. I had to examine all the negative messages I had absorbed and determine how much they were still affecting me. I had to learn to see myself as part of the White race, whether I liked it or not.

My family, church, and the media were major influences on me. I went to a church that was entirely White and remember watching how any Black families that would come to visit would have it made clear to them that they weren't welcome. They were treated much like I was when I went to the Black dance club, except they didn't end up having fun and meeting nice people. The stares and whispers didn't end; the shared laughter never started.

I was affected by hearing my brothers talk about "niggers," or more often about "Black bitches." I remember my parents not allowing one of my brothers to go play basketball at a certain court because it wasn't safe around "those" people. I remember my father pointing out what we thought was a garishly painted house and saying "colored" people have no taste. I also remember him making it clear that he didn't want me ever to bring home a Black man. As much as I want to believe I never accepted these attitudes, I know they influenced me and what I believed. I came to believe that "they" were different from "us."

The process of acknowledging what was meant by "us," of owning my own racial heritage, included owning all the history that goes with being White. During this process, the only part of that history I could see was its shame: slavery and genocide of Africans, American Indians, Asians, and Mexicans. There didn't seem to be any horror that wasn't committed in the name of the "manifest destiny" and superiority of European Whites. My reaction was to feel an incredible amount of guilt and shame; I didn't want to be White, didn't want to belong to this group, didn't want to be part of this "us."

Even more painful than that was having to examine how I had benefited from racism. I had to question how I could hold so much anger toward those who were wealthy (or male) because they didn't recognize their privileges but had never acknowledged the privileges I enjoyed from my skin color. It had never crossed my mind that there was a way in which I was privileged. I didn't come from money, I wasn't born beautiful, my family life had been far from perfect, and I had struggled to get where I was.

It wasn't easy to look at the probability that I had struggled less than if I were a person of color. That maybe my White skin had allowed me access to the upper-level college preparatory classes despite being working class, which, in turn, probably increased my test scores, which opened doors to receive academic scholarships and, basically, gave me the opportunity to achieve a level beyond where I was born. I'd like to think that I earned everything I have, but I can no longer tell myself that. I earned some of it, and some of it was very likely given to me because of being White. I have grown to recognize the privileges I receive every day for being White.

It was during this time of feeling overwhelmed with guilt and shame about my race that I worked for a year as the only White person in an all-

African American agency. It was not a job I had applied for or wanted; it was a job I was requested (and eventually forced) to accept. I didn't want the job because I was afraid the staff would hate me. I remember talking with my boss about my fears. He was an African American man with whom I'd worked before and who had requested my placement in the position. He never denied that hostility was possible, but he never let me off the hook regarding my responsibility. He made it clear that it was my place to deal with any prejudice directed at me and that he would support me in that process, but that it was something I would have to face. He also reminded me that it was something minorities face on a daily basis. Again, in having to walk through my fear, I enjoyed a wonderful experience. There was only one person who made it clear she didn't want me there, and even she taught me a valuable lesson. She taught me how subtle sabotage can be. I would miss meetings because I never received the memorandum informing me of them. I wouldn't receive phone messages. I'd receive paperwork late or not at all, and I could *feel* her dislike emanating from her. It was through this experience that I learned to be very hesitant to question the experiences of persons of color who feel they are being discriminated against but can't name anything grossly inappropriate.

My professional life has moved me farther in my journey to overcome racism. A large part of that has come from my close work and friendship with an African American lesbian, Jan. We connected immediately when I came to interview and quickly became friends. We have done numerous programs together focusing in general on oppression issues and, often, specifically on race. We have had to struggle together with issues of race more so than any other issue. What has saved our relationship is our willingness to talk about race, to put our "raggedy selves" on the table.

Many of these struggles have come from my desire not to have race separate us and Jan's desire to keep part of her personal space monoracial; that is, sometimes she just wants to hang with the Black folks. Intellectually, I understand this. I sometimes don't want men around because there is a comfort in groups of women that doesn't exist with men present. It has nothing to do with disliking men; it's simply a different vibe that exists. But on a personal level, it continues to hurt. I struggle with feeling rejected, separated because of my skin color, not seen as the person who is Jan's friend but as a representative of the White race. She knows this because we've talked about it at length. She struggles with it as well because she knows it hurts me, but she wants to have her needs met too.

I now understand why I sometimes feel closer to, and more connected with, some people of color than with many White people. My understanding came through viewing oppression as encompassing all the different groups experiencing it. Having been born into a working-class family, I share many cultural dynamics with people of color also born into this economic sphere. It is often difficult for me, and apparently others, to figure out how to separate race from class. My sensitivity to how I've experienced oppression personally, through class, body size, and gender issues, has allowed me to have some sense of perspective on the pain of racism. Finally, my willingness to admit to and name privileges that I experience because of my race seems to afford me some credibility with people of color....

My conclusion, sadly, is that most people of color simply don't expect much from White people. They don't expect us to be open, to have thought about these issues, to have thought about ourselves (rather than them) in terms of these issues, to be working against racism inside and outside of the therapy room. I believe it is my responsibility, as a member of the majority group, to fight racism. As I benefit and derive increased societal rewards from racism's existence, perhaps my voice may reach other White ears that refuse to listen to the voices of people of color. I believe this as passionately as I believe that men must speak to other men about sexism, that heterosexuals must speak to members of their own group about homophobia, and so on.

Those of us committed to being allies must be willing to persevere in this struggle. People of color do not have the option of ignoring racism and its effects; therefore, we must not ignore it either. We must choose to persevere in the face of rejection, criticism, and suspicion from members of majority and minority groups. Not everyone wants Whites to be involved in this struggle, and I understand this lack of trust. But racism is the problem of the racists, not those who are oppressed by it. As a part of the problem group, I must be involved in eliminating the problem itself.

Some say that no one willingly gives up power, and while members of majority groups refuse to see any benefit to themselves for changing the system (personal and institutional), progress will be slow and painful. But when majority group members can see that *their* lives will improve, *their* accomplishments will be seen as more completely due to merit rather than privilege, that the quality of life will improve for all of us, then, perhaps, change will be possible.

• • • • • • • • • • • • • • • • • • • •

 Discussion Questions

1. What do these five personal statements have in common?
2. Each of these essays considers diversity from a different kind of concern. Are they equally important concerns? If you had to rank them, how would you select the one or two that truly matter? If you find you cannot rank them in importance, why not?
3. Do these authors raise issues of political correctness? Or is that too narrow a way of viewing their experiences?

4. What other groups—minority or majority—might put forward similar experiences and draw similar conclusions from them?

5. Federal, state, and local laws now identify specific groups of people as "protected classes." These usually include groups defined by characteristics shared in common such as religion, race, gender, physical disability, and Vietnam-era veteran status. Should these be legally "protected" classes? Explain.

Suggestions for Your Journal

Most of us identify with many different groups. Thus a single individual college student might consider herself a member of all the following: her family, her church, her nationality, her race, her athletic team, her first-year class, her sorority, her armed forces unit, and many more. What groups do you identify with? How have you come to develop that many-faceted sense of identity? Rank those groups in order, from the ones you feel most closely tied to, to the ones that seem most distant to your feelings.

Have you ever felt that others discriminated against you as a member of some group? Write about that feeling and how you dealt with it. Is there a lesson in your personal experience for future action?

A university is a specialized kind of institution. In a journal entry or essay, write about the ways in which the specific character of a university does or should have implications for issues of discrimination.

I Have a Dream

Martin Luther King Jr.

On August 28, 1963, Dr. Martin Luther King Jr., the preeminent civil rights leader in America during the 1950s and 1960s, delivered this speech as the keynote address of the March on Washington for Civil Rights. His widow, Coretta Scott King, has said of that occasion: "At that moment, it seemed as if the kingdom of God appeared. But it lasted for only a moment." This speech is one of the enduring documents of 20th-century American history.

• • • • • • • • • • • • • • • • •

I am happy to join with you today in what will go down in history as the greatest demonstration for freedom in the history of our nation.

Five score years ago, a great American, in whose symbolic shadow we stand today, signed the *Emancipation Proclamation.* This momentous decree came as a great beacon light of hope to millions of Negro slaves who had been seared in the flames of withering injustice. It came as a joyous daybreak to end the long night of their captivity.

But one hundred years later, the Negro still is not free; one hundred years later, the life of the Negro is still sadly crippled by the manacles of segregation and the chains of discrimination; one hundred years later, the Negro lives on a lonely island of poverty in the midst of a vast ocean of material prosperity; one hundred years later, the Negro is still *languished* in the corners of American society and finds himself an exile in his own land.

So we've come here today to dramatize a shameful condition. In a sense we've come to our nation's capital to cash a check. When the architects of our republic wrote the magnificent words of the Constitution and the Declaration of Independence, they were signing a *promissory note* to which every American was to fall heir. This note was a promise that all men, yes, black men as well as white men, would be guaranteed the *unalienable* rights of life, liberty, and the pursuit of happiness.

It is obvious today that America has defaulted on this promissory note insofar as her citizens of color are concerned. Instead of honoring this sacred obligation, America has given the Negro people a bad check, a check which has come back marked "insufficient funds." But we refuse to believe that the bank of justice is bankrupt. We refuse to believe that there are insufficient funds in the great vaults of opportunity of this nation. And so we've come to cash this check, a check that will give us upon demand the riches of freedom and the security of justice.

We have also come to this hallowed spot to remind America of the fierce urgency of now. This is no time to engage in the luxury of cooling off or to take the tranquilizing drug of gradualism. Now is the time to make real the promises of democracy; now is the time to rise from the dark and desolate valley of segregation to the sunlit path of racial justice; now is the time to lift our nation from the quicksands of racial injustice to the solid rock of brotherhood; now is the time to make justice a reality for all of God's children. It would be fatal for the nation to overlook the urgency of the moment. This sweltering summer of the Negro's legitimate discontent will not pass until there is an invigorating autumn of freedom and equality.

Nineteen sixty-three is not an end, but a beginning. And those who hope that the Negro needed to blow off steam and will now be content, will have a rude awakening if the nation returns to business as usual.

There will be neither rest nor tranquillity in America until the Negro is granted his citizenship rights. The whirlwinds of revolt will continue to shake the foundations of our nation until the bright day of justice emerges.

But there is something that I must say to my people who stand on the warm threshold which leads into the palace of justice. In the process of gaining our rightful place we must not be guilty of wrongful deeds.

Let us not seek to satisfy our thirst for freedom by drinking from the cup of bitterness and hatred. We must forever conduct our struggle on the high plane of dignity and discipline. We must not allow our creative protest to degenerate into physical violence. Again and again we must rise to the majestic heights of meeting physical force with soul force.

The marvelous new militancy which has engulfed the Negro community must not lead us to a distrust of all white people, for many of our white brothers, as evidenced by their presence here today, have come to realize that their destiny is tied up with our destiny, and they have come to realize that their freedom is inextricably bound to our freedom. We cannot walk alone.

And as we walk, we must make the pledge that we shall always march ahead. We cannot turn back. There are those who are asking the devotees of civil rights, "When will you be satisfied?" We can never be satisfied as long as the Negro is the victim of the unspeakable horrors of police brutality.

We can never be satisfied as long as our bodies, heavy with the fatigue of travel, cannot gain lodging in the motels of the highways and the hotels of the cities. We cannot be satisfied as long as the Negro's basic mobility is from a smaller ghetto to a larger one.

We can never be satisfied as long as our children are stripped of their selfhood and robbed of their dignity by signs stating "for whites only." We cannot be satisfied as long as a Negro in Mississippi cannot vote and a Negro in New York believes he has nothing for which to vote. No, we are not satisfied, and we will not be satisfied until justice rolls down like waters and righteousness like a mighty stream.

I am not unmindful that some of you have come here out of excessive trials and tribulation. Some of you have come fresh from narrow jail cells. Some of you have come from areas where your quest for freedom left you battered by the storms of persecution and staggered by the winds of police brutality. You have been the veterans of creative suffering. Continue to work with the faith that unearned suffering is redemptive.

Go back to Mississippi; go back to Alabama; go back to South Carolina; go back to Georgia; go back to Louisiana; go back to the slums and ghettos of the northern cities, knowing that somehow this situation can and will be changed. Let us not wallow in the valley of despair.

I say to you today, my friends, that even though we must face the difficulties of today and tomorrow, I still have a dream. It is a dream deeply rooted in the American dream. I have a dream that one day this nation will rise up, live out the true meaning of its creed—we hold these truths to be self-evident, that all men are created equal.

I have a dream that one day on the red hills of Georgia, sons of former slaves and sons of former slave-owners will be able to sit down together at the table of brotherhood.

I have a dream that one day, even the state of Mississippi, a state sweltering with the heat of injustice, sweltering with the heat of oppression, will be transformed into an oasis of freedom and justice.

I have a dream my four little children will one day live in a nation where they will be not be judged by the color of their skin but by the content of their character. I have a dream today!

I have a dream that one day, down in Alabama, with its vicious racists, with its governor having his lips dripping with the words of interposition and nullification, that one day, right there in Alabama, little black boys and black girls will be able to join hands with little white boys and white girls as sisters and brothers. I have a dream today!

I have a dream that one day every valley shall be exalted, every hill and mountain shall be made low, the rough places shall be made plain, and the crooked places will be made straight, and the glory of the Lord will be revealed and all flesh shall see it together.

This is our hope. This is the faith that I go back to the South with.

With this faith we will be able to hew out of the mountain of despair a stone of hope. With this faith we will be able to transform the jangling discords of our nation into a beautiful symphony of brotherhood.

With this faith we will be able to work together, to pray together, to struggle together, to go to jail together, to stand up for freedom together, knowing that we will be free one day. This will be the day when all of God's children will be able to sing with new meaning—"my country 'tis of thee; sweet land of liberty; of thee I sing; land where my father died, land of the pilgrim's pride; from every mountainside, let freedom ring"—and if America is to be a great nation, this must become true.

So let freedom ring from the prodigious hilltops of New Hampshire.

Let freedom ring from the mighty mountains of New York.

Let freedom ring from the heightening Alleghenies of Pennsylvania.

Let freedom ring from the snow-capped Rockies of Colorado.

Let freedom ring from the curvaceous slopes of California.
But not only that.
Let freedom ring from Stone Mountain of Georgia.
Let freedom ring from Lookout Mountain of Tennessee.
Let freedom ring from every hill and molehill of Mississippi.
From every mountainside, let freedom ring.

And when we allow freedom to ring, when we let it ring from every village and every hamlet, from every state and every city, we will be able to speed up that day when all of God's children—black men and white men, Jews and Gentiles, Protestants and Catholics—will be able to join hands and sing in the words of the old Negro spiritual, "Free at last, free at last; thank God Almighty, we are free at last."

• •

 Vocabulary

As you think about this essay, these definitions may be helpful to you:
1. **Emancipation Proclamation**   issued by President Abraham Lincoln in 1862 freeing all slaves in all territory still at war with the Union
2. **languished**   suffering neglect
3. **promissory note**   a pledge to pay a debt; an "I.O.U."
4. **unalienable**   incapable of being surrendered or transferred

 Discussion Questions

1. What does King mean by the phrase "the tranquilizing drug of gradualism"?
2. King argues that physical force must be countered by "soul force." What does he mean?
3. Using the language of his own time, King speaks of "the Negro." Today's authors would probably not use this word. Why?
4. Discuss the ways in which repetition of key words and phrases plays a part in making this an effective speech.
5. As a Christian minister, King drew heavily on the language of the Bible, which was natural to him. What effect does including such language ("we will not be satisfied until justice rolls down like waters and righteousness like a mighty stream," "every valley shall be exalted, every hill and mountain shall be made low") add to this speech?

 Suggestions for Your Journal

Write about the social or political cause for which you would be willing to demonstrate in a public way. In your comments, describe how you came to feel as strongly as you do about this cause.

Martin Luther King Jr. is closely related intellectually and historically to another great social leader, India's Mahatma Gandhi. Both were known for a form of, in King's words, "militant nonviolence." King expressed his admiration for Gandhi by arguing: "We must forever conduct our struggle on the high plane of dignity and discipline. We must not allow our creative protest to degenerate into physical violence." Write an entry in which you agree or disagree with King's statement.

Affirmative Action
and Multiculturalism

David Bruce Ingram and Jennifer A. Parks

David Bruce Ingram is a professor of Philosophy at Loyola University in Chicago. He is
the author of 4 books on philosophy and ethics and 23 books in the area of business
ethics. Jennifer A. Parks is an assistant professor of Philosophy at Loyola University and
the co-director of programs in healthcare ethics.

I still get misty-eyed when I read Martin Luther King Jr.'s famous "I Have a
Dream" speech, which he delivered in front of the Lincoln Memorial on August 28, 1963, at the height of the Civil Rights Movement. Here's King, dreaming
about the day when people in America "will not be judged by the color of their
skin but by the content of their character"; when "the jangling discords of our
nation will be transformed into a beautiful symphony of brotherhood"; when
"black men and white men, Jews and Gentiles, Catholics and Protestants, will be
able to join hands and to sing in the words of the old Negro spiritual, 'Free at
last, free at last; thank God Almighty, we are free at last.' "

We've come a long way since King delivered those mighty words. We've
outlawed segregation and legal discrimination and our society has made tremendous strides in racial healing. But I wonder whether we have gone far
enough in eradicating racial injustice and bringing about equal opportunity for
all. Blacks as a whole lag far behind whites economically (the typical black family has one-tenth of the assets of a typical white family); they continue to be
underrepresented in legislatures and on corporate boards; they have a lower life
expectancy and suffer a higher rate of infant mortality; and they continue to
face discrimination at all levels of life, from police profiling to discrimination in
securing loans and real estate "red-lining."

In Census 2000, the U.S. Government tried to take a nose count of all
Americans, including asking each of us to identify what race and ethnicity we
belong to. Persons were asked if they are Hispanic or not, and then they were
invited to pick one or more (up to six) racial categories that best described
them. What was remarkable about this approach was that it recognized that racial identification is not an all-or-nothing affair—none of us, in fact, is racially
pure when it comes right down to it. Furthermore, it *tacitly* recognized that race
itself is largely a matter of personal preference.

Not so long ago Americans thought that race was an all-or-nothing affair—something fixed in nature, having to do with the blood you inherited from
your parents. For example, among whites it was assumed that if you inherited
even a drop of "black" blood from, say a great-great-grandparent, then you were

totally black. Modern genetics has totally refuted this biological notion of race. A person's racial features express his genetic make-up, which in turn is the product of recombining the genes he inherited from his parents. Depending on how his genes are recombined, persons may or may not look very much like their parents. Genetically speaking persons who look racially alike are as different as, or more different from, each other than persons who don't look racially alike.

If race doesn't exist in any biological sense, should people still think of themselves racially? Perhaps in an ideal society they wouldn't. Racial distinctions are a modern invention. Prior to the European conquest of the New World, people divided themselves mainly on the basis of religion and culture. Religious and cultural conversion on the part of the heathen/barbarian was almost always possible. The only differences that were regarded as natural were differences between the sexes and, to a far lesser extent, differences between nobles and commoners.

So you see, we didn't always divide the world along racial lines. Racial distinctions were invented to justify the enslavement of Africans and Native Americans by Europeans. Perhaps in an ideal world, differences in skin pigmentation would matter about as much as differences in eye pigmentation.

We often think of cultural differences as forming the basis for ethnic identifications and biological differences as forming the basis for racial identifications. Reality is more complicated than this. Members of the same ethnic group often share overlapping physical features; and members of the same racial group often share overlapping cultural traits. This isn't surprising, since both physical and cultural traits are passed down from generation to generation, the former through genes, the latter through *socialization.*

If race and ethnicity are so closely linked together, then it seems that what applies to one ought to apply to the other. For instance, if we think that an ideal world would be a world without racial distinctions, then it seems that we should also think that an ideal world would be a world without ethnic differences. In fact, if you consider some of the changes that would have to happen in order for racial thinking to disappear, such as complete residential and occupational integration of all races—it becomes clear that these changes would have deep cultural repercussions as well. For many aspects of ethnic culture are also cultivated in relatively tight-knit and geographically bonded racial communities.

This takes us to a very hard question. Is complete racial and ethnic integration a desirable ideal to strive for? We think that racial integration is desirable for fighting racism. However, even after the elimination of legal segregation we see that many blacks prefer to live in black communities because they feel more welcome there. Even after all traces of racism are gone, some blacks may still prefer to live among blacks for cultural reasons. For example, although certain aspects of the African American spiritual tradition can be (and have been) transported into all cultures, the black church as the bedrock of a distinctive black identity can't be. Some blacks might still prefer to live in predominantly black communities in order to preserve this identity.

The problem of integration suggests two ways of fighting discrimination against religious, ethnic, and racial groups:

- anti-racism
- multiculturalism

Anti-racism targets racial segregation, and so promotes the aim of racial integration at all levels of life. It reminds us of our common humanity, and the universal rights we share with all others. Its ideal is that of a raceless society, where physical differences between people are as insignificant as differences in eye color.

Multiculturalism, by contrast, targets cultural domination—or the attempt by a dominant culture to eradicate, assimilate, or otherwise integrate subordinate cultures to the point where they no longer exist as distinct and independent. As a positive agenda, multiculturalism encourages us to respect all cultures as equals. Unlike anti-racism, it sees positive value in preserving and promoting differences, even if this requires granting special exemptions and privileges to minority cultures that are endangered.

So where does affirmative action fit into all this? Affirmative action initially meant actively recruiting qualified minorities—mainly blacks. Good faith recruitment policies didn't work very well, so the government asked businesses to set deadlines for hiring a certain number of blacks. This didn't work very well either, so the government started imposing quotas—a set number or percentage of jobs—that had to be filled by blacks. Along the way, women and other minorities were added to the list of protected classes. Courts have since ruled that the use of affirmative action quotas in college admissions is unconstitutional and that their use in government contracting is highly suspect.

Affirmative action now effectively protects most of the American population. In 1996 the Clinton administration expanded the list of affirmative action beneficiaries of federal contracts to include small businesses owned by women, the disabled, and the socially disadvantaged, in addition to those owned by blacks, Latinos, Indians, Asians, Eskimos, and Native Hawaiians.

In order for affirmative action to be an effective tool for leveling the playing field it must be administered in a way that is sensitive to individual differences in comparative disadvantage. This will be difficult to do, although not entirely impossible. For example, being a woman today is much less of a disadvantage that it was thirty years ago (in fact, women have made the greatest strides in educational and economic advancement of any group and now comprise a solid majority of all students attending institutions of higher education). Being a Native American resident of an impoverished reservation, by contrast is still (at least in most cases) a very serious disadvantage.

Does affirmative action elevate the less qualified over the better qualified? Yes, if you think that the only relevant qualifications for measuring future job performance are things like where you went to school, what grades you got, and how well you performed on standardized tests. Surely these qualifications matter. The question is, how much?

Pronounced differences in test scores and grades may sometimes predict different levels of job performance. In some cases, grades and test scores might be irrelevant—you don't need to be a literary genius or mathematics whiz to be a good electrician. Other kinds of qualifications—such as speech, appearance, friendliness, and so on—are more subjective, and therefore more prone to racial biases. Experience is an important qualification but it, too, can sometimes mask true ability. And let's not forget that some qualifications are not at all related to future performance. Princeton University admits 40 percent of all admissions applicants whose parents were former students of the university in comparison to just 15 percent of the regular applicant pool. Last but not least, race itself might be a relevant qualification when filling a high-profile post in a Black Studies Program at a university; for typically, such positions involve role modeling and mentoring as well as teaching and research.

Affirmative action is indeed a strategy for "leveling the playing field," but unlike past forms of racial discrimination, it doesn't try to accomplish this by dragging one segment of the population down to the level of oppressed populations. Rather, its aim is positive: to compensate for the continuing effects of sexual and racial discrimination. In other words, its aim is to elevate the oppressed populations to the current, privileged status enjoyed by all the rest.

 Vocabulary

As you think about this essay, these definitions may be helpful to you:
1. **tacitly**   expressed silently or understood without the use of words
2. **socialization**   the process of becoming part of a group and fitting in with that group's culture and values

 Discussion Questions

1. Ingram and Parks ask what they consider to be "a very hard question"—namely, "Is complete racial and ethnic integration a desirable ideal to strive for?" How do they answer that question? How would you answer it?
2. In your experience, is it true, as Ingram and Parks assert, that "experience is an important qualification but it ... can sometimes mask true ability"? Give some examples to support your response.

3. Ingram and Parks comment parenthetically that "being a woman today is much less of a disadvantage that it was thirty years ago. In fact, women have made the greatest strides in educational and economic advancement of any group and now comprise a solid majority of all students attending institutions of higher education." Assuming that this claim is true, can you identify some reasons that such a considerable change should have happened?

 ## Suggestions for Your Journal

It is difficult for students just entering their college years to imagine what was true of students at the same age 20 or 30 years ago. Interview someone who is at least 20 years older than you are and a college graduate. Summarize their sense of how the world has changed in the intervening years.

Ingram and Parks suggest that there have been improvements related to many of the social problems they talk about and that Dr. Martin Luther King Jr. addressed in his famous 1963 speech "I Have a Dream." Is there still a need, in your view, for affirmative action programs? How do they affect you personally? How would discontinuing affirmative action affect you?

UNIT SUMMARY

The essays in this unit discuss some of the conditions necessary to ensure that the pursuit of truth, identified in Unit 6 as the defining characteristic of a university, can be carried out by all participants in the university community without interference. Some observers believe that university faculty and students are just trying to be "politically correct" when they acknowledge and try to protect diversity. However, the essays in this unit are not grounded in the relatively recent notion of "political correctness." Instead, these essays address contemporary topics of concern within the framework of a vision of all individuals exercising their freedom to express ideas—a freedom that is essential to, and therefore precious within, the university.

Summary Questions

1. Were you surprised by any of the conclusions that these writers defended? How do they differ from your own current, or previous, beliefs?
2. Can you give examples of finding value in diversity—examples that have made a difference in the way you think or behave?
3. Many people would comment that visions of the future like that presented by Martin Luther King Jr. are attractive and useful as a goal but too idealistic to be realized in a complex society. Do you agree? How might we go about preparing the kind of world that King envisioned in his dream?

Suggested Writing Assignments

1. Do you tend to make judgments about any group of people (for example, a nationality group, a fraternity or sorority, or a religious group) based on membership in that group? If so, write a short essay explaining why you do this. Are there any times when *group* characteristics appropriately outweigh individual character?
2. Have you ever been the object of bigotry? Write an essay describing how you were singled out and suggest a plan for responding to such behavior.
3. Whose job is it to ensure that, within a university, people are judged only on the basis of their ability? Write an essay identifying those who need to act on this matter and specify the most important steps they should take.

Suggested Readings

Bowen, William G., and Derek Bok. *The Shape of the River: Long-Term Consequences of Considering Race in College and University Admissions.* Princeton, NJ: Princeton University Press, 1998.

Fisk, E. B. "The Undergraduate Hispanic Experience." *Change* (May/June 1988), 29–33.

Haley, Alex, and Malcolm X. *The Autobiography of Malcolm X.* New York: Grove Press, 1976.

Halpern, J. M., and L. Nguyen-Hong-Nhiem, eds. *The Far East Comes Near: Autobiographical Accounts of Southeast Asian Students in America.* Amherst: University of Massachusetts Press, 1989.

What Should I Know About Careers?

According to many students, one of the main purposes of acquiring a college degree is to prepare for a career. And yet this process remains a mystery to many students. The concepts of work, job, and career, although often used interchangeably, are very different. Work can be defined as an activity that accomplishes a task. Career is a lifelong process that usually includes many jobs. Work in our culture is often synonymous with one's identity. Even small children are asked what they "want to do" when they grow up. By the time students enter college, they have some idea of general areas of study they might want to explore or pursue. How work is valued by the individual shapes the perceptions of and attitudes about the meaning of a career as the exploration and planning process is engaged.

In their book *Careerism and Intellectualism Among College Students,* Katchadourian and Boli state that there has been an increase in careerism among college students

Our road to success is currently under construction.

—Anonymous

233

since the late 1970s. This trend has been documented in surveys of entering first-year students who indicated that "becoming an authority in my field" and "being well off financially" were of greater importance to them than other nonwork-related goals. Students' choices of major have also changed. Whereas students wanting business degrees peaked in the late 1980s, other majors, such as the health professions and computer science, have increased.

Students entering college in the 21st century face a bewildering array of issues concerning their choice of career. Economic shifts, societal and environmental concerns, and the increased complexities of business because of new technologies create a volatile job market. Career-planning professionals encourage students to assess their personal strengths and limitations and base their choices on this knowledge rather than rely on external forces over which they have little control.

The readings in this unit represent a wide array of opinions and attitudes toward work and related issues. Do you expect to "do the work you love" after graduation? If so, Boldt explains how you will be part of a new social movement. Goal setting is difficult for many people but is a critical aspect of career planning. Lore provides some specific ways to accomplish this important task. Sherry and Ballard both write about searching for a job. Sherry writes about the process and Ballard provides some practical insights into how to prepare throughout the college years for the day after graduation.

Peggy Simonsen, looking ahead, points out that traditional career paths no longer dominate the future of new graduates. She describes career patterns for the new century that will require different strategies for success.

All these thought-provoking ideas about work will offer a sense of how important identifying one's work values and purpose is. The college years are a time to explore, gather information, test alternatives, and finally make the first of many career decisions. Although most students approach this process from a very practical perspective, the readings in this unit should also help you think about your personal definition of work and how it will influence your ultimate career decisions.

Doing the Work You Love

Laurence G. Boldt

Laurence G. Boldt is a nationally known writer and career consultant based in the
San Francisco Bay Area. He has given speeches and conducted workshops across
the country and has been featured in such publications as *Newsweek* and *New
Age Journal.*

A powerful new social movement is transforming the way people live and
work. For years, virtually invisible to those not directly involved, this movement has been quietly building momentum. Today its impact is no longer in
doubt. In recent years, it has become the subject of a spate of newspaper and
magazine articles and has been featured in a variety of television and radio programs. Truly grass-roots, this is a social movement without political action committees, paid lobbyists, or effective national or international organization. It is a
bottoms-up movement in which people are transforming society not by mass
political action but by reorienting their own lives. It is a broad-based movement
affecting men and women of all ages, races, and socioeconomic backgrounds
in many nations.

At the heart of this emerging social movement is a fundamental redefini-
tion of work and success. For a variety of reasons, people's expectations of what
their work life can and should be have been dramatically and irrevocably altered in recent years. While throughout most of the twentieth century, work was
viewed principally as a means to an end—be it survival, security, status, or
power—today it is increasingly being valued on its own terms. More and more
people are coming to expect that their experience of work should include
meaning, challenge, self-expression, and joy. More and more, people are looking
for ways to integrate their values and talents into their everyday experience of
work. And more and more, they are finding them—discovering that it really is
possible to earn their way in the world without compromising, indeed by celebrating, the promptings of their hearts and souls. The cat is out of the bag and
there is no putting it back. The "work-for-love" movement has caught on.

Today, many people are waking up to the need for a new, more conscious
approach to work and career. For some, this awakening is coming principally
from their internal alarm, from a deep yearning to express their inborn talents,
gifts, and abilities. Others are motivated primarily by an external alarm. They feel
called to serve humanity, to make a meaningful difference by spreading joy
and/or eliminating suffering in the world. For still others, the awakening is coming from the irritating buzz of the snooze alarm—the recognition that the workplace has fundamentally changed and that, as a result, they must assert greater
control over their own destinies.

In the final two decades of the twentieth century, the entire landscape of work and career changed dramatically. As the president of a leading executive recruiting firm put it, "The way people approached their careers in the past is history. It will never, never, never return." These historic changes in the job environment represent the snooze alarm, the final wake-up call to take responsibility and begin shaping your own career destiny. For today's worker, this alarm is ignored at great peril. The chime of the snooze alarm is loud and clear, ringing out: THE WORKPLACE IS CHANGING . . . THE WORKPLACE IS CHANGING . . . THE WORKPLACE IS CHANGING. There are a number of factors driving these changes. We will explore some of the more important ones below.

Globalization: The global marketplace means different things to and for different people. What it means for American workers is that they are in direct competition with data processors in India and Ireland, with manufacturing labor in Mexico and Indonesia, and with technical experts in Korea and Taiwan. Today, those working in low-skilled manufacturing jobs and in related support industries have borne the brunt of the pain associated with the globalization of trade. As the workforce in the developing world continues to become better educated and as technology continues to break down the barriers of distance, college-educated white collar workers can expect to experience in this new century the kinds of job losses that their less-educated blue collar counterparts did in the last two decades of the twentieth.

Merger Mania: Today, big business is more concentrated than ever. In the last twenty years, the banking, insurance, pharmaceutical, media, publishing, transportation, healthcare, utility and retail industries—to name only a few of the more visible ones—have seen merger on top of merger. Many of these mergers have united companies across international boundaries. For workers, mergers and acquisitions are virtually synonymous with layoffs. Moreover, mergers spark more mergers, which in turn bring even more layoffs. Even companies that manage to avoid being gobbled up by bigger ones feel increased pressure to slash labor costs in order to remain competitive.

The Electronic Revolution: The new electronic technologies are significantly less labor-intensive in manufacturing, management, data collection, and processing than were the old technologies of the industrial era. In some fields, one person with a computer can do the work formerly done by half a dozen. In other fields, new technologies are on their way to replacing some positions altogether. Bank tellers are being replaced with automated tellers; receptionists, with voice mail; gas station attendants, with self-serve and electronic pay-at-the-pump sites. In the early years of the twenty-first century, the electronic revolution is expected to make an even greater impact on middle-management white collar workers.

Out-sourcing: Another trend reshaping the workplace is the rise in temporary, part-time, and independent contractor work. Today, nearly 25 percent of the U.S. workforce, or one in four American workers, is a temporary, part-time, or contract worker. Providing a variety of services to large organizations has been one of the major growth areas for new small business. At the same time, the out-sourcing phenomenon has displaced thousands from once-secure jobs within large corporations and will likely continue to do so.

Mass Retail: In many small towns across America, factory outlets and discount superstores have all but eliminated local retailing. In urban centers and small towns throughout America and Europe, large superstores, factory outlets, or franchise chain stores have replaced independent bookstores, hardware stores, office supply stores, grocery stores, barbershops, restaurants, and locally-owned department stores. In many sectors, the small independent retailer is going the way of the small independent farmer. While mass retail has eliminated many small businesses, it has also been a major source of new jobs. Unfortunately, many of these jobs are part-time, low-paying, and not particularly challenging or rewarding.

Coming all at once, these and other trends have in a few short years radically and *inexorably* transformed the American workplace. While echoes from the snooze alarm are sending waves of anxiety and fear throughout the modern workplace, they are also providing the impetus for a variety of creative responses. Fifteen or twenty years ago, the individual with the dream of pursuing a more independent career path looked at the risks involved versus the security of their corporate jobs and decided that they were better off staying where they were. Today, many people are recognizing that it is at least as risky *not* to follow their dreams and begin charting their own destinies. Whether we choose to work for ourselves or for the small business organizations that are providing most of the new jobs, the qualities necessary for success are precisely those that doing the work one loves is likely to possess, namely: self-motivation, a high level of energy, a willingness to learn and grow, and *perseverance*.

While we cannot predict with any certainty how the nature of work will change in the coming century, it seems at this point inevitable that the work-for-love movement will continue to grow. Certainly the three wake-up calls discussed above will go on sounding, and there is every reason to believe that people will go on listening to them. This is truly an exciting time to be alive and one pregnant with possibilities. By making the commitment to follow your heart and do the work you love, you are part of a truly historic social transformation, one that has the potential to make the world a more just, humane, and beautiful place. Best of luck on your quest!

• •

 Vocabulary

As you think about this essay, these definitions may be helpful to you:
1. **inexorably**   relentlessly
2. **perseverance**   steadfastness

 Discussion Questions

1. How has the fundamental definition of work and success changed in the last 10 or 20 years, according to Boldt?
2. What is the "work-for-love" movement that the author describes?
3. What are some of the societal forces at work prompting a change in attitude toward taking control of one's own destiny?

 Suggestions for Your Journal

Record some of your thoughts about your future career. What type of work would you love to do? Is it different from the type of career you are currently preparing for educationally? Discuss how they are the same or different. The author indicates that the qualities necessary for success are self-motivation, a high level of energy, a willingness to learn and grow, and perseverance. Which of these qualities do you have? Which ones do you need to develop further? Do you think Boldt's movement survived the bursting of the dot-com bubble?

How to Get There from Here

Nicholas Lore

- Nicholas Lore is the founder of Rockport Institute, an international career counseling
- network that has coached thousands through first-time career and midcareer decisions.
- He has worked with students, business executives, artists and musicians, government
- officials, technical people, support staff, and professionals in all fields. Nicholas Lore has
- been commended for excellence by two U.S. presidents.

I once saw a TV news feature story about two professional golfers. They were the same age, looked alike, had gone to PGA school together, each had 2.2 children, cute wives, were best friends, and had the same stroke average. Two people could not be more alike unless they were twins. One of them had won several major tournaments that year and was raking in high sums of money. The other was working as a golf pro at a country club and had never won anything, even though he had participated in tournaments. The point of the feature story was supposed to be something about the fickle finger of fate. But as they were interviewed, it became evident that there was one big difference between the two golfers. The winning golfer, when asked about his future goals, said his goal was to be the best and most successful golfer in the world. The other fellow said his vision for the future was to make a living playing golf. One had created an extraordinary vision for the future and was going for it 200 percent. The other was happy to putt around in the comfort zone.

It does not make you a better person to have bigger goals. It simply makes life a more exciting game that stretches your very being. You may be happy in the comfort zone. You may just want to have a decent career, 2.2 kids, retire to Florida, and watch TV until one day you don't wake up. If so, I suggest that you really swing out and set some goals that will create an exciting vision for your future. Whatever you want, being clear about your goals makes it much more likely that you will get it.

Principles of Goal Setting

1. Understand that there are three different levels of goals. At the highest level are big comprehensive *meta-goals*. The word *meta* means "transcending or more comprehensive." These goals usually express large, abstract ideas, like health, contribution, love, ecstasy, pleasure, security, self-expression, prosperity, satisfaction. From these meta-level goals flow *specific goals*. Falling under the broad comprehensive goal of prosperity, you might set specific goals concerning income, saving, investment, retirement, controlling impulse buying, etc. Finally, at the lowest level are the items on your to-do list. Some of these are *action steps*. They are the nitty-gritty, step-by-step plans to make your dreams come true.

Other lower-level goals could be thought of as mileposts. They are markers along the path to completing a project that fulfills a goal. They tell how far down the trail you have gone.

Most people's meta-goals are not something they created. In fact, most of us have had no say in choosing our meta-level goals. Remember that advertising psychologists say that what motivates us is looking good, feeling good, being right, feeling safe, and avoiding pain. With the exception of "being right," these are powerful *motivators* for our nonhuman friends as well. They are already programmed into our internal wiring. If "feeling safe" is a meta-goal, you may have some choice about how to realize this goal, choices about what "safety" means to you, for example. But, you don't have any more choice about the goal itself than you do about your shadow. Like your shadow, meta-goals follow you around everywhere. You can live in the dark and deny they exist, but they will spring forth every time the light shines on you. Many of these higher-level goals will be the same as some of your most important and deepest held values. Once you are consciously aware of the extraordinarily powerful role these meta-goals play in your life, new possibilities arise: perhaps you could start to invent some new ones, alter, transform and even abandon old ones.

The most conscious, evolved people create their own meta-goals rather than just run the software program built into them. For example, Gandhi's nature was deeply sensual, which he abandoned because he thought this meta-goal detracted from his life's purpose. Imagine what people would have thought if he spoke and spun from the grounds of the Himalayan Hedonism Hideaway. When you create a purpose for your life, what you are actually doing is creating the highest form of meta-goal possible. Living from a purpose is essentially surrendering to a meta-goal that you invented which you elevate to a higher position than the ones already programmed in, and which serves some purpose larger than your self-fulfillment.

2. Make your goals correspond with what you really want. If your goals represent what you think you should want, what would please your parents or your cultural identity but are not authentically your own, you will have great difficulty achieving them. Align your goals with your deepest principles and values and with your most genuine dreams and desires. Wanting something passionately does not necessarily mean you must have it. If you do not have the passion, the desire for something, don't turn it into a goal. Life is short. You don't have time to waste going after things you really don't want.

3. Create goals for every important area of your life. Remember that each part of your life is *interwoven* with everything else. Don't stop with career goals. Create goals for your relationships, your hobby, or your community involvement. Make up some health and fitness goals, satisfaction and well-being goals. Parents should not make up goals for their children but should encourage them to become masterful at setting their own goals.

4. Understand that well-founded goals contain some specific ingredients that boost their effectiveness. Fuzziness is the enemy of productivity that moves your goals along to completion. When you are slogging through waist-deep mud along the path to fulfilling a goal, it is amazingly easy to forget why you were in the mud in the first place. All of your goals should be *highly specific*. Whenever possible, make your goals *measurable*. If they are not measurable, how will you be able to tell if you are achieving them? Don't worry about attempting to make your meta-goals measurable. They are usually too abstract to hone into measurability. Goals should have a *definite completion date*, if possible. The whole reason to set goals is to have something specific to shoot for. Goals are an active intention, not a prediction. They focus your energy and direct your attention toward things you desire to accomplish.

5. Write them down. Your brain is a bad place to keep your goals. Goals are more valuable than anything you have, except your health. Your brain is too much like a pocket with many holes in it, too susceptible to hypnotism, *somnambulism*, and storms of uncertainty and doubt to be the best place to store your goals. If you manage a Goals List you will be able to simply cross off a goal you have accomplished or are abandoning. If you keep your goals in your head, you will have to deal with your psychology and your memory in addition to your goals.

6. Create both short-term and long-term goals. Effective goal setting involves creating a comprehensive life plan as well as deciding what to accomplish next week or tomorrow.

7. Manage your Goals List. Revisit your goals often. At the beginning of each year, go over your long-term goals, create new ones, revise the existing ones, and toss out the ones you decide not to aim for. Go over the goals you set for the year just ending. Complete each goal by marking it done, transferring it to a time in the future, or declaring it complete as it is, even if you failed to get the result you wanted. Go through the same process at the end of every month and every week, focusing on goals you set for those time periods. The most effective people I know complete their Goals List for the day that is ending, create new goals for the next day, and then spend a few minutes looking for ways to improve their efforts tomorrow.

8. Set goals that take you as far as you are willing to stretch to make your wildest dreams come true, but not farther. Most people set goals that do not require much of a stretch. If they wanted to buy a house, they would go after reasonable goals, such as features that fit their price range. Their main criterion is that their goals be sensible, reasonable. If you want a reasonable degree of success and satisfaction, by all means, create reasonable goals. If you want more than that, being reasonable will constantly block your path.

When you come up with a good idea for a possible goal, treat it with respect. Whether it is an idea that solves one of the world's great problems or is just an idea for something wild to do with a friend this weekend, it doesn't matter. Your ideas deserve your respect because they are the output of your internal creative nature. Without them, life would just creep on and on and on. Make a conscious decision about what to do with each idea. Are you going to commit to making it happen, abandon it, delegate it, forget about it, or what? You want your accomplishment cycles to get off to a good start, to be intentional, not accidental.

If you sit down and write out your goals, you will wind up with a nice list. If you want your life to rock and roll, begin to manage the entire cycle of accomplishing those goals. Choosing your future career is a project that is an important part of that accomplishment cycle.

 Vocabulary

As you think about this essay, these definitions may be helpful to you:
1. **meta-goal**   a goal that is transcending, comprehensive
2. **motivators**   incentives or influences that get you started and keep you going
3. **interwoven**   mixed or blended together
4. **somnambulism**   walking in your sleep

 Discussion Questions

1. Are most people aware of the "meta-goals" that influence their lives? How does the author define them? What role do these higher order goals play in one's life?
2. Why is it important to set goals for yourself rather than accept those that others set for you?
3. Why does Lore insist that you write down your goals in specific, measurable terms? Why is setting time limits important?
4. Do you think the suggestions he gives for managing your goals are realistic? How do you manage your goals?
5. Are most of your goals reasonable and sensible? If so, are you satisfied with them? If not, what can you do to stretch them? How flexible are you if they don't turn out the way you desire?

 Suggestions for Your Journal

Do you think goal setting is important? Think about what you want to accomplish in your studies one month from now. If you have never written down a short-term goal before, write down one specific, measurable academic goal that you would like to complete in 30 days. What action steps will you need to take to accomplish it? If you are an experienced goal-setter, have you incorporated all of Lore's principles in your experiences? Which ones need to be improved?

Do you have difficulty thinking long-term? Why? What specific steps can you take to improve the way you set goals? Do you disagree with any of Lore's activities? If so, explain why.

Job Search: Chance or Plan?

Mark R. Ballard

Formerly the director of career services in a liberal arts college, Mark R. Ballard is currently director of human resources development at Victoria's Secret Catalogue, where he continues his work in career planning and organizational career development. In this essay, Ballard offers some excellent advice for initiating the job-search process and delineates specific career-planning tasks for each year of student life. He believes his advice, if followed, will generate good job prospects upon graduation.

● ● ● ● ● ● ● ● ● ● ● ● ● ● ● ● ● ● ●

I want to tell you about Terry—the alumnus who "chanced" his career. His story can provide important insights for your own career planning.

Terry was a popular student in high school, was involved in many activities, and graduated in the top 25 percent of his class. Terry could hardly wait to leave his hometown to become a college student at the university. His academic performance was quite respectable. He could not believe how quickly the years passed. They elapsed so fast that he did not get involved in any structured *co-curricular* activities because he was "too busy" with school, sports, and friends. For spending money, Terry worked, but his employment experience, for the most part, consisted of being a lifeguard during the summers at his hometown pool and a cashier in a fast-food restaurant.

The quarter before Terry was slated to graduate, he decided to visit the Career Services Office. (He remembered hearing about this resource in his freshman orientation class.) Terry eagerly signed up for several on-campus interviews with companies that came to campus to interview students.

Terry bought a suit, had someone prepare a resume for him, and interviewed with several company representatives. He was confident that he presented himself well in the interviews and would most assuredly get an offer from one of the employers with whom he interviewed. After all, he had never had difficulty finding part-time jobs.

Graduation came and went for Terry. Summer came, and Terry began to panic. Mid-summer, Terry returned to Career Services since the anticipated job offers did not materialize out of his interviews. Terry came back to the office looking for additional companies who were coming on campus to interview students and alumni. But there were none during the summer, since companies who do come to college campuses to interview students generally complete their hiring visits during April. Terry was unaware of this fact since he did not attend the on-campus interviewing orientation session: he was "too busy." Terry left the office disappointed, failing to take advantage of the many other employment resources. He vowed to return "sometime," but he never got around to it.

In the follow-up questionnaire mailed to alumni six months after graduation, we received a letter from Terry. Good news: he had landed a job! Well,
maybe not good news. The job, which he stumbled on by "accident," was not the
kind of position Terry thought he would land with a college degree. Sadly, his
college education would not be fully utilized, and his salary was not comparable to similar college graduates.

Here's the moral of Terry's tale: Finding meaningful employment *commensurate* with one's educational level is not an event that occurs at the end of
one's final term in college. It is a process that begins early in one's collegiate career. Making the transition from academics to the work world does not begin
with writing a resume, buying a new suit, or getting that first job interview. It begins with thought, research, and goal setting.

To secure employment upon graduation, begin with the process of self-
assessment. As a part of this process, you need to be able to answer such questions as, "What do I want to do for work?" and "Where do I want to do it?" In other
words, what are your abilities, strengths, assets, gifts, talents? What is it that you
are interested in, enjoy, are curious about, are motivated by, or get pleasure from?
What are your values—those needs that you want satisfied by your work (recognition, independence, money, prestige, social status, uncovering knowledge)?
What are the job tasks or activities of the careers that you are considering, the
types of organizations that employ individuals in these occupations, the job out-
look/forecast, salary ranges, entrance requirements, and lifestyle issues associated with the vocations you are considering? What are the steps necessary to
undertake the decision-making process related to your career? Do you know
where to go to find out how to write a resume, interview for job offers, and to
learn strategies to find jobs? If you can answer these questions, you will increase
your prospects for success in the job search.

As an entering student, you may find it easy to say: "I'll deal with those job-
related questions and issues during my senior year, or when I'm ready to graduate." "It's too early now." "I don't have time." "I'm just a freshman." "I'll figure it out.
After all, I figured out how to apply to and get accepted to college."

But consider the following. Suppose you were to interview today for the
job of your dreams, and the interviewer said to you, "Tell me about yourself and
why you want this job. You have thirty minutes. I'll begin timing when you begin
talking." How would you respond? What would you say? That is a common open-
ing statement for an employer to make in a job interview.

To land the job of your dreams, you will first need to know about yourself.
Do not confuse starting the process with implementing your career decision.
You don't need to choose a career now, just to begin to think about, and to get
actively involved in, the process during your early years of college. That way,
early in your senior year, you can reflect on the self-assessment and the career
exploration tasks that you addressed and the career decision that you made
early in your college years. Your senior year is also the time for you to focus attention on *transitional* issues that will take you from academics to the work
world, or on to graduate or professional school. Career planning is working

through the many tasks associated with finding employment through planning—rather than through chance.

Career planning is the developmental, systematic process of

1. learning about yourself (for example, your interests, abilities, and values),
2. identifying occupations that correspond to your assessment of self,
3. exploring the occupations that you are considering,
4. selecting an occupation to pursue,
5. readying yourself for the job search process (resume and application letter writing, job interview skill development, job finding techniques and strategy knowledge), and
6. securing satisfying employment.

Does it seem that the process of career planning could be simplified by proceeding directly to step six—finding a job upon graduation? If so, remember Terry. That is exactly what he did. He jumped into the job search without establishing the foundation of the first five stages. He landed a job, but a job in the ranks of the underemployed, and that can have *ramifications* for a lifetime.

Your career process will be easier if you fully use the career planning and placement services provided at your university. There, staff members can help you answer the all too familiar question, "What can I do with a major in . . . ?" and assist you in finding purposeful, gratifying employment.

As a career services professional, I have worked with thousands of students, employers, and alumni. When I survey employers and alumni for their perspective on how students can best prepare themselves to make the transition from academics to the work world, they usually give five recommendations for students entering a university.

1. Choose a major in a subject that interests you—one that really gets you excited. Do not rely on your parents, peers, or counselors to make the choice for you regarding your academic major or the occupation to pursue. Make the decision yourself. As a related note, given the difficulty of predicting which skills will be in demand even five years from now, not to mention in a lifetime, your best career preparation is one that emphasizes broad skills (for example, social, communication, analytical, logical, leadership, human relations), intellectual curiosity, and knowledge of how to learn.
2. Strive for a rigorous academic program and high grades. Yes, grades are important to employers. Job candidates are often rejected from interviews due to low GPAs.
3. Develop your leadership, communication, human relations, and time management skills by taking active roles of responsibility in student organizations and activities. This involvement will provide you with an opportunity to put knowledge from the classroom into practice.
4. Get career-related experience prior to graduation (through part-time positions, *cooperative education,* internships, and volunteer work). The benefits of such experience go well beyond making money. You will have a chance

to sample a variety of jobs and work settings, make valuable contacts with professionals for future networking, develop self-confidence, and gain insight when choosing elective courses in your academic program.
5. Use the career planning and placement services on campus early in your academic experience to help you with your career decision making and your job search. By doing so, you can get a head start on your employment future.

You can take the above recommendations a step further by following a year-by-year plan for your job search. Use this scheme as a general strategy to increase the likelihood of your landing the job of your dreams upon graduation.

As a Freshman . . .

The goal of your freshman year should be to learn as much as you can about yourself and the relationship this information has to careers. Consider the following:

In your academic course work, use the required general education courses and other college courses to help you explore your potential. You might wish to take courses and explore subjects that have always been of interest to you but that you never before had an opportunity to take.

Visit the career services office (sometimes referred to as the Placement Office) on your campus and get acquainted with the services and resources of that office. Your academic adviser can direct you to the right place.

Explore your interests, abilities, and values. Identify appropriate career choices by using the computerized career guidance systems (DISCOVER and SIGI-PLUS are two that are commonly available), meeting with a staff member of the career services office for a career counseling session, attending any career awareness workshops offered on campus and sharing your goals with your academic adviser.

Find out about cooperative education and internship opportunities through your intended college of graduation.

Analyze job descriptions in the career services office and ask yourself how these positions fit with your identity profile.

Begin investigating and getting involved in at least one of the student organizations and activities on campus to develop your leadership, communication, human relations, and time management skills.

Find a summer job that will provide you with an opportunity to learn or refine skills that will be attractive to a prospective employer (e.g., communication, responsibility, ethical decision making, and human relations—learning to work with individuals of differing backgrounds).

As a Sophomore . . .

During your sophomore year, your goal should be to concentrate on identifying careers that appeal to you and to begin testing them out.

Use the career books and other references in the career office and elsewhere on campus to research career options.

Learn to begin the process of informational interviewing—contacting and talking with people employed in fields you are considering. For example, if you are interested in chemistry, dietetics, or nutrition as a major, consider conducting an informational interview with a nutritional researcher at an area business or hospital. Career services staff members can help you identify professionals working in occupations that are of interest to you.

Take active roles of responsibility in clubs, organizations, and activities.

Cultivate relationships with faculty, counselors, and others who can help in answering questions that relate to careers and the relationship of course work to careers.

Take time to attend the "career days" held on campus and in the area. These events provide you with the opportunity to meet representatives from major U.S. organizations. Be sure to ask about cooperative education and internship opportunities.

Find out about summer internships and cooperative education opportunities through the career services office.

Begin developing a resume as well as job interviewing skills. Workshops on these topics are conducted regularly through many career services offices.

As a Junior . . .

During your junior year, your goal should be to obtain career-related experience.

Prepare for the job search by attending workshops and individual counseling sessions on resume writing, application letter writing, job search strategies, and interviewing skills.

Develop a network of contacts in the field of your choice through continued informational interviewing, involvement in professional associations, and cooperative education or internships.

Continue to attend the "career days" held on the campus and in the area. Continue to ask the company representatives about internships and cooperative education opportunities.

Research job leads and make initial contacts early in winter for sources of possible employment that have some relationship to your tentative career choice. Gather letters of recommendation written on your behalf from past employers, current employers, professors, teaching associates—professionals who can vouch for your skills and abilities. Open a credentials file if your career services office has such a service.

As a Senior . . .

Your senior year is the culmination of your college education and is the launching pad for your future. Your goal is to secure satisfying employment or to get accepted to graduate or professional school if your career interest indicates the need for an advanced degree.

Learn the procedures for interviewing with the various career placement offices on campus should you wish to interview with organizations that come on campus to interview graduating students.

Research the organizations with which you wish to interview by using the career services office's company literature libraries.

Attend "career day" events that are held on the campus and in the area and actively participate by distributing resumes to the company representatives and telling them about who you are and the type of position you are seeking.

Interview for jobs during the year with employers who come on campus through the career services office. Note: they are not likely to be there during the summer. (Remember Terry's disappointment?)

Continue collecting letters of recommendation written on your behalf by people who can attest to your skills and abilities. Keep these letters on file in your college's career services office.

Explore, in consultation with career services personnel, other strategies to find employment for your field of interest, such as using the many job listings that are published through career services offices, making use of computerized listings of positions, enrolling in national employment databases through career services offices, and learning the process of networking (getting involved with professionals in the field you wish to enter and learning where the hidden job market is). **The best job search strategy is to use a variety of job search strategies simultaneously; do not rely solely on one strategy to find employment.**

Choosing a career and finding a professional job take a lot of time and effort. You need to find out as much as you can about what interests you, what you do well, and what you want out of life. Even after you have decided on your career direction, you will find a wide range of job options available to you. There may be occupations that you have never even heard of that would suit your education, interests, values, and abilities perfectly. It is important to find out about them as early as possible. By waiting too long to begin proper planning and preparation for a successful career, you run the risk of embarking on the job search scene unaware of what field to pursue, getting frustrated, giving in, giving up, and taking any job you are offered.

The staff members of your career services office can help you with every phase of the career planning and employment process. It is not a magical, quick process, and the staff will not find a job for you. What you can expect, however, are informed professionals who will guide your career decision making and your job search process.

The valuable information you will receive from these offices will prove beneficial to you for the rest of your life. Make a commitment to get a head start on your career. Visit your career services office today. You owe it to yourself.

Reprinted by permission of the author.

• •

 Vocabulary

As you think about this essay, these definitions may be helpful to you:
1. **co-curricular** being outside of but complementary to the regular curriculum
2. **commensurate** equal in measure or extent
3. **transitional** in the process of passing from one state, stage, or place to another
4. **ramifications** consequences or outgrowths
5. **cooperative education** a program that combines academic studies with actual work experience

 Discussion Questions

1. What is the first important step in the job search process, according to Ballard?
2. What would you tell an employer about yourself in 30 minutes during a job interview?
3. What are the six steps that Ballard outlines to systematically begin the career planning process?
4. What type of work experiences can students engage in prior to graduation?
5. What are some strategies students can use during their first year to enhance the career planning process? As sophomores? Juniors? Seniors?

 Suggestions for Your Journal

Describe your dream job. Where would it be? What tasks would you be involved with all day? How would it fulfill your work values? How would it affect your family? How could it affect your lifestyle? Paint a picture of what a typical day would be like.

Which of the tasks or activities on Ballard's list for the first-year college student have you accomplished? What specific steps can you take to complete them by the end of the year?

Discuss the differences between the practical suggestions for career planning in this reading and the ones suggested by Burtchaell in Unit 3. How can you accomplish both?

Postgraduate Paralysis

Mary Sherry

- Mary Sherry owns a firm that publishes research reports for architects and real estate
- developers. In this essay, which first appeared in *Newsweek* magazine, Sherry offers a
- parent's perspective on an offspring's job search. When she realized her daughter was
- looking for a career, not a job, her perspective on how to help changed.

• • • • • • • • • • • • • • • • • • •

Thousands of college graduates took their diplomas this year in fear or even embarrassment. They were not proud of themselves, nor eager to take on the real world. Instead, they thought of themselves as failures. These are the graduates who have not been offered fat salaries and generous benefits. They are the ones who won't be going to work as lawyers, investment bankers and engineers. They have taken the right courses, gotten good grades and gone through some on-campus job interviews. But because they weren't offered the perfect job—no, that exciting career—seemingly guaranteed to all those who make the right moves, they are sitting at home, victims of postgraduate paralysis.

This may come as a surprise to anyone who has read about the fabulous job offers tendered to recent graduates. However, those of us who are parents of children in this age group know that such offers are relatively rare and that many liberal-arts students graduate with the belief that the work world may not have a place for them.

Consider my daughter; she graduated from college with a degree in economics two years ago. She was offered a job by a *recruiter* who came to her campus—but it was with a trucking firm in South Carolina, as a dispatch-management trainee. She turned it down. It was her parents' first clue that she had a problem.

It seems economists don't work for trucking firms. Nor do Midwestern children want to live in the South before they become arthritic. Yet even at home in Minneapolis, our daughter couldn't seem to find anything to apply for. Her father told her to make the rounds of the personnel agencies. But she was so horrified by the *demeaning* atmosphere at one that she refused to visit any others.

Then one day, when she was looking at the Sunday paper and complaining that there was nothing in it, I told her that there had to be something. "Look at this," I commanded. "And this! And this!" I circled a number of jobs in the first two columns I skimmed. But Maureen protested: "I don't want to be an administrative assistant."

It was then that her father and I realized that she had been looking in the paper for a career, not a job. And ever since, we have watched the children of friends suffer from this same *delusion.* No one, it seems, has told them that a career is an *evolutionary* process.

When I graduated from college 25 years ago, I never expected to find a job that was in itself a career. In those days, we were told we knew nothing, but that upon graduation we would have the tools to learn. And learn we did—on the job. I began by doing grunt work in the customer-service department at *National Geographic* magazine. In due time, I wound up with a career, indeed, owning and running a firm that publishes research reports for architects and real-estate developers.

Apparently, schools have changed their approach. Today's students are told they know everything in order to succeed in a career. Career talk often begins in seventh grade or earlier, and the career is offered as the reward one receives upon graduation. No one is satisfied with this system. Businesses complain that they get new graduates who are unhappy with anything less than high-level, decision-making jobs as their first assignments. And parents are shocked that the child without a job can graduate traumatized by the fear of rejection.

As I see it, parents are a principal cause of the problem. Who among us hasn't thought, "What's wrong with that kid?" when we hear that a recent college graduate is a checker at a grocery store because "he can't find a job." At the same time, how many of us can put the screws on a recruiter's reject and convince him that he must abandon his idea of a career and take up the idea of finding work?

This is a distasteful task, especially when we have shipped our children off to expensive colleges, believing that simply by footing the tuition bill we are making them economically secure. The kids believe this, too, but the reality is that when they graduate, they are no more prepared for careers than we were.

Entry-level positions: It is not a disgrace to go out and pound the pavement. I used just this expression the other day with a friend of my son who, though he had graduated in December with a degree in philosophy, has not yet found a job. He had never heard the saying before. He is bright, personable and would do well in almost any kind of business. But he complains that he can't find work in the want ads—he has not visited any personnel agencies—and so he talks about going to law school instead. He was crushed by not having been recruited before graduation.

Which brings me back to my daughter. After some yelling and screaming by her parents, she did make the rounds of *headhunters* and found one who specialized in entry-level positions. This gentleman was wonderful; he helped her assess her skills and prepared her for interviews. She also read the newspapers and answered different types of ads. Not surprisingly, she got many responses. After a few weeks she had the exhilarating experience of having three job offers at once. Two were the products of answering newspaper ads and one came through the headhunter's efforts. She landed an excellent position as an insurance underwriter—a job she didn't even know existed when she graduated.

Happy in her job, Maureen also fell in love; and when she began to look for employment in Chicago where she and her husband will live, she needed no help from her parents. She was confident and aggressive. She used headhunters, the want ads, her friends and ours. She had a new resource—business contacts. Yet as she was typing letters one day, I offered some sympathy about how hard it is to hunt for a job.

"It's OK, Mom," she said. "This isn't like the first time. Now I know how to look for a job!"

And she found one as a senior underwriter. She'll make more money and more decisions.

It's beginning to look like a career.

From Mary Sherry, "Postgraduate Paralysis," from *Newsweek*, July 11, 1998. Reprinted by permission of the author.

 Vocabulary

As you think about this essay, these definitions may be helpful to you:
1. **recruiter**   a representative of a company or organization who is seeking to secure the services of or hire individuals to work for that organization
2. **demeaning**   degrading
3. **delusion**   something that is falsely believed
4. **evolutionary**   characterized by a process of change in a certain direction
5. **headhunters**   paid recruiters of personnel

 Discussion Questions

1. Why do some students feel like failures if they do not have a job at graduation, according to Sherry?
2. How did Sherry's daughter approach the job-search process?
3. What is the difference between a job and a career?
4. What advice does Sherry give for finding entry-level jobs? Do you agree?
5. How did Sherry's daughter finally find her first job? Subsequent jobs?

 Suggestions for Your Journal

Do you know any college graduates who are still searching for a job? If so, what have you learned from their experiences?

What type of entry-level job are you preparing for when you graduate? What kinds of experiences (such as internships, volunteer work, co-op or work experiences) would enhance your chances of getting the job you desire? What resources exist on your campus to help you obtain these experiences? What other steps can you take to make yourself more marketable when you graduate?

Career Patterns for the 21st Century

Peggy Simonsen

- Peggy Simonsen is president of Career Directions, Incorporated. She designs and
- implements career development and performance management systems and training
- for corporations. Simonsen is a nationally prominent speaker and frequent contributor
- to numerous journals and newsletters. In this essay she describes the career patterns
- that will emerge in the new century and how these will be different from old ways of
- thinking about career patterns.

Up is not the only way.
—Beverly Kaye

Managing your career strategically in the new century will require new ways of thinking....A variety of career patterns are evolving. There may be flatter, team-based environments where expectations of upward progression are limited and limiting. A career pattern driven by internal choice rather than external structure will be the most valuable to individuals and will therefore add the most value to the employing organization. Newer employees in organizations today recognize this and aren't as likely as their predecessors to create careers based on incompatible structures or outdated expectations and reward systems. As one employee learning new ways to think about careers said, "You mean it's OK not to want to move up?"

Portfolio Careers

The career pattern most different from the traditional upward career path is that of the *portfolio* career, such as freelance writer. Not employed by a single organization, a freelance writer might have regular assignments with one publication, occasional articles published by others, and some consulting work creating PR campaigns or brochures. In addition, he or she might write and lay out a newsletter and perhaps take on a large one-time assignment to create a policy manual. This writer would be creating a portfolio of work he or she has done.

Today, portfolio careers have expanded to encompass more than one field. Sometimes used to build expertise while planning a career change, the portfolio career can give more autonomy, time, freedom, and opportunity for creativity and diverse activities. People with portfolio careers might be managing a traditional assignment in a large organization while building a small business on the side. An engineer might prefer to work for a job shop, taking on assignments that last from six months to two years, building a variety of experience, and having the freedom to leave when the project is completed or gets too routine. Someone with a love for a field that doesn't pay well might add another type of work to add more income, without giving up the work he or she loves. . . .

Portfolio careers might be driven by *"contingency* work"—that is, employment by a company as long as necessary, but not full-time, permanent employment. To remain flexible and avoid creating new bureaucracies, downsized companies are increasingly using contingency workforces. For a person wanting to hold on to the work patterns of the twentieth century, contingency work seems like a step down the ladder, with no chance for advancement and typically no company-paid benefits. However, for individuals who choose to build portfolio careers, the advantages are autonomy in selecting assignments, variety of work, time freedom, higher hourly pay than for the same work that is salaried, and the chance to build a greater *repertoire* of skills.

This career pattern requires individuals to recognize that they must market their capabilities. They need to be aware of the value of their skills in the marketplace and present themselves as people who can solve others' problems. While this may sound like the essentials of a job search, it must become a regular course of action for a successful portfolio career.

Lifestyle-Driven Careers

Women balancing family and work have been the primary practitioners of lifestyle-driven careers. Taking the primary responsibility for raising children, the wife and mother would work at a part-time job that wouldn't interfere with her home responsibilities. This career pattern is evolving and becoming a choice for men, too. With more two-career households, many couples are finding themselves with little time to build and enjoy their life together and with their families. Others have strong outside interests or *avocations,* so they want to balance their workloads to allow time for these. Still others find their lives out of balance because of excessive work demands after organizational downsizing. People are insisting that work be a subset of life, not all of it. So individuals are making choices about careers on the basis of life needs. The labor shortage gives individuals some leverage by causing employers to create more flexible policies and practices. Companies are recognizing the value of lifestyle-friendly policies, especially when retention of educated and skilled workers is a goal. But organizations are also recognizing that a culture of support for individuals—making work time more satisfying and less stressful—makes good business sense. . . .

Research on career motivation shows that lifestyle-driven careers are the fastest-growing pattern. People with this motivation say career is important, but more important for career decisions is having a balanced, fully satisfying life. The demands of many work environments make a lifestyle-driven career pattern difficult to implement.

Emerging workers, who may be willing to work eighty-hour weeks to meet critical deadlines, expect reciprocation and a break when the crisis passes. Without loyalty to an organization, they will pack up and leave when work demands become unreasonable.

Mature employees, who have lived through downsizing changes—and perhaps personal burnout from excessive time and work demands—often feel less commitment to their work and talk about leaving. Some are too risk-averse to take action to leave, but their work is likely to suffer. These are the people who need to take action, for their own good and that of their employers. Employers who don't recognize the validity of a lifestyle-driven career pattern will lose good people.

Linear Careers

Linear careers are the closest to the traditional career path. However, linear careers in the twenty-first century are not likely to be with only one organization. Rather than going to work for a good company and expecting to be employed for life, employees will avoid much of the frustration experienced upon reaching a level in the organization beyond which they cannot move. Individuals who expect to move up in responsibility and compensation in the future will change organizations when they reach a plateau or growth slows. People managing their careers strategically will not have the expectation that a linear career can happen in one organization. They will be more *proactive* to make it happen.

Organizations will still need leaders willing to take on greater responsibility. They will need to build commitment to the company's success. But they won't be able to take this commitment for granted, assuming loyalty at all costs. The mutual benefits of shared responsibility for organizational development and career success will be recognized by both organizations and employees.

Even today, after excessive downsizing, many organizations are recognizing the need for succession planning and workforce planning. They recognize the disruptive nature of constantly hiring from outside instead of developing from within. There is a growing trend to design systems to develop competencies in internal candidates for assignments as they become available.

Conversely, individuals cannot assume that length of service alone will determine career progression. They must constantly add value, build networks, and overcome barriers to their development. People who will build successful linear careers will take a broader, organizational perspective rather than a personally driven perspective. With flatter organizations, self-directed teams, and therefore fewer management positions, promotions will rarely occur through a person's being in the right place at the right time. They will more likely be based on proven ability to lead. People who fit this career pattern are motivated by achievement, power, and ambition and are willing to pay the dues necessary to achieve success the way they define it....

Expert Careers

Perhaps the only recognized alternative to moving up in the past was the role of individual contributor who chose not to become a manager. A career pattern that has existed forever but often was not valued in traditional organizations is that of the expert. I say "not valued" because rarely was a skilled expert compensated as well as a mediocre manager. The whole structure was designed to support linear careers, so people who turned down promotions because they preferred their technical tasks often felt like second-class citizens. As technology demanded expertise, some organizations created dual-ladder career paths to reward people who were individual contributors, not managers. However, most dual-ladder models still rewarded upward paths—for example, from junior engineer to senior engineer to group leader to project manager.

A few organizations whose success depended on superior individual contributions created rewards for exceptional outcomes, such as patents, scientific breakthroughs, journalistic awards, and record-breaking sales records. This latter pattern will continue into the next century. Led by young firms, without the baggage of the old corporations (especially compensation systems), the expert career pattern is coming into its own. People are rewarded with stock, profit sharing, or substantial bonuses when the project is completed successfully, not because it is the end of the year. Hard work and capability are not only valued, they drive the organization's success. As organizations require fewer managers but need all the state-of-the-art skill they can get, this career pattern may become predominant.

If an expert career pattern is right for you, it will require continuously developing your expertise. It will mean running fast to keep abreast of changes in your profession. The very traits that drive individuals to become experts might frustrate them when the work is changing so fast that it is impossible to maintain an expected level of expertise. It certainly is not a career pattern that allows one to slack off and trade on previous successes, as it might have been in an era of slow change. People whose career pattern is based on expertise need passion for their work, desire always to learn more, ambition to make significant contributions to their fields, and satisfaction from their technical competence. ("Technical" here means task specific, not necessarily electronic. An editor has technical competence in language use; a sales representative has technical competence in both the sales process and the products he or she sells.)

Like a linear career, an expert career probably will not happen in just one organization. It is up to individuals not only to manage their own growth in the field but also to be proactive about the environment in which the work is performed. The company might sell off the division that requires their particular set of skills and knowledge, so while the work doesn't change, the employer does. Technology might suddenly move a generation ahead, leaving experts' work obsolete or declining in value. Or the employer might not choose to move forward in technology, so experts might need to leave in order to continue growing in their areas of expertise. Organizational priorities might change in response to market demands, leaving a previously valued area of expertise now less important—and therefore with fewer resources to support the work. Expert employees might realize the unique nature of their expertise and decide to create their own organizations, to specialize in the work they have been paid to do as employees. While expertise may be seen as a career pattern out of the past, the circumstances in which it is applied will be more dynamic in the future. . . .

Managing your career strategically might mean recognizing the contribution you make and the satisfaction you derive from being an expert at what you do—and turning down a promotion. It is possible to take on management responsibilities and still maintain expertise, but the focus changes. In our fast-changing environments, it is hard enough to maintain expertise without having it be secondary to getting work done through others, but some highly competent individuals manage both roles well. . . .

Sequential Careers

A growing approach to managing your career strategically is the choice of a sequential career. Rather than involving simultaneous career activities, as in the portfolio career, in a sequential career one role ends before another is launched. As people retire from a primary career earlier in life, and as life expectancy is extended, the twenty-first century will see more sequential career patterns. In some cases, the second career is less demanding or not as well compensated as the first, but often it is just different.

We are seeing a substantial increase in the number of people choosing sequential careers because of the decline of the old career patterns. People who bought into the concept of a job for life—even if it was one they didn't choose or want to be in—are suddenly free to make other choices. Either because their job ended or because the paradigm changed and they are thinking about work differently, many are changing careers at midlife or beyond. Some have the opportunity for an early-retirement severance package, which leaves them with the financial base to make choices that are based on fit rather than compensation. Some who have been in the business environment are choosing new work in the not-for-profit sector, intentionally choosing to make income and lifestyle changes. . . .

Younger people are purposely building sequential careers because of the variety they allow. They work in one field for a while, building a level of competence or experience, and then when the challenge begins to wane they decide to pursue work in another area of interest. As long as they move from strength and not from unsatisfactory performance, the building of a sequential career is not seen as negative. Sometimes they move to completely different areas for the sake of new experience, which typically requires starting in a lower-paying job than the one they left. To avoid stepping back, sequential career builders often move to a related area where their background is valued, though not a direct contribution to the new field. For example, a financial analyst in a sales department who knows the company's products moves into a sales support position, then into marketing with another company, and finally into strategic planning, each time adding new skills and experience to her work history.

Sequential career builders may not stay long enough at one organization to build a strong reputation for expertise or to position themselves for promotions, but that isn't what's driving them. Change, variety, and challenge are their drivers, and they definitely don't want linear careers. However, it's important to distinguish between a successful sequential career and job-hopping. A sequential career is successful if the person attains some expertise, competence, and acknowledgment in each job. Young people, particularly, may go from one field to another without gaining any expertise. Then they find themselves at the age of thirty without a portfolio of well-honed skills and with an image of moving away from unsuccessful attempts. In some cases, they even turn down promotions, which might have been important for moving into higher-level situations. . . .

Entrepreneurial Careers

Some people seem to be born entrepreneurs. Creative, independent, driven by their own goals and passions, they need the autonomy of their own companies. These types have always existed, so what is different now? The career patterns we've discussed are enabling entrepreneurial types to start their own businesses in different ways:

- Portfolio careers, where people juggle paid employment with a fledgling business—perhaps in the same field, perhaps in a new area
- Lifestyle-driven careers, where some start their own businesses to get more time flexibility, or to reduce a commute, or to be less tied to a demanding environment
- Linear careers, when the move up has been derailed or a plateau has been reached; capable women who have hit the glass ceiling in a large organization often opt to start a business where their leadership skills can be maximized
- Expert careers, where people feel they can use their expertise better with fewer limitations in their own businesses, or where the expertise is no longer needed by an employer and so a former employee becomes self-employed to provide the same service or product to the market
- Sequential careers, where an entrepreneurial drive has been squelched for security reasons and now can emerge as the next career

Obviously, not all entrepreneurs are from the same mold—if they were they wouldn't be entrepreneurs. But there are some whose very nature is entrepreneurial. They are risk-taking, goal-oriented, creative, hard-driving, persevering, competitive, and challenge-driven. . . .

Not all entrepreneurs are driven to start more than one business. Some land at the helm by happenstance (as when they inherit a family business) and make a commitment to grow the business over many years. Some entrepreneurial people never start a business at all but become equity partners in small, already established operations, where they contribute to growth and success. These aren't people who need structure and a predictable paycheck; they can create their own systems and take financial risks because of the potential payoffs.

Many new companies in the field of technology are launched because their founders have the expertise and because they can be so much more responsive to market opportunities than old, bureaucratic organizations.

Increasingly, larger organizations are recognizing the value of entrepreneurial traits to innovation and creative problem solving inside the company.

Gifford Pinchot (1985)[1] calls this "intrapreneuring": the company provides the equivalent of venture capital, and a small group of employees creates a business plan for an innovative product or service to be developed in-house and brought to market.

Pluralistic Career Cultures

With the old "employment contract" an artifact of the twentieth century, something is needed to replace the way we define careers. Instead of shifting from the old, relatively stable structure to one of free-form *pandemonium,* organizations will need to recognize and support multiple career patterns. Brousseau, Driver, Eneroth, and Larsson[2] make a plea for organizations to adopt a pluralistic approach to career management and to develop a pluralistic career culture as a way to cope with change and the diverse needs of organizations and people. Encouraging and including a variety of career patterns can realign individuals and organizations.

We can hope that in the coming century, both individuals and organizations will value a variety of career patterns. Individuals will need to know which types of careers are appropriate for them at any point in time, and organizational practices will reward those patterns that serve their purposes and keep the company on track to achieve business goals. Today only slightly more than half of all work options are derivatives of traditional work arrangements (that is, full-time positions at the same workplace for a long time). The variety will expand as the new century grows. . . .

• •

 Vocabulary

As you think about this essay, these definitions may be helpful to you:
1. **portfolio**   a selection of representative work
2. **contingency**   the state of happening by chance or unforeseen causes
3. **repertoire**   a supply of materials, skills, or devices
4. **avocation**   a hobby or occupation pursued for enjoyment
5. **proactive**   taking the initiative
6. **pandemonium**   wild disorder

[1] G. Pinchot III, *Intrapreneuring: Why You Don't Have to Leave the Corporation to Become an Entrepreneur* (New York: HarperCollins, 1985).
[2] K. Brousseau et al. (1996), "Career Pandemonium: Realigning Organizations and Individuals, " *Academy of Management Executives, 10*(4), 53.

 Discussion Questions

1. In what ways do these new career patterns differ from the old, more traditional ones?
2. What, according to Simonsen, are the characteristics of the "lifestyle" career pattern?
3. How do modern linear careers differ from those in the past?
4. Why might an "expert" career pattern be difficult to maintain in work that changes rapidly?
5. Why are younger people purposely building sequential careers, according to Simonsen?

 Suggestions for Your Journal

How do you define "career"? Will you want to change careers often or will you feel more secure working in the same career for a long time? Which of the six career patterns that Simonson describes appeals the most to you?

What reward systems are most important to you? How would your choice of career pattern provide the rewards you desire? How do your current ideas about your education fit into what you most desire in a career?

UNIT SUMMARY

The readings in this unit provide a wide variety of opinions about work and workers. Reflect on your own ideas about your place in the work world and how these writers have added to your understanding of its complexities and challenges.

Summary Questions

1. Responding to a recent poll, younger workers indicated that they care more about job satisfaction than job security. How do you think that knowing this might influence what employers offer new workers?
2. Describe how you have searched for a job in the past and the differences having a college degree might make.
3. How do you think the American workplace has changed in the last 20 years? How will your work life be different from that of your parents? How will these differences, if any, affect your life in a way different from theirs?

Suggested Writing Assignments

1. The readings in this unit explore several beliefs, attitudes, and perspectives about work. Select one and write a brief essay on why the ideas in this reading agree or disagree with your own ideas about work.
2. Write a brief essay on what you want in your future career (e.g., independence, creativity, security, high salary) and why these work values are essential to you.
3. Write a brief essay about how you are currently approaching the choice of academic major and career field and what you still need to do in order to make an initial decision or confirm one you have already made.

Suggested Readings

Bolles, Richard. *What Color Is Your Parachute?* Berkeley, CA: Ten Speed Press, 2004.
Gordon, Virginia, and Susan Sears. *Selecting a College Major: Exploration and Decision Making.* Upper Saddle River, NJ: Prentice Hall, 2004.
Terkel, Studs. *Working.* New York: Pantheon, 1974.

Life After College: Future Success or Future Shock?

I magine the day you will be wearing a cap and gown and receiving the diploma that attests to your status as a college graduate. What does the future hold for you? Several readings in previous units offered visions of the future from different perspectives. These can stimulate your thinking about what you might hope to accomplish during your college years so that your college education can prepare you for both the workplace and your life in general.

In Unit 1, several authors described the value of a college education and emphasized the importance of taking advantage of the opportunities offered through the experience of higher education. You were asked to examine your reasons for being in college and how these might affect your initial goals for the college experience itself. The beginning of your college life is a good time to set some tentative goals to reach by the day you are ordained a college graduate. Through your college career, you will want to broaden those goals to

Climb high
Climb far
Your goal the sky
Your aim the star.

—INSCRIPTION ON JOHNS HOPKINS MEMORIAL STEPS

263

include specific actions to prepare for the future lifestyle you desire. Some of your ideas might change very much.

You will also want to set goals related to the type of work you want to do and the type of worker you want to become. These should take into account both the type of job and quality of work life you hope to obtain after college. Thoughtful planning now can also improve your effectiveness as a worker later in life.

A commission established by the Secretary of Labor in 1990—the Secretary's Commission on Achieving Necessary Skills (SCANS)—defined the skills that young people need in order to succeed in the workplace of the future. The SCANS report outlined five competencies and other basic skills and personal qualities essential for future workers. Among these are the abilities to use resources productively, to acquire and use a wide variety of interpersonal skills, to learn to use information effectively, and to use technological and organizational systems. Future workers will also be expected to demonstrate such critical basic skills as effective reading, clear writing, and computational expertise. Oral communication skills will also be important. Computer literacy will be an absolutely required skill in the future workplace. Certain personal qualities such as integrity, effective self-management, responsibility, and sociability were also named essential for success in the future workplace.

It is during the college years that many of these foundational skills and personal competencies can be acquired and practiced, usually in a nonthreatening environment. The quality of your life after college will depend on how well you take advantage of the opportunities presented to you during your college years.

The essay by Pellegrino was a commencement address in which the speaker distinguished receiving a baccalaureate degree from being educated. Levine and Cureton compare the current generation of college students with those of the past and suggest four attributes today's students need to possess to live successfully in the new century. The reading by Howe and Strauss describes their vision of the Millenial Generation, who they insist might be the next great one. Christopher Reeve urges college students to maintain their integrity "in a culture that has devalued it" and describes how his injury has helped him live a more "conscious" life.

In addition to discussing these issues in class and writing about them in your journal, you might want to talk to family, friends, and others to whom you look for guidance. Examining what is important to you now and in the future is a first step in setting thoughtful, realistic goals for your life after college. Don't wait until the day you march down the graduation aisle to consider who you are and where you want to be when that day arrives.

Having a Degree and Being Educated

Edmund D. Pellegrino, M.D.

Edmund D. Pellegrino is the director of the Center for Clinical Bioethics at Georgetown University, where he is the John Carroll Professor. This essay was a commencement address given by Dr. Pellegrino at Wilkes College.

Few humans live completely free of illusions. Reality is sometimes just too harsh to bear without them. But comforting as they can be, some illusions are too dangerous to be harbored for very long. Eventually they must meet the test of reality—or we slip into psychosis.

I want to examine a prevalent illusion with you today—one to which you are most susceptible at this moment, namely, that *having* a degree is the same as *being* educated. It is a bit *gauche,* I admit, to ask embarrassing questions at a time of celebration. But your personal happiness and the world you create depend on how well your illusion is brought into focus. And this *emboldens* me to intrude briefly on the satisfaction you justly feel with your academic accomplishment.

The degree you receive today is only a certificate of exposure, not a guarantee of infection. Some may have caught the virus of education, others only a mild case, and still others may be totally immune. To which category do you belong? Should you care? How can you tell?

The illusion of an education has always plagued the honest person. It is particularly seductive in a technological society like ours. We intermingle education with training, and liberal with professional studies, so intimately that they are hard to disentangle. We reward specific skills in politics, sports, business, and academia. We exalt those who can *do* something—those who are experts.

It becomes easy to forget that free and civilized societies are not built on information alone. Primitive and despotic societies have their experts too! Computers and animals can be trained to store and retrieve information, to learn, and even to out-perform us. What they can never do is direct the wise use of their information. They are imprisoned by their programmers and their own expertise. The more intensive that expertise, the more it cages them; the less they can function outside its restricted perimeter.

In a technological society experts proliferate like toadstools on a damp lawn. Some are genuine. Others are quick studies specializing in the predigestion of other people's thoughts. They crowd the TV screens, the radio waves, the printed page, eager to tell us what to believe and how to live—from sex and politics to religion and international affairs. They manufacture our culture, give us our opinions and our conversational *gambits.*

Now that you have a degree in something, you are in danger of stepping quietly into the cage of your own expertise—leaving everything else to the other experts. Whether they are genuine or phony makes little difference. If you do, you sacrifice the most precious endowment of an education—the freedom to make up your own mind—to be an authentic person. Knowledge, as Santayana said, is recognition of something absent. It is a salutation—not an embrace—a beginning, not an end.

You cannot predict when you will be brutally confronted by the falsity of your illusion like the juror who was interviewed following a recent murder trial. He was responding to one of those puerile how-does-it-feel questions that is the trademark of the telecaster's *vacuity*. "Being a juror was a terrible thing," he said. "I had to think like I never thought before. . . . I had to understand words like justice and truth. . . . Why do they make people like us judges?"

This is the pathetic lament of a sincere, sympathetic, but uneducated man. He was surely an expert in something but he could not grapple with the kind of question that separates humans from animals and computers. Justice and truth are awesome questions indeed. But who should answer those questions? Is being a juror another specialty? Do we need a degree in justice and truth? Does not a civilized and democratic society depend upon some common comprehension of what these words mean?

These same questions underlie every important public and private decision—from genetic engineering to nuclear proliferation, from prolonging human life to industrial pollution. They determine *how* we should use our expert knowledge, *whether* we should use it, and *for what* purposes. The welfare of the nation and the world depend on our capacity to think straight and act rightly—not on the amount of information we have amassed.

To be a juror, to be a person, to live with satisfaction, requires more than a trained mind—it requires an educated one, a mind that does not parrot other men's opinions or values but frames its own, a mind that can resist the potential tyranny of experts, one that can read, write, speak, manipulate symbols, argue, and judge, and whose imagination is as free as its reason.

These attributes are not synonymous with simple exposure to what is *euphemistically* called an education in the humanities or liberal arts, even when these are genuine—as often they are not. That belief only piles one illusion upon another. Rather than courses taken, or degrees conferred, the true tests of an educated mind are in its operations. Let me suggest some questions that indicate whether your mind operates like an educated one—no matter what your major may have been.

First, have you learned how to learn without your teacher? Can you work up a new subject, find the information, separate the relevant from the trivial, and express it in your own language? Can you discern which are your teacher's thoughts and which are your own? Your first freedom must be from the subtle despotism of even a great teacher's ideas.

Second, can you ask critical questions, no matter what subject is before you—those questions that expose a line of argument, evaluate the claims being made upon you, the evidence adduced, the logic employed? Can you sift fact from opinion, the plausible from the proven, the rhetorical from the logical? Can you use skepticism as a constructive tool and not as a refuge for intellectual sloth? Do you apply the same critical rigor to your own thoughts and actions? Or are you merely rearranging your prejudices when you think you are thinking?

Third, do you really understand what you are reading, what people are saying, what words they are using? Is your own language clear, concrete, and concise? Are you acquainted with the literature of your own language—with its structure and nuance?

Fourth, are your actions your own—based in an understanding and commitment to values you can defend? Can you discern the value conflicts underlying personal and public choices and distinguish what is a compromise to principle and what is not? Is your approach to moral judgments reasoned or emotional? When all the facts are in, when the facts are doubtful and action must be taken, can you choose wisely, prudently, and reasonably?

Fifth, can you form your own reasoned judgments about works of art—whether a novel, sonata, sculpture, or painting? Or are you enslaved by the critic, the book reviewer, and the "opinion makers" vacillating with their fads and pretentiousness? Artists try to evoke experiences in us, to transform us as humans. Is your imagination free enough to respond sensitively, or are you among the multitude of those who demand the explicitness of violence, pornography, dialogue—that is the sure sign of a dead imagination and an impoverished creativity?

Sixth, are your political opinions of the same order as your school and athletic loyalties—rooting for your side and ignoring the issues and ideas your side propounds? Free societies need independent voters who look at issues and not labels, who will be loyal to their ideals, not just to parties and factions. Do you make your insight as an expert the measure of social need? There is no illusion more fatal to good government!

If you can answer yes to some of these indicators, then you have imbibed the essence of a liberal education, one which assures that your actions are under the direction of your thought, that you are your own person, no matter what courses you took and what degree you receive today. You will also have achieved what is hoped for you:

> Education is thought of as not just imparting the knowledge of a professional
> discipline, but also as demonstrating a certain way of life—a way of life which is
> humane and thoughtful, yet also critical and above all rational.

If your answers are mostly negative (and I hope they are not), then you are in danger of harboring an illusion—one that is dangerous to you and society. The paradox is that the expert too has need of an educated mind. Professional and technical people make value decisions daily. To protect those whose values they affect, to counter the distorted pride of mere information, to use their capabilities for humane ends, experts too must reflect critically on what they do. The liberal arts, precisely because they are not specialties, are the indispensable accoutrements of any mind that claims to be human.

There are two kinds of freedom without which we cannot lead truly human lives. One kind is political and it is guaranteed by the Bill of Rights. The other is intellectual and spiritual and is guaranteed by an education that liberates the mind. Political freedom assures that we can express our opinions freely; a liberal education assures that the opinions we express are free. Each depends so much on the other that to threaten one is to threaten the other.

This is why I vex you with such a serious topic on this very happy occasion. The matter is too important for indifference or comfortable illusions. My hope is that by nettling you a bit I can prevent what is now a harmless illusion from becoming a delusion—firm, fixed belief, impervious either to experience or reason.

May I remind you in closing that the people who made our nation, who endowed it with the practical wisdom that distinguished its history, were people without formal degrees. One of the best among them, Abraham Lincoln, went so far as to say: "No policy that does not rest upon philosophical public opinion can be permanently maintained." Philosophical public opinion is not the work of information or expertise but of an educated mind, one that matches the aim of Wilkes to impart a way of life that is "...humane and thoughtful, yet also critical and above all rational."

T. S. Eliot, in his poem "The Dry Salvages," said: "We have had the experience of an education—I hope you have not missed the meaning." You have had the experience of an education—I hope you have not missed the meaning.

Reprinted by permission of the author.

● ● ● ● ● ● ● ● ● ● ● ● ● ● ● ● ● ●

Vocabulary

As you think about this essay, these definitions may be helpful to you:
1. **gauche**   (pronounced gōsh) lacking social experience or grace
2. **embolden**   to instill with boldness or courage
3. **gambits**   in this essay, remarks intended to start a conversation or make a telling point
4. **vacuity**   the state of being empty or lacking content
5. **euphemistically**   substituting an agreeable or inoffensive expression for one that may offend or suggest something unpleasant

 # Discussion Questions

1. Why does Dr. Pellegrino think it is an illusion that having a degree and being educated are the same?
2. What is an uneducated person, according to Pellegrino?

3. How does Pellegrino define "knowledge"?
4. List six ways that, according to Pellegrino, the mind works. Why?
5. What are the two kinds of freedom needed to live "truly human lives," according to Pellegrino?

 ## Suggestions for Your Journal

How do you view a college degree? As a piece of paper that can get you a job or as a symbol of the years when you learned to become "educated"? What is your definition of being educated? Do you think it is important to think about how an educated mind works? Why?

What are some specific actions you can take to master the six ways the mind of an educated person operates during your college career? When you graduate, how will you, as Pellegrino states, use your knowledge "to think straight and act rightly," not just the information you have accumulated in your mind?

A Time of Discontinuity

Arthur Levine and Jeanette S. Cureton

Arthur Levine is president and professor of Education at Teachers College, Columbia
University. Jeanette S. Cureton is an academic researcher, formerly of the Harvard
Graduate School of Education. This reading is taken from the authors' 1998 book,
When Hope and Fear Collide: A Portrait of Today's College Student.

• • • • • • • • • • • • • • • • • • •

There are rare times in the history of a society in which rapid and profound change occurs. The change is so broad and so deep that the routine and ordinary cycles of readjustment cease. There is a sharp break between the old and the new. It is a time of *discontinuity*. In the history of this country, there have been two such break points.

The first was the Industrial Revolution, which began in earnest in the first decades of the nineteenth century. It brought about a transformation in the United States from an agricultural to an industrial society. For those who lived through it, everything appeared to be in flux. The nation's economy was turbulent and uncertain, with wide swings both up and down. New technologies with the capacity to remake the nation's daily life, ranging from steamboats and canals to railroads and mechanized factories, were burgeoning. Old industries were dying, and new industries were being born. Demographics were shifting dramatically as the population moved west and south, from rural to urban areas. Large numbers of immigrants, with relatively little formal education, were coming to America. All of the country's major social institutions—church, family, government, work, and media—were being transformed. Reflecting on the vastness of the changes, Henry Adams concluded that "the old universe was thrown into the ash heap and a new one created."

Adam's assessment was very close to the mark. The effects of industrialization have been well documented. Among the consequences are family disorganization, *attenuation* of kinship ties, and a splintering of connections between generations. Mate selection and marital patterns are retarded. Gender roles change. Homogeneity gives way to heterogeneity. Apathy and alienation grow. New and higher literacy levels are required to function in society, causing sharp differentiation in the wealth and status of the populace. Mass communication expands, and isolation within society declines. Interest groups and associations multiply....

The second break point or time of discontinuity is occurring now. The United States is currently undergoing profound demographic, economic, global, and technological change. Demographically, the U.S. population is aging, changing color, coming from other countries, and redistributing itself across the country at astounding rates....

For today's college students, this world of change dominates their lives. The cycles of community and individualism have given way to a world of unceasing, unknowable change.

This reality is compounded by the enormous size of the population attending college today. As a consequence, the benefit of a college education has diminished. When only a small proportion of an age group graduates from college, they are virtually guaranteed the best jobs a society offers. When the majority attend college, this is no longer possible. The guarantee of the best jobs expires along with the guarantee of any job. In short, the students who attended college at the turn of the century were shopping at the educational equivalent of Tiffany's. Today's undergraduates are at something much more akin to Kmart. The multiplication in size of the college student population means they are subject to exactly the same social forces as the rest of the nation's population. A smaller, more *elite* group might have been protected from the waves of change crashing upon the rest of the country. The college *cohort* is simply too large today to be sheltered in any fashion....

The consequence of rapid social change and shifting conditions in higher education today is a generation straddling two worlds, one dying and another being born. Each makes competing and conflicting demands on today's college generation; they are torn between both. A dying world makes them want security, and a world being born makes urgent their call for change. In the same fashion, pragmatism wrestles with idealism, doing well with doing good, and fear with hope. They are, above all else, a transitional generation, not unlike the young people of Henry Adams's day, and they are experiencing the same symptoms as did those who lived through the Industrial Revolution.

Education for a Transitional Generation
As a group, current undergraduates might be described as having the following characteristics. They are

- Frightened
- Demanding of change
- Desirous of security
- Disenchanted with politics and the nation's social institutions
- Bifurcated in political attitudes between left and right; the middle is shrinking
- Liberal in social attitudes
- Socially conscious and active
- Consumer oriented
- Locally rather than globally focused
- Sexually active, but socially isolated
- Heavy users of alcohol
- Hardworking
- Tired
- Diverse and divided
- Weak in basic skills and able to learn best in ways different from how their professors teach

- Pragmatic, career oriented, and committed to doing well
- Idealistic, altruistic, and committed to doing good
- Optimistic about their personal futures
- Optimistic about our collective future
- Desperately committed to preserving the American dream

This generation is no better and no worse than any other generation, but, like every other generation before, it is unique. As a result, this generation requires a unique brand of education that will enable it to attain its personal dreams and to serve the society it must lead. The education we offered to previous generations, whether successful or not, will not work for these students. They are different, and their times are different. Above all, current undergraduates are in need of an education that provides them with four things.

Hope

The first is hope. When we speak about hope, we do not mean the flabby or groundless, rosy-eyed, Pollyannaish brand. Rather, we mean the kind of conviction that allows a person to rise each morning and face the new day. It is the stuff Shakespeare talked of when he wrote, "True hope is swift and flies with swallow's wings; / Kings it makes gods, and meaner creatures kings" (*Richard III* 5.2.23). Current students profess to being optimistic about the future; but that optimism is frail.

By way of example, in the course of our research we talked with a student who told us she was majoring in business. We asked how she liked it. She said she hated it. We asked what she would rather be majoring in. She said dance. We asked, Why not major in dance? She looked at us the way one would look at a dumb younger sibling and said, "Rich is nice. Poor is not nice. I want nice," and she walked off. We had no answer that day, but over time we have thought about that student a lot. She gave up all of her dreams to study a subject she hated. If she follows a career that flows from her major, she will probably dislike that too. The saddest, saddest part of the story is that she did not have to make the choice she did. This student may not have become a professional dancer, but she could manage a dance company, or be a dance teacher, or a critic, or perhaps operate a store selling dance equipment. The tragedy of the story is not that she made a bad selection. It is that the young woman gave up her hope. It was so tenuous that she dared not hold onto it....

Responsibility

The second *attribute* is responsibility. Despite all we said about the adversities this generation is facing, current college students are still among the most fortunate people in the world. They owe something to others. Indeed, they are more involved in service activities than their predecessors, but at the same time they are not convinced that they can both do good and do well. Many feel that when it comes to security and responsibility, a choice must be made.

At a New England liberal arts college, all first-year students were required to participate in an exercise called "Freshman Inquiry." Students were required to prepare an essay talking about what they had learned and not learned in college so far, their hopes and aspirations for the future, and how they planned to use the remainder of their college education. After the essay was written, each student met with a panel composed of a faculty member, an administrator, and a fellow student to discuss it. One student submitted an essay to a panel, saying when she grew up she wanted to be CEO of a multinational corporation, become a U.S. senator, head a foundation that provided scholarships for college students, and work for nuclear disarmament. The student was asked what she needed out of college to accomplish all this. After a little thought, she answered, "A killer instinct." Her listeners sought clarification. She said this meant the ability to step on people or walk over them when necessary to get what she wanted. She was asked about altruism. This time she asked for clarification, and the word was defined for her. She said that was not part of her game plan. The panel reminded her of her desire to work for nuclear arms control. Surely that was altruistic. She told the panel they did not get it: "If there were a nuclear war, I would not get to be CEO of a multinational corporation." Three years later, the student graduated, plans and opinions intact. Her grades were high, and several years later she was attending one of the nation's better business schools. All of her dreams may come true, but one is forced to conclude that her college experience was inadequate. It never taught her about responsibility, what she had an obligation to do for others.

Appreciation of Differences

The third attribute is understanding and appreciation of differences. Today's undergraduates are living in a world in which differences are multiplying and change is the norm, but they attend colleges that are often segregated on the basis of differences and where relationships between diverse populations are strained.... It is imperative that college students learn to recognize, respect, and accept their differences.

Efficacy

The final attribute is efficacy, that is, a sense that one can make a difference. Here again, current undergraduates affirmed this belief at the highest rates recorded in a quarter-century.... It brings to mind a group we met at a well-known liberal arts college. The college had created a special program for its most outstanding seniors to prepare them for the nation's most prestigious graduate fellowships. Levine [a co-author of this essay] was asked to talk to the students about leadership. After a few minutes of watching the students squirming in their seats, looking out the windows, and staring at their watches, he concluded the talk was not going well.

He told the group what he suspected; they agreed. They traded hypotheses back and forth about what had gone wrong. Finally, one student said, "Life is short. This leadership stuff is bullshit. We could not make a difference even if we wanted to." Levine took a quick poll of the group to see how many agreed with the student. Twenty-two out of twenty-five hands went up.

Today's students need to believe that they can make a difference. Not every one of them will become president of the United States, but each of them will touch scores of lives far more directly and tangibly—family, friends, neighbors, and coworkers. For ill or for good, in each of those lives students will make a difference. They need to be convinced that making a difference is their birthright. They should not give it away. No one can take it away. . . .

From Arthur Levine and Jeanette S. Cureton, *When Hope and Fear Collide.* Copyright © 1998 Jossey-Bass, Inc. This material was used by permission of John Wiley and Sons, Inc.

● ● ● ● ● ● ● ● ● ● ● ● ● ● ● ● ● ●

 Vocabulary

As you think about this essay, these definitions may be helpful to you:
1. **discontinuity**   lack of continuity or cohesion
2. **attenuation**   weakening
3. **elite**   a powerful minority group
4. **cohort**   in statistics, a group of individuals having a great deal in common
5. **attribute**   an inherent characteristic

 Discussion Questions

1. According to the authors, what are the two periods in history when profound change occurred? What do these two periods have in common?
2. Why do the authors claim the benefit of a college education has diminished?
3. Do you agree with the authors' description of current undergraduates? Why or why not?
4. What four attributes must a college education provide? Do you agree these are the most important for the future? Why or why not?
5. What can college students do to make sure they will "make a difference"?

Suggestions for Your Journal

Are you feeling the "time of discontinuity" that the authors describe? If so, in what way? Do you think you are getting a Tiffany or a Kmart education? Why? What would you add to or subtract from the list of characteristics that these authors attribute to current undergraduates? Do you personally believe that you can make a difference in the world? Do you really want to? Why or why not?

The Next Great Generation

Neil Howe and William Strauss

Neil Howe and William Strauss, the authors of *Generations, 13th Gen,* and *The Fourth Turning,* write and lecture frequently on generational issues. They host active discussions with readers (at www.millennialsrising.com and www.fourthturning.com) and run LifeCourse Associates, a strategic planning consulting firm.

• • • • • • • • • • • • • • • • •

"We're the Millennial Generation," asserts 17-year-old Tyler Hudgens of McLean, Virginia. "We're special, one of a kind. It's our turn, our time to shine."

"Kids Today," answers the "buzz" page in *Newsweek.* "They're just no good. No hardships + no cause = boredom, anger, and idiocy."

Who's right—Tyler Hudgens, or *Newsweek*?

Until very recently, the public has been accustomed to nonstop media chatter about bad kids—from mass murderers, hate criminals, and binge drinkers to test failers, test cheaters, drug users, and just all-around spoiled brats. To believe the news, you'd suppose our schools are full of kids who can't read in the classroom, shoot one another in the hallways, spend their loose change on tongue rings, and couldn't care less who runs the country. According to a national survey, barely one adult in three thinks that today's kids, once grown, will make the world a better place.

As for Miss Hudgens, where could she look to find allies? She won't find them among hard-line culture warriors, whose agenda for moral renewal feeds on the supposed *depravities* of youth, nor among those on the other side, whose plans for expansive government depend upon youth's supposed pathologies. She won't find them in business, which has learned how to target the hard youth edge so well that it would rather avoid the risk of trying anything new. Only among Tyler's teenage peers will she find an unwavering optimism to match her own. Even there, one can imagine a well-trained note of irony: *We're special? Oh. And on whose planet?*

Yet, the central message is that *Newsweek* is wrong and Hudgens is right.

A new generation is rising.

Meet the Millennials, born in or after 1982—the "Babies on Board" of the early Reagan years, the "Have You Hugged Your Child Today?" sixth graders of the early Clinton years, the teens of Columbine, and the much-touted high school classes of the new century, now invading the nation's campuses.

As a group, Millennials are unlike any other youth generation in living memory. They are more numerous, more affluent, better educated, and more ethnically diverse. More important, they are beginning to manifest a wide array of positive social habits that older Americans no longer associate with youth, including a new focus on teamwork, achievement, modesty, and good conduct.

Only a few years from now, this can-do youth revolution will overwhelm the cynics and pessimists. Over the next decade, the Millennial Generations will entirely recast the image of youth from downbeat and alienated to upbeat and engaged—with potentially *seismic* consequences for America.

Look closely at the dramatic changes now unfolding in the attitudes and behaviors of today's youth, the 18-and-unders of the new century. The evidence is overwhelming—and just starting to attract notice. In the spring of 2000 newsweekly magazines with "good news" youth stories marked a possible turning of the media tide.

That's not all. When you fit these changes into the broader rhythms of American history, you can get a good idea of what kind of adult generation the Millennials are likely to become. You can foresee their future hopes and fears, strengths and weaknesses, as they rise to adulthood and, in time, to power. You can understand how today's kids are on track to become a powerhouse generation, full of technology planners, community shapers, institution builders, and world leaders, perhaps destined to dominate the twenty-first century like today's fading and ennobled G.I. Generation dominated the twentieth. Indeed, Millennials have a solid chance to become America's next great generation, as celebrated for their collective deeds a hundred years from now as the generation of John Kennedy, Ronald Reagan, Joe DiMaggio, and Jimmy Stewart is celebrated today.

By that time, no one will recall the *Newsweek*-styled cynical barbs that greeted Tyler Hudgens as she, along with millions of other young people, began setting a new tone for America. And by that time, perhaps Miss Hudgen's sunny opinion of her generation will be widely shared, reinforced by the enduring memories of heroic achievements.

Is this possible? Yes. Is it certain? No.

While the outlook for this generation is largely positive, dangers abound, given its enormous potential power. Millennials do pose a threat to the future of this nation and the world. But if danger arrives, it won't come from the direction today's adults worry about—in the form of a selfish, alienated rabble of disaffected Ultra-Gen-X hyperslackers. Imagine, instead, an unstoppable mass hurling down the track in the opposite direction, a *cadre* of young people so cohesive and so directional that, if their aspirations are thwarted, they might overwhelm the political defenses of their elders and mobilize around a risky, even destructive agenda.

For decades, Americans have been wishing for a youth generation that would quit talking and start doing. Now that older generations are starting to produce kids like this, a new generation arises: OK, Boomers and Gen-Xers, now that you've got them, can you handle them?

Over the coming decade, the Oh-Ohs, this rising generation will introduce itself to the nation and push the nation into a new era. Once this new youth persona begins to focus on convention, community, and civic renewal, America will be on the brink of becoming someplace very new, very "millennial" in the fullest sense of the word. That's when the "end of history" stops, and the beginning of a new history, their Millennial history, starts.

Some *pundits*—marketers, especially—dub these kids "Generation Y," as though they were a mere Generation X2, *South Park* idiots beyond redemption, the ultimate price for America's post-60's narcissism. Others, giving them names such as Generation Dot Com, depict them as an exaggerated extension of America's current mood of self-oriented commercialism.

How utterly depressing. And how utterly wrong.

Yes, there is a revolution under way among today's kids—a *good news revolution*. Their generation is going to rebel by behaving not worse, but better. Their life mission will not be to tear down old institutions that don't work, but to build up new ones that do. Look closely at youth indicators and you'll see that *Millennial attitudes and behaviors represent a sharp break from Generation X, and are running exactly counter to trends launched by the Boomers.* Across the board, Millennial kids are challenging a long list of common assumptions about what "postmodern" young people are supposed to become.

Are Millennials another "lost" generation?

No. The better word is "found." Born in an era when Americans began expressing more positive attitudes about children, the Millennials are products of a dramatic birth-rate reversal. During the Gen-X child era, planned parenting almost always meant contraceptives or abortions; during the Millennial childhood, it more often means visits to the fertility clinic.

Are they pessimists?

No. They're optimists. Surveys show that—compared to Xer teens a decade ago—today's teens are more upbeat about the world in which they're growing up. Nine in ten describe themselves as "happy," "confident," and "polite." A rapidly increasing share say that growing up is easier for them than it was for their parents. Teen suicide rates are now falling for the first time in decades.

Are they self-absorbed?

No. They're cooperative team players. From school uniforms to team learning to community service, Millennials are gravitating toward group activity. According to a recent Roper survey, more teenagers blamed "selfishness" than anything else when asked, "What is the major cause of problems in this country?" Unlike Gen Xers, they believe in their own collective power.

Are they distrustful?

No. They accept authority. Most teens say they identify with their parents' values, and over nine in ten say they "trust" and "feel close to" their parents. The proportion that report conflict with their parents is declining. Half believe that lack of parental discipline is a major social problem and large majorities favor tougher rules against misbehavior in the classroom and society at large.

Are they rule breakers?

No. They're rule followers. Today's kids are disproving the experts who once predicted a tidal wave of juvenile crime during the late 1990's. Over the last five years, the rates of homicide, violent crime, abortion, and pregnancy among teens have all plummeted at the fastest rate ever recorded. Even including the

Columbine massacre, there were only half as many violent deaths at schools nationwide in the late nineties as there were in the early part of that decade.

Are they neglected?

No. They're the most watched over generation in memory. Each year, adults subject the typical kid's day to ever more structure and supervision, making it a nonstop round of parents, relatives, teachers, coaches, baby-sitters, counselors, chaperones, minivans, surveillance cams, and curfews. Over the last decade, time spent on homework and housework is up, while time spent on weekday TV watching is down.

Are they stupid?

No. They're smarter than most people think. During the 1990's, aptitude test scores rose within every racial and ethnic group, especially in elementary schools. Eight in ten teenagers say it's "cool to be smart," while a record share of teenagers are taking AP tests and say they "look forward to school" and plan to attend college.

Have they given up on progress?

No. Today's kids believe in the future and see themselves as its cutting edge. They show a fascination for, and mastery of, new technologies—which explains why math and science scores are rising faster than verbal scores. Teens rank "scientists" and "young people" as the two groups that will cause "most changes for the better in the future."

Why is the image of this generation so off the mark? For the simple reason that the predictive assumption is wrong. Whatever the era they are living in, Americans habitually assume that the future will be a straight-line extension of the recent past. But that never occurs, either with societies or with generations.

Millennials resemble a fully charged rocket—or to use Ortega y Gasset's classic definition of a generation, "a species of biological missile hurled into space at a given instant, with a certain velocity and direction." So long as Millennials can wheel themselves onto the right launchpad and point themselves in the right direction, they can deliver excellent results. They represent an opportunity, that once fully understood and appreciated, must be acted on by people of all ages.

● ●

 Vocabulary

As you think about this essay, these definitions may be helpful to you:
1. **depravities**   corrupt acts or practices
2. **seismic**   earthshaking

3. **cadre**   a nucleus or core group
4. **pundits**   those who give opinions in an authoritative manner

 Discussion Questions

1. How have the media portrayed the "Millennial Generation" in the past and how is that image changing? Why is this image so "off the mark," according to Howe and Strauss?
2. What characteristics do the authors attribute to the Millennials? Which of those characteristics describe you? Which do not?
3. What are some of the dangers the Millennials will face?
4. How are the Millennials different from Generation X, according to Howe and Strauss? Do you think the authors have created stereotypes that aren't necessarily true? Explain your thinking.
5. Do you agree that Millennials are going to change things? What kind of changes do you hope will take place? What changes do you think will take place?

 Some Suggestions for Your Journal

To which generation do you belong (i.e., Boomers, Xers, Millennials)? Do the characteristics attributed to your generation seem too stereotypical? How do they seem to reflect the history of our society?

If you are of the Millennial Generation, do you like the portrait that the authors have painted of your peers? How are your perceptions different from theirs? The same? If you are of another generation, what is your perception of the Millennials you know? Do you agree with the authors' description of them? Why or why not?

Do you think categorizing generations as this essay does is meaningful? To what extent?

To the Graduates

Christopher Reeve

- Christopher Reeve gave this commencement address to the graduates of a large
- Midwestern university in June, 2003. Reeve is an actor with many movie credits, but
- perhaps he is best known as "Superman." He was paralyzed after a riding accident in
- 1995 and speaks to that change in his life in this address.

I am extremely honored to address so many of you who are graduating today. I wanted to be here to pay tribute to the long standing ideals of this university: compassion for our fellow human beings, the aspiration to be champions in all arenas of life, and the desire to make a difference.

At this university, students and faculty understand the importance of public service on both a local and global scale. Some focus on the environment, others on community outreach, education, social programs, health research, and many other programs. I salute these points of pride to congratulate you for your outstanding achievements. But I also want to sound a note of caution as you leave this sanctuary of learning, self-discovery, and ethical conduct to make your way in the outside world.

You have been taught to work hard, not to cheat, and balance your own advancement with service to others. But when you look beyond this campus, you witness seemingly endless examples of questionable conduct in government, religion, business, the media, and even sports. Our intelligence agencies are being challenged to explain their recommendation for the invasion of Iraq. The Catholic Church is embroiled in a crisis of misconduct and cover-ups. CEOs of major corporations are facing fines and imprisonment for their greed at the expense of the employees who helped create their success. The reputation of one of the most respected newspapers in the country has been severely damaged by a reporter who could not resist plagiarizing in his zeal to succeed. Even the achievements of one of our favorite baseball players will probably be eclipsed by controversy over his use of an illegal bat.

The challenge before you will be to maintain your integrity in a culture that has devalued it. You will have to bring your own personal and professional ethics with you on the journey when you leave here today, because you may not find anyone to guide you. Living a moral life in an indifferent world is likely to be more difficult than you can imagine. How will you succeed?

The answer may be found in a few simple words written by Abe Lincoln: "When I do good I feel good. When I do bad I feel bad. And that is my religion." All of us have a voice inside that will speak to us if we let it. Sometimes it is easy to hear; sometimes we have to turn down the volume of distracting noise around us so we can listen. That voice tells us if we are on the right track. It lets us know if we give as much as we take, if we welcome the opinions of others, and at least accept diversity even if we are not able to embrace it.

As you go forward, hopefully that inner voice will remind you of some of the points of pride that bring such distinction to your university. You will discover that you can go far by being conscientious, but you will go farther and find true satisfaction by being conscious. If you have already achieved self-awareness and set specific goals for yourself, that is fine. If you don't know who you are or what to do next, don't worry about it. Your life should not run on a schedule, and you may go down some dead end streets until you find the right road. Don't be afraid to question assumptions you may have lived with since childhood. Take your time and seek true independence as you search for meaning and fulfillment.

Perhaps the greatest reward for living a conscious life is that it prepares you to cope with adversity. If you are open to change and new experiences, if you are accustomed to self-discipline, if you respect others and nurture your relationships, then you will have built a solid platform that will support you and help you deal with anything that comes your way. I'm not saying all of that is easy. But sitting here today I can honestly tell you that you don't need to break your neck to learn the value of living consciously. I was lucky to grow up unthreatened by change and eager for new experiences. Thirty years as an actor before my injury taught me self-discipline and helped me cope with rejection and failure. My marriage and my relationships with friends and family were alive and well before the accident. Since then they have grown even stronger and given me the ability to recover and go forward.

That catastrophic event also changed my perspective about other things in life. Outside of my circle of family and friends, I didn't appreciate others nearly as much as I do now. Once I trained with actual paraplegics to portray one in a film. Every evening as I drove away from the rehab center I quickly pushed those suffering patients out of my mind, relieved that I was not one of them. Less than a year later I became paralyzed myself. Did I need to learn something about compassion and humility? No doubt about it.

It was not until I was immersed in my own rehabilitation that I realized an apparent tragedy had created a unique opportunity. Spinal cord patients like the ones I once dismissed were now in the next room, traveling down the same hallways, and struggling right beside me in physical therapy. I came to know people of all ages and from all walks of life that I would otherwise never even have met. For all our differences, what we had in common was our disability and the desire to find a reason to hope. I was inspired by so many and gradually discovered that I had been given a job that would create urgency and a new direction in my life: I could do something to help.

Thanks to the education you have received and the ideals that guide this distinguished university, you have already learned some of the most important principles you will ever need to know: compassion for our fellow human beings, the aspiration to be champions in all arenas of life, and the desire to make a difference. To all of you leaving today I can only say, on behalf of all those who will look to you for guidance and leadership, take those principles with you and hold them close.

Congratulations on all your achievements. I wish you the best of luck.

Used with permission of Christopher Reeve.

 Discussion Questions

1. How does Christopher Reeve define a "moral life"?
2. How does he suggest you can achieve it?
3. What is the difference between being "conscientious" and "conscious"?
4. In what ways has his disability changed Christopher Reeve's life?
5. What is he advising these graduates to consider as they enter a culture that makes it difficult to maintain integrity?

 Suggestions for Your Journal

What emotions did you feel as you read Christopher Reeve's address? How would your life change if you had to face the kind of catastrophe that he suffered? Do you live a "moral life"? If so, how? If not, do you even aspire to one? Explain.

UNIT SUMMARY

In Unit 9 you have read several authors' perceptions of how life after college might be different, along with some of their suggestions for preparing for the day after graduation. The following questions and writing assignments may help you clarify your aspirations for what you want in the future and how you might begin to prepare for it now.

Summary Questions

1. How important is having a degree to you? Do you think it is important to be educated when you graduate? How might your response affect your future career and life?
2. Levine and Cureton describe four attributes that an education must provide. Of these (hope, responsibility, appreciation of differences, and efficacy), which will be the most difficult for you to acquire? Why? The easiest? Why?
3. Briefly compare the portrait of the Millennial Generation drawn by Howe and Strauss with the description of undergraduates given by Levine and Cureton.
4. As you look forward to your years in college, have the authors of the readings in this unit given you any new insights into how you should prepare now for life after graduation? If so, what are they? What steps can you take now to prepare for your life after college (e.g., improve your communication skills or develop technological competencies)?

Suggested Writing Assignments

1. If you wrote an essay in Unit 1 about your reasons for being in college, reexamine these reasons. Are they still the same? Have they changed? Have you added any? What has influenced your thinking the most?
2. How has the prospect of finding a job after college influenced your initial choice of major? Have your experiences so far confirmed that decision? In what way? If you are considering a change, discuss some possible alternatives and why you are considering them.
3. Discuss how you intend to prepare yourself to become an effective worker in tomorrow's workplace. Describe specific ways, such as work and volunteer opportunities, campus involvement, and academic and other experiences, that will help you acquire the general competencies and skills necessary to be effective.

Suggested Readings

Carter, Carol. *Keys to Effective Learning.* Upper Saddle River, NJ: Prentice-Hall, 1999.
Covey, Stephen. *The Seven Habits of Highly Effective People.* New York: Simon and Schuster, 1989.
Mitchell, S. *American Generations: Who They Are, How They Live, What They Think.* New York: New Strategist, 1998.

Author Index

Subject Index